Living the Future:
The Kingdom of God and the
Holy Spirit
in the Vineyard Movement

By

Dr. Douglas R. Erickson, Ph.D.

Living the Future: The Kingdom of God and the Holy Spirit in the
Vineyard Movement

ISBN-13:
978-0692756126
ISBN-10:
0692756124

www.Standuptheology.com

Thank you Douglas Erickson, you've done us an enormous favor! This is a *very* important book for the Vineyard – and for many other Churches and Christians seeking to understand *Jesus' Kingdom message and mission, in the practice of the power of the Spirit.* From its historical development in Wimber and the Vineyard, to its broadening current understanding and practice, Erickson serves us with superb scholarship, diligent research, insightful content, clear communication. Erickson leaves us with the prophetic challenge to grow fully into our Kingdom heritage, with the radical pursuit of the practice of the Spirit.
- Alexander Venter, author of *Doing Church* and *Doing Healing*

Once in a while, in the history of a given movement or tradition a book comes along that defines that movement or tradition. There are a few works written in and for the Vineyard that might fit into this category. This is one of them. This is the first time that the roots, nature and implications of Wimber's theology have been carefully researched and articulated. I predict that it will become one of those books that will be recommended as essential reading for all those who want to really understand where we came from, and what defines us as a movement. All subsequent serious research into the Vineyard will have to take it into account.
-Derek Morphew, Academic Dean, Vineyard Institute

Douglas Erickson has done a great service to the church at large and to the Vineyard. He lays out a clear process concerning the centering influence that the teaching and practice of the Kingdom of God has had in the Vineyard's formation and ongoing life. This will help many understand why we do what we do and how important it is to stay the course. Thank you Doug.
-Phil Strout, National Director, Vineyard USA

Dr. Douglas Erickson has done a great service to the Vineyard worldwide in writing this volume of contemporary historical theology. Erickson carefully interprets the formulations of Vineyard theology in the teaching of John Wimber while simultaneously exegeting Vineyard church practices that continue to this day. Work like this is so helpful — it teaches us where we have come from, helps us to understand who we are, and points forward in the direction of where we may be going as a worldwide movement in the 21st century. For anyone interested in the theology and practice of the Vineyard, this book is not to be missed!

Caleb Maskell, Society of Vineyard Scholars

ACKNOWLEDGMENTS
Douglas R. Erickson, B.A., M.A.C.T. Ph.D.

I am grateful to the Vineyard pastors, leaders and members that have supported and cared for me for more than two decades. A profound thanks is in order to Michael and Brenda Gatlin and the community of the Duluth Vineyard church for "doing the stuff" and incomparable blessings and support given to myself and my family. In the greater Vineyard tribe, countless pastors, practitioners and theologians have supported this project from its inception. I am especially grateful to Bob Fulton, Alexander Venter, the late Bill Jackson, Winn Griffin, Peter Davids and Carl Tuttle for insights and recollections of Vineyard history that have been invaluable. Past U.S.A. director Berton Waggoner, and present director Phil Strout have been encouraging as well. The companionship and kindness of countless members of the Society of Vineyard Scholars has nourished me over the last several years; your imprints can be seen throughout this project. Caleb Maskell's servant leadership during his own studies has been a model of dedication and sacrifice. Cindy Dufty's editing on early drafts of this book were extremely helpful. Innumerable thanks to my editor, Judy Twycross, for her outstanding work making this a better project. All remaining mistakes are mine alone, as Judy did her best.

This project would have never commenced without the friendship and insight of Derek Morphew, who first suggested this as a dissertation topic. Dr Morphew not only suggested the need for such a project for the good of the Vineyard movement, but has also taught me innumerable lessons on what it means to be a follower of Jesus, a practitioner-scholar, and a humble servant of the church.

Finally, to my beloved wife, Sandy, words cannot express my thankfulness for your love and support these many years. Few will know of your selfless sacrifice and unending support that made this whole journey possible. I love you and will be forever in your debt. My children, Zachary, Annika and Soren have probably sacrificed the most of all over the last several years of my writing and study. I love you all deeply.

For John and Carol Wimber

Contents

ABBREVIATIONS

PE	Wimber, John. *Power Evangelism.*
PH	Wimber, John. *Power Healing.*
PP	Wimber, John. *Power Points.*
TWIW	Wimber, Carol. *John Wimber: the Way it Was.*
Quest	Jackson, Bill. *The Quest for the Radical Middle.*
EGTP	*Everyone Gets to Play.* ed. Christy Wimber.
TWIWO	*The Way In is the Way On.* ed. Christy Wimber.
Wimber	*John Wimber: His Influence and Legacy.* ed. David Pytches.
ETS	*Equipping the Saints*
FF	*First Fruits*
VOV	*Voice of the Vineyard*
TPOF	Ladd, George Eldon. *The Presence of the Future; the Eschatology of Biblical Realism.*

INTRODUCTION

I stood amazed in a small auditorium. People all around me stood with hands raised, or held quietly at their sides, singing a soft rock ballad together. Many were weeping, and around the room, groups of people were huddled together, praying for one another. Some were even lying on the ground, or kneeling in prayer. The pastor of this small church had just given a sermon on caring for the poor, and spoke about an outreach that the church was planning for the community in the coming weeks. In response, he had asked all those who felt moved to a deeper concern for the "lost, the least, and the last" to come forward for prayer. A single thought went through my mind as I watched this incredible scene unfold.

I was home.

The Vineyard movement is an emerging Protestant tradition with a global influence far beyond its numerical size. From its beginning in the 1970s, the Vineyard has grown rapidly, and has placed itself as a church movement that seeks to define a "middle way" between American Evangelicalism and Pentecostalism. The Vineyard has enjoyed a growing impact, evidenced by the expansion of the movement across the globe.

The Vineyard movement desires to incorporate the emphasis on conversion and sanctification from Evangelicalism, with the openness to and practice of the charismatic gifts that is the hallmark of Pentecostalism. Despite the influence of this ecclesial expression, there has been little academic work dedicated to the study of the theology and activity of the Vineyard. It is often considered within such categories as "neo-Pentecostalism", "Charismatics" or the even less descriptive, and quite historically naïve, "Third Wave of the Holy Spirit". Missiologists and church historians began to refer to three "waves" or large scale moves of the Holy Spirit in the twentieth century.

1

- The "first wave" was the birth of the Pentecostal movement in the early 1900s.
- The "second wave" was the rise of the charismatic movement in the 1960s.
- The "third wave" was the emergence of churches like the Vineyard in the 1980s.

The pioneer of the Vineyard movement was John Wimber (1934–1997), who enjoyed a successful career as a jazz musician and rock band manager before his conversion to Christianity in a Quaker church. Early in his pastoral career, he discovered the writings of George Eldon Ladd, professor of New Testament at Fuller Seminary in California. His encounter with Ladd's concept of the "already and not yet" kingdom of God dramatically changed Wimber's approach to theology and ministry. This particular understanding of the kingdom of God, borrowed and modified from Ladd, established the ecclesiology, the eschatology, and the Pneumatology of the Vineyard movement. Further, members of these Vineyard churches argue that their theology and practices are unique from both their Evangelical and Pentecostal friends.

For a movement that is better known for its practical emphasis on healing and worship, some might wonder why we should bother to study the theology of the Vineyard. Shouldn't Christians focus on *doing* the works of the Spirit? Is this arguing about minor points of theology even worth our time?

I had a seminary professor who told the following story. When he was a young father, he took his son to a playground, where his son met some other young boys. Soon they were talking about where they lived, what their families were like, whether they had any pets, what superheroes they liked – all the things that are important to kids. One of the boys proudly exclaimed, "My dad's a doctor! He helps sick people get well!" In response, my professor's son replied, "My dad's a doctor too. But he can't help anybody!"

Is this true? Is theological study only fruitless and divisive, or can it actually "help somebody"? If you think that the church would be better off *doing* more and *arguing* less, I would tend to agree with you. However, I would ask for your patience, because most often the things we do are grounded in how we think about the world, faith, and God. That is, almost always, our theology and practice are intimately related. They feed off and influence each other, and thus, it's better to have a firm understanding of the theology that supports or undergirds our church practices. While the theology may get a bit heady at times, it's vitally important to understand both the theology and the practices of the Vineyard movement.

All of us have a theology or background understanding of how we think the church should work, or what's important in the life of a Christian.

On to the theology…

While the idea of the kingdom of God as "fulfillment without consummation", in Ladd's terms, has become the contemporary consensus, this is the culmination of a 200-year quest. Beginning in the modern period with Immanuel Kant, and continuing through Albrecht Ritschl, Johannes Weiss, Albert Schweitzer, Rudolph Bultmann, C. H. Dodd, and Joachim Jeremias, it would be no exaggeration to say that the concept of the kingdom of God has been one of the dominant themes in modern theological and biblical scholarship, as the theme occupies a significant place in the works of nearly all theologians in the modern period. The consensus of the mystery of the kingdom, or fulfillment without consummation, is well understood in many modern church movements, traditions, and communities. One of the primary arguments of this book will be that, while the Vineyard movement has adopted kingdom theology, its practice deeply reflects and reinforces this kingdom theology in a manner that separates the Vineyard from contemporary American Evangelicalism and Pentecostalism.

With this background, a number of questions may be raised. In what sense can it be said that the Vineyard movement is a "kingdom of God" based movement? What is the eschatology that justifies this view of the kingdom of God? Certainly, it is assumed that theological commitments lay in the background of practicing the faith, so in what ways are Vineyard practices influenced by their particular conception of the kingdom of God? The movement claims to be a sort of *"middle way"* between traditional Evangelicalism and Pentecostalism; does this, in fact, hold true among the practitioners of the faith? How can we determine the degree to which theology influences practice, in either the movements under study or their contemporaries? Of particular concern in the light of the "pneumatological turn" in systematic theology, is the question: "What is the relationship between eschatology and Pneumatology in the Vineyard?"

....

To sum up, the guiding question of this book may be stated as this: what distinguishes the Vineyard movement from other Christian communities that also claim to be based on the kingdom of God?

....

In short, what does it mean to "Live the Future"? Notice that I do not say "living in the future", as in what life in the kingdom of God might look like in some future, far-off day. We live, think and minister in the present. Yet somehow, the power of the future, the presence of God's full eschatological victory, has invaded the present. So, we live a future reality in the present. If this is confusing, know that many theologians and pastors have puzzled over this very issue – it is often called "the mystery of the kingdom of God".

There have been numerous academic studies done on the relationship between the kingdom of God and the Holy Spirit. James Dunn's classic essay, *Spirit and Kingdom* (1970), sets the tone for much of this discussion from the Reformed and Evangelical side. Numerous Evangelical authors have offered their contributions from their respective theological perspectives. Pentecostals such as Amos Yong and Steven Land have eagerly embraced the kingdom concept and related it to Pneumatology and classic Pentecostal themes such as Spirit baptism and the operation of the *charismata*. Frank Macchia's wonderful book, *Baptized in the Spirit: A Global Pentecostal Theology*, discusses the kingdom of God concept with

4

the "central Pentecostal distinctive" of Spirit baptism. Missing in the discussion thus far is an investigation of how the kingdom of God concept influences the Pneumatology and practice of the Vineyard. This study seeks to fill that gap.

Given that there has been little academic attention focused on the Vineyard, this study will serve for many as an introduction to the theology and practice of this movement. While numerically the Vineyard cannot compare to the 600 million or more classical Pentecostals in Christendom, the influence of the movement on both Evangelicalism and Pentecostalism is considerable. Unfortunately, there has been little ecumenical dialogue from the Vineyard movement to classical Pentecostalism, and thus this study may also open the way for discussion among theologians and practitioners alike.

First, we will look at the theological and historical background of the Vineyard. This section of the book may be new to many, but it is quite important to understand the history of the Vineyard before we study its theology. Next, we will study the eschatology of the Vineyard; which will be compared to, and contrasted with, the eschatology of Evangelicalism and Pentecostalism. We will also quickly review the twentieth-century kingdom of God studies in order to understand the background of these theologies. Following this, we will move to the exciting recovery of Pneumatology in recent theology. This will lead to an examination of the theology of the work of the Spirit in the Vineyard, again contrasted with their counterparts in other Protestant traditions.

We will then start an investigation of the charismatic experiences of believers within the Vineyard tradition. The majority of this chapter will involve an analysis of the religious experience of Vineyard authors and members to understand more fully our characteristic practices. To be specific, the particular religious experience of the work of the Spirit expressed through the *charismata* of healing, demonic deliverance, and prophecy will be probed through an examination of popular level books, denominational publications, and other sources.

The final chapters will offer some constructive proposals about how the central idea of the enacted, inaugurated, eschatological kingdom of God impacts other topics in theology. This discussion will expand the theological self-understanding of those within the Vineyard as well as provide a way for those outside the movement to understand the theology of the Vineyard movement.

It's important to understand that this study will offer *a* theological understanding of the Vineyard movement, but in no way do I assume that I have captured or set down in writing *the* theology of the Vineyard. It goes without saying that in a globally diverse, ever-developing church movement, a plurality of perspectives and options exist on a great many things. While I have attempted to remain faithful to the theological distinctives of the Vineyard, this work is by no means the final word on these subjects. Many more books on the Vineyard need to be written! It's also important to keep in mind Paul's words that "God has set the members, each one of them, in the body just as He pleased. And if they were all one member, where would the body be?" (1 Corinthians 12:18–19)

This book is *not intended* to show that the Vineyard is better, more godly, or more "biblically authentic" than any other church, movement, or denomination. We will simply discover *what* the Vineyard is. We are *just one member of the body*, and we cannot say to another member that the body doesn't need it, or that is it less important to the body of Christ, his global church. In Vineyard terms, we could say that we are just one vegetable in God's stew, and God certainly loves many diverse flavors in his stew!

At the conclusion of this study, we will see that the inaugurated, enacted, eschatological vision of the kingdom of God is the central theological distinctive of the Vineyard movement. It will become clear that this central distinctive is grounded in scripture and evidenced in practice, and furthermore, this cohesion between theology and action forms a model that is greatly suited to communicate the gospel of Jesus Christ to both Western postmodern cultures, and majority world churches who preach the kingdom of God.

Section I: The Theological Influences of John Wimber and the Vineyard Movement

In order to show the relationship between Pneumatology and eschatology in the Vineyard movement, it is first necessary to understand the theological influences of the pioneer of the movement, John Wimber (1934–1997). The objective of these chapters is to provide an overview of the formative theological influences of John Wimber. This will set the context for the more extensive theological discussion which will follow later.

> An exploration of Vineyard theology is in many ways a study of John Wimber himself.

Wimber joined the young Vineyard movement when it was an informal collection of eight churches. He was quickly recognized as the leader of the movement, and for the next two decades put his stamp on the theology and practice of the Vineyard movement.[1]

First, we will discuss John Wimber's background, conversion, and early theological influences. As he was raised in an atheistic family with no churchgoers in the previous four generations, his perspective of church was largely as an *outsider*, especially to the form of Protestant Evangelicalism in Southern California in the 1960s. The importance of Wimber's not growing up within the evangelical subculture cannot be underestimated; it changed the way he thought about *every aspect of church*. Wimber's phenomenal career in professional music, culminating as the manager and arranger of the popular music group, "The Righteous Brothers", gave him further perspective on worship music in the contemporary churches he became exposed to. His professional music background and understanding of how music influences human behavior continue to impact the worship experience in Vineyard churches to this

7

day.

Next, we will discuss his early exposure to the Evangelical Quaker church where he became a Christian. This formative experience exposed him to doctrine and practices that can be found in Vineyard churches. John's conversion in 1963 at the Yorba Linda Friends Church in Yorba Linda, California, exposed him to the familiar doctrines and practices of the Protestant Evangelical churches in America: the focus on conversion, repentance, sanctification, a high view of scripture, and personal evangelism. These broad evangelical characteristics were combined with the unique Quaker influences of quietude, simplicity, and waiting on the Spirit, which Wimber practiced for nearly a decade.

The third major group of theological influences came to John Wimber as he became exposed to Pentecostal, Charismatic, and Majority World believers at Fuller Seminary. In this chapter, we will discuss how Wimber moved from a position of *cessationism* (believing the charismatic gifts like healing and prophecy have *ceased* with the passing of the apostles, which was the view of Yorba Linda friends Church) to become the leading figure in the "signs and wonders" movement. Exposure to and dialogue with sincere, wise, and mature Pentecostals like Russell Spittler, Peter Wagner and Donald Gee caused Wimber to reconsider his early cessationist positions. As a result of his biblical study and dialogue with these *continuationists*, Wimber began to change his position on the presence of the charismatic gifts in the contemporary church.

Finally, we will see how these formative theological influences set in place what would be later called "The Vineyard Genetic Code", which is crucial to understanding the character and theology of the contemporary Vineyard movement. Similar to my experience, many people have discovered their spiritual "home" in the Vineyard movement. Many people have said over the years that

"You don't join the Vineyard, you discover you are Vineyard".

This book hopes to reveal what is used to construct that home, and how it was built.

ONE

John Wimber and the Vineyard

Conversion and Early Years

John Wimber was born on February 25th, 1934 in Kirksville, Missouri and was the only child of his mother, who was abandoned by John's father on the day he was born.[2] The family was not religious and did not attend or participate in any church. John was a musical prodigy, and, as an only child, spent long hours learning and practicing musical instruments. In 1953, as an eighteen-year-old, Wimber won first prize at the prestigious Lighthouse International Jazz festival competition.[3] After graduating from high school, John pursued a career in the music industry, writing, playing, and arranging jazz music, and winning numerous awards and recognitions. He married his wife Carol in 1955, and they soon had three kids, while living in Las Vegas, Nevada. In 1962 Wimber became the manager of an up-and-coming popular music band named "The Righteous Brothers", for whom he also arranged music and played saxophone. While his music career was skyrocketing, his personal life fell into despair. The couple was separated for some time, with Carol living in Los Angeles, and John in Las Vegas, before Carol began divorce proceedings in 1962.[4]

In a fit of desperation, John went out into the desert one morning to search for answers. He recounts that after crying out to God for help, Carol called him the next morning, asking to give the marriage one more try. John moved his family from Las Vegas to Orange County, California, in the hope that a more stable setting would help them straighten out their marriage problems. In December of that year, John and Carol met with one of John's oldest friends and fellow musicians, Dick Heying. Dick and his wife, Lynne, informed the Wimbers that they had become Christians, and were part of a local church, Yorba Linda Friends Church, an Evangelical

9

Friends gathering.[5] In 1963, John and Carol went to Yorba Linda Friends Church, where they began attending a small Bible study led by a layman, Gunnar Payne.[6] Gunnar would become a foundational person in John Wimber's spiritual quest. For many months, John would badger Gunnar with many questions related to faith, the Bible, Christianity and Jesus. Eventually in that year, first Carol, then John, made faith professions and became Christians.[7]

In December of 1963 the Wimbers faced a crossroads: in the midst of his newfound Christianity, John had been slowly letting his music career slide away, but Bill Medley of "The Righteous Brothers" called John and begged him to produce a Christmas Album. John eventually refused his offer. In the winter of 1964, Bill called again, this time informing him that they needed John on board because "The Righteous Brothers" had been tapped to headline for the Beatles' upcoming tour. Again, John Wimber refused, sensing that this was a temptation to re-enter his former life of music, drug and alcohol consumption and decadence. This decision proved to be John's final break with the professional music business.

The Yorba Linda Friends Church 1964–1977

Wimber began to explore his new faith in earnest. He became a disciple of Gunnar Payne, following Gunnar as he evangelized and ministered to the community of Yorba Linda, eagerly absorbing all he could from his mentor. John was a quick student, and soon began to lead Bible studies and evangelistic outreaches. The church experienced explosive growth in this period, and outgrew their facilities several times. In working with Gunnar, the classic evangelical characteristics of Bible study, personal evangelism, conversion, sanctification, and church life became second nature to John. His leadership abilities were obvious, so in 1970 John was asked to join the pastoral staff at Yorba Linda Friends Church, a position that he held until 1974. In these years, John would later recall that he and Carol had led hundreds, perhaps thousands, of people to Christ.[8]

It is interesting to note that at this time, the Evangelical Quaker church was cessationist in regard to the operation of the charismatic gifts.[9]

10

What is Cessationism?

Cessationism is the theological belief usually attributed to B.B. Warfield that hold that miracles, signs and wonders were primarily given to authenticate the ministry of Jesus and the Apostles. Once the Biblical canon was completed, there was no longer any need for miracles or signs and wonders and so these were withdrawn from the Church by the Holy Spirit.

The Wimbers had some exposure to various individuals who expressed the charismatic gifts, such as speaking in tongues and divine healing, and even had several experiences themselves, but owing to their theological convictions, rejected these gifts as normative.[10] In a following section, we will trace the greater influence of Evangelical Quaker theology on Wimber. John enrolled in Azuza Pacific College in 1970, earning a two-year certificate in Biblical Studies.[11] He was given the position of co-pastor of Yorba Linda Friends Church and was soon teaching 11 Bible studies and overseeing more than 500 people.

The Fuller Institute of Church Growth 1974–1978

In 1975, John Wimber was asked by Dr C. Peter Wagner to establish the Charles E. Fuller Institute of Evangelism and Church Growth at Fuller Evangelical Seminary in Pasadena, California. [12] The two men had met earlier, as Wimber had enrolled in a doctoral ministry Church Growth course taught by Wagner in 1974. In Wimber, Dr Wagner perceived exactly what he had needed in a partner: a practitioner who had a great deal of experience with the everyday practicalities of running a church. Wimber was at the point of burnout in his pastoral ministry, and welcomed the opportunity for a career change.[13]

At the Institute of Church Growth, Wimber began to travel across the U.S. visiting churches and studying their leadership structures and growth patterns. During this time, Wimber consulted with hundreds of churches from 27 denominations, and met over 40,000 pastors.[14] He and Carol maintained their membership at Yorba Linda Friends Church, but stepped away from most of their leadership obligations.

Several significant events at Fuller served to change the course of Wimber's ministry philosophy, and consequently shaped the eventual character of the Vineyard. First, Wimber came into personal contact with academics from Pentecostal and Charismatic backgrounds such as Michael Green, Russell Spittler and Donald Gee.[15] Secondly, Wimber developed friendships with many non-Western students and professors who had experience in foreign missions. These students and scholars such as C. Peter Wagner and Charles Kraft had robust understandings of the *charismata,* especially healing, deliverance and spiritual warfare, which challenged Wimber's cessationist paradigm.[16]

Finally, Wimber encountered the teachings of George Eldon Ladd, who synthesized the twentieth-century theological concept of the kingdom of God as being present, but not completely consummated. As a result of these influences, John began to question his cessationist position. Unknown to him, Carol had begun to do the same. In a small group of the Yorba Linda Friends Church, the Wimbers and close friends, including Carol's sister Penny and her husband, Bob Fulton, began experimenting with praying for the sick. As the group grew in numbers and influence, they began to welcome and accept other manifestations of the Holy Spirit such as tongues and prophecy.[17] This move eventually drew them into conflict with the leadership of the Friends Church. In April of 1977, both parties agreed that the small group of people in relationship with John and Carol should part from Yorba Linda Friends Church, so that they would be free to continue their pursuit of the *charismata.*[18] It was a very difficult time for both the Wimber group and Yorba Linda Friends Church.

Calvary Chapel Yorba Linda

In 1977, Wimber began leading a small group of believers that would eventually become Calvary Chapel Yorba Linda.[19] Initially, this group numbered over 100 people. Because of a connection with John McClure, John Wimber's assistant at Fuller, the new group affiliated with Dr Chuck Smith's Calvary Chapel group and constituted themselves as Calvary Chapel Yorba Linda on Mother's Day, 8 May 1977.[20]

Chuck Smith had started the Calvary Chapel movement after

12

ministering to thousands of young people during the Jesus Movement of the late 1960s and early 1970s.[21] By the time Wimber joined the movement, Smith was leading a group of churches that were exploding in membership, even though they were primarily composed of teenagers and young adults – the so-called "hippie culture" of Southern California. One of the early leaders of the "Jesus People" movement of the sixties and seventies, Smith attracted numerous young leaders to his ministry.

At first, this was a good fit for the group gathered by the Wimbers and the Fultons. John served as the de facto pastor. However, the harmony would prove to be short-lived. As the Yorba Linda Calvary Church continued to pursue the charismatic gifts of the Holy Spirit, they came into increasing conflict with other pastors and the leadership of Calvary Chapel. John increasingly incorporated time for healing prayer into their services, which had never been practiced in Calvary Chapels before.[22] John welcomed and accepted other charismatic manifestations, including speaking in tongues, prophecy, and deliverance from evil spirits. Further, Calvary Chapel had an expressly dispensationalist eschatology, that taught the end-times rapture of the Church.[23] This doctrine was in stark contrast to Wimber's view, which fully accepted the non-dispensationalist (even *anti-dispensationalist*) "already and not yet" kingdom theology of G.E. Ladd. These two sources of conflict, dispensationalism and cessationism, caused increasing tension between the two groups.[24]

The conflict grew and eventually proved to be too great a divide between the groups. The group around the Wimbers and Fultons, now numbering over 1500 people, was blessed by Chuck Smith and sent out from the Calvary Chapel association in May, 1982.[25]

The Vineyard Movement Begins

John Wimber had become close friends with Kenn Gulliksen, a Calvary Chapel pastor. By 1982, Kenn had over seven churches gathered in what he had named "the Vineyard". Originally, Gulliksen had not envisioned that the Vineyard Churches would separate from the Calvary association; rather he considered the Vineyard churches under his care to be a subset or movement within the larger Calvary Fellowship. However, as Wimber and Gulliksen separated themselves from their Calvary peers by encouraging the operation of the *charismata* within the Vineyard Churches, their parting with Chuck Smith was inevitable. When the Wimber group came out of Calvary Chapel in 1982, Gulliksen and Wimber immediately brokered a partnership, with Gulliksen giving Wimber the leadership of the fledgling Vineyard Churches. Thus, in May 1982 Wimber's group became known as the Vineyard Christian Fellowship of Anaheim. Within a year, over 30 other Calvary Chapels would change their affiliation to the Vineyard Movement.[26]

According to Bill Jackson, in his history of the Vineyard entitled *The Quest for the Historical Middle: A History of the Vineyard,* many of these pastors were attracted to Wimber's openness to charismatic gifts, and his experience and knowledge of church planting and church growth that he had gained in his years at Yorba Linda Friends Church. John Wimber stepped away from the Fuller Institute of Church Growth in 1980, but continued his close relationship with Dr C. Peter Wagner. In January of 1982, Dr Wagner called on Wimber to join him in co-teaching a new course at Fuller Theological Seminary. The course, which was destined to make history, was entitled "MC 510: Signs, Wonders, and Church Growth". In a quote made famous in Vineyard and Fuller Seminary circles, the Dean at Fuller Seminary at this time, Dr Robert Meye, reportedly said, "I know of only two seminary courses which have become famous…the first was the course on dogmatics taught at Basel by Karl Barth, and the other is MC 510 taught by John Wimber here at Fuller".[27]

Dr Wagner was the professor on record, but the course was largely run by Wimber. Wagner would often lecture on missiological or pneumatological issues, then would turn the classroom over to John Wimber for 'clinic time', at which point Wimber would begin to minister to those in attendance, all the while describing the process and phenomena that he observed.[28] MC 510 became one of the most successful (and controversial!) courses in Fuller's history, and put John Wimber, and the Vineyard Movement, on the national stage.

Signs, Wonders, Church Growth: the Beginnings of a Distinct Theology

As early as 1964, John and Carol had experienced healing prayer when their son Sean, who was three-years-old at the time, had wandered into a bees' nest and received dozens of stings. Sean came running back to the yard crying "Flies! Flies!" His body was covered in red welts from the stings. John, who at this point had only been a Christian for a short time, began praying for his son even though he had no theological grid that would support such prayer. To his surprise, Sean was healed instantly and all of the welts disappeared.[29] However, Wimber recounts in *Power Healing* that, even though he did not have a theological system that allowed for the operation of the *charismata,* he continually had charismatic experiences such as praying in tongues, healing, and prophetic insight.

In August of 1977, Wimber had been teaching through the book of Luke at the Yorba Linda Friends church. He was thus forced to teach on the topics of healing and deliverance, even before he or the church engaged in the work of healing. He wrote that the congregation began to pray for the sick before he did, because they practiced what he was preaching! At one point, the church had been actively praying for healing for over eleven months without experiencing a single instance of divine healing. During this time, Wimber read countless books from church history to contemporary writers in the Pentecostal and Charismatic movement. They finally experienced a breakthrough when John prayed for a woman with a fever and she was healed instantly.[30] After this experience, the church continued to experience successful healing prayer on a frequent basis.[31]

....

"power evangelism" is the dramatic conversion of individuals, families, or groups that sometimes occurs after an instance of divine healing or other displays of the Holy Spirit's power.

....

As noted above, when Wimber came to Fuller Seminary as a student, his cessationist position was forcibly challenged by some of the faculty and his fellow students. Wimber notes that some of the students from Majority World countries introduced him to the idea of "power evangelism"; that is, they told him stories of dramatic conversions of individuals, families, and groups that had occurred after an instance of divine healing.

After he became the leader of the fledgling Vineyard movement, Wimber faced a dilemma. Since 1977 he had been convinced that the gifts of the Holy Spirit were meant to be operative in the church. His early exposure to some of the more flamboyant and popular Pentecostal "faith healers" and evangelists had at one time turned him off to the *charismata* entirely. His Quaker sensibilities caused him to be skeptical of dramatic and flamboyant presentations and appearances that were often the hallmark of the popular "faith healers". However, his interest and training in church growth drove him to explore the connection between miracles, evangelism, and church growth. This quest would eventually become one of the principal features of the Vineyard "DNA".

Establishing the Vineyard Genetic Code

While he was at Fuller Seminary, Wimber became intrigued by a concept of sociology called *set theory*, which was introduced to him by Dr Paul Hiebert. Hiebert spoke of organizations forming under three different models: bounded sets, centered-sets, and fuzzy sets.[32] A bounded set is one in which the "boundaries" of who is in or out of the set are clearly revealed in the form of creeds, articles of commitment or even birthplace, race, or genetics. In contrast, *centered-sets* have no such clear markers, as all subjects are oriented towards a commonly agreed upon center.

The Vineyard has often been thought of as a centered-set movement

Thus, the main question in a centered-set is not, "Who is in or outside the set?", but rather, "What is the trajectory of a particular member – towards the center or away from the center?" Wimber was attracted to this concept, perhaps due to his Quaker influence, because he saw it as allowing more freedom within diversity for both individual believers and churches.[33] Alexander Venter, a South African Vineyard pastor who served as John Wimber's research assistant for several years, states it this way:

16

The centered-set is a paradigm or frame of reference that is responsibly liberating. It is a flexible, value-driven society. The idea is that people are drawn to a set of values with which they identify, represented by the center...who the leaders are, and what they represent, attract others, who see in them the kind of life that they would like to live.[34]

Soon after Wimber became the leader of the Vineyard movement, he set out what he described as the Vineyard "genetic code"; that is, the essential characteristics that he hoped would be true of every Vineyard church. The immature genetic code was first presented by John Wimber at a conference for Vineyard pastors in 1983.[35] It was Wimber's desire that the genetic code would become the distinguishing marks of Vineyard churches worldwide, even if expression or presentation of the code may vary owing to cultural or societal conditions.[36] The formal development and declaration of the code became a necessity as the Vineyard movement grew, and more churches chose to "adopt in" to the movement. Venter contends that Wimber realized that the code needed to be formally declared after the controversy with the "Kansas City Prophets" in 1991.[37] Wimber relayed the code often "in formal services, when adopting a church into the Vineyard, when ordaining a new pastor, or when commissioning a new Vineyard that had been planted and was now a fully-fledged church".[38] Venter states the following items as principal elements of the genetic code: teaching and valuing the scriptures, worship, small groups, spiritual gifts, training, ministry to the poor, evangelism, church planting, and ecumenical relationships.

....

The Vineyard "genetic code" as taught by John Wimber had the following elements: Scriptures, worship, small groups, spiritual gifts, training, ministry to the poor, evangelism, church planting, and ecumenical relationships.

....

As we study John Wimber, it will become clear that identifying "what

John thought" is no easy matter. Not only did Wimber change his mind on a number of issues as he grew in understanding, his willingness to give the Spirit room to work also led him to hold many apparent contradictions. Many Vineyard leaders that I have spoken with, identified this ability to hold issues *in tension* as one of Wimber's greatest strengths. These factors place a great deal of importance not just on *what* Wimber thought of any given issue, but *when* and under *what circumstances* his thoughts were captured. Wimber's amazing ability to hold seemingly-contradictory ideas in tension can make understanding his theology quite difficult at times, as we will see. Not only was he able to hold views in tension with one another, he was actually comfortable *in the tension itself.* In order to understand the Vineyard movement, one must understand this willingness to live in a "both/and" existence allows for disagreement, process, and relationship to take pride of place, at times, over hard-and-fast doctrinal stands. This is why the Vineyard has attracted folks from both Reformed *and* Wesleyan backgrounds. Some Vineyardites have a very casual, "low church" approach; others greatly value the sacraments.[39] The Vineyard crosses many social, political, and ethnic lines. Beyond the commitment to inaugurated eschatology, Wimber sought to make room for believers from many backgrounds, beliefs and experiences. It seems like the Vineyard identity, expressed through the DNA and a commitment to be centered-set, is more an *ethos or approach* than a set of rules, doctrinal beliefs, or demands. Once again, many people don't "become" Vineyard; they discover that they "are" Vineyard.

If this is true, then where did this ethos come from? A number of places certainly, but the first formative influence for John Wimber was the little Quaker church where he came to faith. For this reason, it will be these Quaker influences that we will examine first to determine how the Vineyard developed its unique identity.

TWO

The Influence of the Evangelical Friends Church on John Wimber

Evangelical Friends in America

To understand the influence of Quakerism on John Wimber and the Vineyard, it is necessary to understand the place of Yorba Linda Friends Church within the larger historical tradition of the Society of Friends and then, within the particular stream of evangelical American Friends.[1] Quakerism, or the Religious Society of Friends, as they prefer to be called, is a broad and diverse movement that has evolved into numerous groups across the globe.[2] In North America, there are currently four major groups within the Friends tradition.[3] The four groups all trace their heritage to the historical Friends like George Fox, William Penn, Robert Barclay, and the Puritan Movement in England during the seventeenth and eighteenth centuries.[4] During the nineteenth century, however, a major division occurred which created two major streams within the modern Society of Friends.[5] This split occurred primarily as a reaction to, or an embrace of, the dramatic growth of evangelical revivalism in American Protestantism during the middle of the century. As Methodist revivalism swept first across England, and then across the American frontier in the Second Great Awakening, American Quakers were increasingly affected by the theological and practical implications of the "revived" faith.[6] For many, the call to renewal, to holiness, and to a return to the teachings of scripture, was a call to return to the Quaker roots of Fox and Barclay. For many others, however, revivalism – and its theological sister, the holiness movement – represented a grave threat to historical Friends theology and practices. For American Friends, this controversy would cause the "great separation" of 1827–28, which eventually created a divide within the Society of Friends that exists to the present day.[7]

19

In 1887, Quaker representatives from various groups met in Richmond, Indiana to confer and dialogue over issues that had divided them. Delegates of the conference produced the "Richmond Declaration of Faith", which was largely evangelical in its tone and doctrine.[8] In 1947, the Association of Evangelical Friends was formed from groups still associating with yearly meetings in the Gurneyite or revivalist traditions.[9] This group was later reformed as the Evangelical Friends Association, of which Yorba Linda Friends Church was a member. In 1989, the Evangelical Friends Church International was birthed, which included Friends meetings from countries outside the United States. It's important to understand how Yorba Linda Friends Church gave Wimber's churches both Evangelical and Quaker characteristics.

Quaker influences on John Wimber

It is quite obvious that John Wimber was greatly influenced by his Friends heritage and, more specifically, Yorba Linda Friends Church. It is important to understand how and to what degree they influenced Wimber, and then the consequent development of Vineyard theology and activities. To answer these questions, we will consider a number of characteristics of the Friends heritage that greatly impressed Wimber and, in turn, have become foundational characteristics of the Vineyard movement. We will also see that Wimber rejected or heavily modified certain beliefs and practices of Yorba Linda Friends church as well.[10]

Wimber picked up a number of influences from his Quaker church experience that persist in one form or another in the Vineyard to this day. Some of these are:

- a de-emphasis of the clergy-laity distinction
- a low key, non-hyped expectation of the Spirit's working
- caring for the poor and working for justice
- a refusal to treat other Christians, even strong critics, as enemies.

Recalling that John and Carol Wimber's early exposure to faith was not through a "professional" minister, but through Gunnar Payne, a lay leader, it is not surprising that the democratization of ministry, or *de-emphasis of the clergy-laity distinction*, became an essential element of Wimber's approach to ministry.[11] Wimber later canonized this in the Vineyard as "everybody gets to play". In their time at Yorba Linda Friends Church, John led groups, Bible studies, and meetings well before he was recognized as an official church "pastor". Wimber did hold that there were offices of church leadership such as pastors and elders; he recognized that these designations should be given to those who *perform the work* of the office. In his famous response to a Vineyard pastor who questioned him on how to choose elders for his church, Wimber replied: "Elders are those who *Eld*".[12] This commitment to "everybody gets to play" means that *all believers*, not just the professional paid clergy, are called do the work of the ministry. *All* are called to witness and evangelize, *All* are called to pray for the sick, *All* are called to serve and care for the poor.

....

"Everybody gets to play" means that every member of the church is called to evangelize, heal the sick, and serve the poor. These are not just the tasks of the paid clergy, but for all of the believer's in the church.

....

Wimber's early exposure to what he referred to as a Pentecostal extremism and emotionalism caused him to neglect the gifts of the Spirit for many years. When the small group at Yorba Linda Friends Church did begin to experience a move of the Spirit, a simple, yet profound waiting in quietude and expectation characterized their meetings.[13] At the birth of the Vineyard, Wimber would instill this simple, yet bold expectation as a foundational element of Vineyard worship. He avoided any attempt to manipulate, emotionally charge, or "hype up" worship times; in his view this blocked the work of the Spirit and created false expectations and hollow worship. Carol Wimber writes of these early days:

No theatrics, nothing staged....casual and simple. Unpretentious and culturally current. Non-religious and transparent and honest. A 'come as you are' gathering where anyone would fit in, where one wouldn't have to 'dress up' to go to church. Where the leader doesn't look any different than the rest of the people.[14]

Many years later, the Vineyard is still recognized for its simple, casual approach to worship that still expects the Spirit to "show up".[15] Although Yorba Linda Friends had been heavily influenced by Evangelical cessationism and dispensationalism, and so had moved from its "Quaker" roots, Wimber's group found in the tradition the evidence of supernatural phenomena that gave birth to the term, "Quakers".[16] The early Quaker meetings were characterized by a habit of waiting expectantly in silent prayer for the Holy Spirit to fall. When the power of the Holy Spirit fell on them, they often physically trembled or "quaked". Very similar phenomena began to occur in the early Vineyard meetings, and Wimber began to recognize these physical responses as potential signs of the Spirit's presence. We will investigate these physical phenomena in detail a bit later.

Wimber often encouraged preachers or worship leaders that the more the Spirit showed up in power, the more they should "tone down" the emotional hype, energy or language. The reason for this was that Wimber strongly believed that the Spirit of God was enough, and did not have to be assisted by human emotional manipulation. His early experience with flamboyant Pentecostal preachers was in stark contrast to the expectant, quiet, and relaxed approach of the Friends.

From the very early days of the Vineyard, Wimber instilled the values of caring for the poor, working for justice, and feeding the homeless or destitute.[17] If anything, the Friends tradition is most known for its concern for prisoners and the poor, and its work against institutional injustice and racism. Carol Wimber recalls John's sincere desire to serve the poor before they had become a Vineyard when he told her: "If God ever has me pastor a church again, I pray we will devote ourselves to the poor".[18] While at the Anaheim Vineyard, Wimber established one of the largest food shelves in the area. Since then, numerous Vineyard churches have established food shelves, language training programs, even job training and employment counseling.

Historically, the Friends have been both criticized and honored for their commitment to pacifism and non-resistance. [19] While Wimber did not embrace pacifism *per se,* he at times did embrace the idea of pacifism, especially in responding to his critics or enemies. In the 1990s, when he came under significant personal and corporate attack, he published an *Equipping the Saints* article titled: "Why I don't respond to criticism".[20] According to Carol Wimber, this conviction came to Wimber at a Friends camp in 1976, where John became convicted that he should not openly defend himself against public attack, but instead, let his public actions and reputation speak for itself.[21] Wimber was fond of telling his pastors, "Your enemy is never your real enemy...even when he acts like it".[22]

THREE

The Influence of Evangelicalism and Pentecostalism on the Vineyard

The Impact of Evangelicalism on John Wimber

As mentioned earlier, Yorba Linda Friends Church identified itself with the evangelical Friends movement, an identification that continues to this day. It is clear, then, that much of John's Wimber's early theological formation was influenced by Evangelicalism, first by Gunnar Payne, and then YLFC. This influence began very early in his conversion process – the interactions with Gunnar, John and Carol's subsequent participation in the Bible study group led by Payne, and the conversations with his sister-in-law and her husband significantly formed Wimber's mature philosophy of ministry. From this early connection to Payne, Wimber *experienced* numerous Protestant Evangelical practices, even before his conversion to Christianity.[1] Some of these influences that worked their way into the Vineyard identity are:

- a focus on conversion, repentance and sanctification
- a high view of the Bible for edification and instruction
- culturally-relevant mission

The first evangelical trait that Wimber observed, and later embraced, was the focus on the "new birth", or the process of conversion, repentance, and sanctification.[2] Wimber observed this process in his close friends Dick and Lynn Heying,[3] and then among other people that attended Gunnar Payne's Bible study. It is impossible to overestimate the influence of these early evangelical experiences on the development of Wimber's thought. His later involvement with Calvary Chapel, his association with the Fuller Institute of Church Growth, and his inclusion of these evangelical characteristics within the Vineyard "DNA" are all natural outcomes of his early experiences at YLFC and his relationship with Gunnar Payne.[4] As Wimber matured in his leadership skills, he was given more responsibility at YLFC. He personally led numerous small groups, and taught in larger gatherings. However, evangelism was always a significant element of his life during this period.[5] His proficiency in this task led to his becoming a paid staff pastor at YLFC in 1970.[6] Evangelism, the new birth, sanctification, and the fulfillment of the "great commission" (Matthew 28), continued to be a significant element of his ministry throughout his tenure at YLFC, in Calvary Chapel and into the Vineyard.[7]

In the Bible studies led by Gunnar Payne, Wimber was exposed to another significant hallmark of evangelical identity, namely a high view of the Bible, signified by the expectation that each believer read and study the scriptures to seek understanding, in order to maintain a relationship with Jesus. This act was to happen in both individual, small group, and corporate gatherings. When John and Carol Wimber interrogated Gunnar Payne about the person and mission of Jesus, and the reality of personal conversion, Payne's reliance on the scriptures provided Wimber with a model that he would never waver from. Even many years later, when he was speaking before crowds of thousands as the leading figure of the signs and wonders movement, Wimber was still essentially an expository preacher. In the early days of the Vineyard movement, Wimber's emphasis on "equipping the saints" for ministry was grounded in his robust reading and application of the Bible. His teaching ministry, first at Yorba Linda Friends Church, then at Calvary Chapel and in the Vineyard, was all built upon the foundation that was laid in his life in those early days of learning from Gunnar Payne.[8]

After Wimber left YLFC in 1975, and began to attend Calvary Chapel, he became an eager disciple of Chuck Smith's approach to ministry.[9] Smith had intentionally designed his ministry outreach to be attractive to the hippie culture of Southern California. Services were often casual, open-air affairs, sometimes on the beach. Music was generally built around the rock music culture – the worship music often sounded like soft-rock songs that could be heard on the radio. Attire was casual, even "beach wear", and there was very much a "come as you are" ethic.[10] For youth that were turned off to the formalistic and staid mainstream church culture, the casual and contemporary style of the Calvary Chapels presented fewer barriers to their religious searching.

Wimber was obviously impressed with this intentional value of being culturally relevant, considering his previous experiences of churches being extremely out of step with culture as we previously discussed.[11] Calvary's emphasis on being culturally engaged is a long-held feature of Evangelical Protestantism in America. In contrast to Protestant Fundamentalism, early Evangelicals sought to *critically engage* with secular culture, rather than withdraw and disengage from secular culture as fundamentalists had in the early decades of the twentieth century.[12] In his attempt to create a church culture that would be attractive to the hippie generation, Smith had continued in the trajectory. When Wimber began leading the Vineyard movement, *Culturally Relevant Mission* became one of the movement's key values.[13]

....

Culturally Relevant Mission has become one of the hallmarks of the Vineyard movement- this does not mean changing the Gospel to fit the expectations of the culture, but communicating the Gospel in ways that make sense to the culture.

....

The Impact of Pentecostalism and the Charismatic Movement on John Wimber

As John Wimber began to shed his cessationist ideas he realized that he had come to his belief, not from a careful and reasoned study of the Bible or theology, but rather from his personal distaste of popular faith-healing personalities.[14] Thus, it wasn't the gift of divine healing that he rejected; rather it was the *models of healing* that he had been exposed to that he believed to be strange, culturally or socially inept, or, in his words, not "with it". As a former professional musician and jazz player, the

27

Pentecostal healers he had seen or heard of were simply "uncool".[15] Despite his occasional experiences with divine healing, such as the healing of his son Sean[16], Wimber was still quite skeptical; that is, until he met what he considered to be reliable, trustworthy models – first at Fuller Seminary, and then in the Charismatic and Pentecostal world.

Wimber's cessationist ideas were first challenged by missionaries and students at Fuller Seminary who had witnessed significant charismatic experiences of physical healing. Recalling this time in his book, *Power Healing,* Wimber wrote:

> I met professors like Donald McGavran, Chuck Kraft, Paul Hiebert, and the School of Theology's Russell Spittler. Their courses and reports of signs and wonders from the Third World once again softened my heart toward the Holy Spirit and divine healing. I was especially impressed by the relationship between charismatic gifts like healing and church growth in Third World countries. Not only was there numerical growth, there was vitality and integrity in many Third World churches.[17]

Because these reliable witnesses challenged his presuppositions, he began an urgent study of the Bible to understand all that he could about the charismatic gifts. Once he was convinced that his early cessationist views were suspect, he began to eagerly and regularly pray for the sick in order to develop patterns and practices that would reflect his convictions. He also began to seek out and read popular authors that practiced divine healing, in order to glean as much as he could from their experiences. Wimber became personal friends with many of the leaders of the Charismatic Movement of the 1960s and 1970s. The "Charismatic Movement" refers to the dramatic rise in charismatic experiences within traditional Catholic, mainline, and Evangelical Protestant churches in the latter half of the twentieth century. [18]

Unlike classical Pentecostalism, Charismatics chose to stay *in* their denominations, and yet seek charismatic experiences, rather than leave these churches and traditions and form new ones, as many Pentecostals had done in previous generations. [19]

···

The Charismatic movement or the "Second Wave of the Holy Spirit" differed from Pentecostalism in that Charismatics chose to stay in their existing churches and denominations, even as they sought out powerful charismatic experiences of the Holy Spirit.

···

Wimber found solid teaching and much common ground with practitioners from many theological backgrounds. Father Francis McNutt, a Catholic, became a mentor and a dear friend.[20] The Episcopalian priest Dennis Bennett was also a strong influence.[21] Other notable Charismatic authors that influenced Wimber as he studied the topic of divine healing include Ralph Martin, Michael Green, Martin Lloyd-Jones, Donald Gee, and Russell Spittler.[22] It is important to note that what Wimber sought from these authors was not a *theology* of healing, but rather, techniques, insights, and experiences related to the actual *practice* of divine healing. Because he considered the Charismatics to be closer to him theologically than the Pentecostals he knew at the time, Wimber made many enduring friendships among the Charismatic practitioners.[23] He willingly had Charismatic leaders submit articles to *First Fruits* and *Equipping the Saints*,[24] allowing them to teach at conferences on healing, and he became a frequent guest on Charismatic-oriented television shows like *The 700 Club* and the Christian Broadcasting Network.

As Wimber enthusiastically embraced his new theology and practice of healing, he then went back into the Pentecostal tradition; this time with his eyes more open. Although he still had some reservations about certain unusual approaches to healing,[25] he now understood that the practice could be real and vital to the church. So he began to investigate the healing ministries of famous Pentecostals such as Oral Roberts, Aimee Semple McPherson and Kathryn Kuhlman.[26] However, he did so with eschatology from Ladd firmly in place; thus, while he accepted and borrowed the practices of many Pentecostal healers, he rejected certain aspects of their Pneumatology, such as their conception of the baptism of the Holy Spirit, the so-called Second Blessing, and their doctrine of tongues being the initial evidence of that baptism.[27]

....

Wimber disagreed with Pentecostal theology on three major areas: The "second blessing" or "subsequence" view of the baptism of the Holy Spirit, speaking in tongues as evidence of that blessing, and healing being "guaranteed" in the atonement.

....

As Wimber studied these sources, he realized that divine healing of the body had been operative throughout church history up until the post-Reformation period, when the so-called "mystical" practices of the Catholic Church were called into question.[28] While most Pentecostals at the time held a "constitutional" view of the gifts, Wimber's experience caused him to question this. The *constitutional* view, refers to a person's "constitution" or innate ability, like an athletic, musical, or mathematical talent.

He began to understand that not only physical healing, but healing from emotional wounds, and even deliverance from the influence of demonic spirits could be *taught and developed* in the church; that is to say, these were gifts that could be *learned* and therefore the practices themselves could be *studied, practiced,* and therefore *improved upon.*[29]

....

The Constitutional view of the gifts teaches that the gifts of the Spirit are similar to how we would say "She is a natural musician" or "He is a gifted athlete".

....

He later wrote: "I also read every Christian book about healing I could find. My motive was not only to learn how I could pray effectively for the sick, but to *learn how I could learn to train and equip every member of my congregation to pray for the sick*".[30] My personal history in the Vineyard bears this out. Before I came into the Vineyard, I had assumed that the gifts were expressed by people who had been given the gift – much like someone might have natural musical or athletic talent, or the ability to understand mathematics. Hence, just as people were "natural athletes", I thought some people were "natural" healers, prophets, or so on. When I read and heard Vineyard teachers declaring: "everybody gets to play" and speaking of the *situational* view of the gifts, I realized that this made much more scriptural and theological sense. (We will discuss these issues in more detail in a following chapter). I began to learn as much as I could about praying for the sick and prophecy, and began to *practice* the use of these gifts. Like many people, this new perspective completely overturned my view of ministry and the work of the Holy Spirit.[31]

....

Because Wimber had a situational, rather than a constitutional, view of the gifts of the Spirit, he understood that the use of the gifts could be taught and built up in the church, as he had done at Fuller with MC 510.

....

Wimber's new journey brought him into familiarity with other *charisms* that he had formerly rejected, such as speaking in tongues and prophecy. Once again, he turned first to the scriptures, and then to contemporary sources to understand these phenomena. While he would never place the importance on tongues that the Pentecostals had, he did come to recognize the gift as a legitimate charismatic expression. He embraced prophetic gifting as well, which would eventually, for better or for worse, be nearly as well known in his ministry as healing.

Finally, he did come to appreciate and value historic Pentecostalism as an authentic, biblical and timely expression of the global church, even as he maintained significant theological disagreements over certain aspects of their practice and theology.[32] Furthermore, he counted many Pentecostals as close friends, and developed lifelong ministerial and professional relationships with many Pentecostal ministers, theologians, and healers. In many ways, he saw his calling as the "Pentecostalizing" of the traditional Evangelical church, or restoring the appreciation and practice of the *charismata* in mainstream Evangelical churches.

The Worldwide influence of the Vineyard Movement

John Wimber's untimely death in 1997 was not only a blow to the Vineyard, but to countless churches, groups, and denominations that had come to embrace his model of church renewal.[33] Wimber's ecumenical sensibilities and his willingness to love and accept the whole range of historical Christian expression had been birthed at Fuller, expanded in his renewal ministries, and evidenced by the pastors and leaders from many dozens of denominations and traditions that attended his funeral. After his passing, the Vineyard movement reorganized itself again, and named a young protégé of Wimber, Todd Hunter, to be his successor as National Director of the Movement in the U.S.A. It remained to be seen, however, if the theology, values, and practices put in place by Wimber would remain after his formidable presence was gone. In the popular press, there was certainly some speculation about whether the movement would survive once Wimber's forceful personality and brilliant mind had passed from the scene.[34]

However, there was even more complexity, as Wimber's travels worldwide, and the emphasis on overseas church planting in the 1990s onwards, began to show results. By the year 2000, only three years after Wimber's death, there were national or regional Vineyard bodies all across the globe, with growing churches and influential leaders in Scandinavia, Great Britain, Europe, Africa, Asia and Latin America.[35]

Wimber's ecumenical sensibilities bore fruit beyond the worldwide Vineyard movement. In Great Britain, his ministry partnerships birthed a new expression within the Anglican Communion, namely the New Wine Movement. Wimber had traveled to London as early as 1981, where he held renewal meetings at Anglican churches led by David Pytches, David Watson, and Sandy Millar.[36] Wimber's desire to renew Evangelicalism, which Peter Wagner had coined "The Third Wave", continued to develop after his death as well. While there is no official "Third Wave" association per se, numerous prominent Evangelical churches in America function quite like Wimber's vision of renewal, and yet do not affiliate with the

Vineyard Movement.[37] These Evangelical congregations have rejected both cessationism *and* core Pentecostal doctrines like the baptism of the Holy Spirit being a separate, identifiable experience subsequent to conversion with speaking in tongues as initial evidence of this baptism. Formal membership in organizations such as the Christian Churches Together, as well as the National Association of Evangelicals is further evidence of Ecumenical participation of the Vineyard movement.[38]

As the Vineyard was faced by ecclesial and ethical issues in the post-Wimber era, the theological responses were developed out of the theology, values, and priorities established by Wimber and the early leadership of the Vineyard. However, it became evident that tensions in these values created issues that could not be ignored. For example, the solid evangelical background of the Vineyard led to a commitment to the teachings of scripture, and yet, the value of culturally-relevant mission often revealed a struggle between interpreting scripture and communicating the truth of scripture in a way that was understandable by the surrounding culture. What is more, the commitment to being a centered-set, rather than a bounded set movement, created pressures about defining the boundaries of the Vineyard movement; that is, as the movement sought to define itself in the post-Toronto period,[39] one of the difficulties was doing so from a bounded set perspective, and understanding exactly how – and if! – Toronto had betrayed the Vineyard DNA.[40]

While numerous specific issues have come to the fore in recent years that were only marginally present in the Wimber years, the issue of women's role in ministry was the first major test of the post-Wimber process of corporate leadership and discernment. No longer would one dominant voice rule the conversation, namely that of Wimber's, but more remarkably, Wimber's "voice" was only one voice among others; the question of "What was John's view" was no longer the definitive answer to any particular question.[41] In place of Wimber's dynamic presence, arose a diverse, corporate and communal decision-making process, based on dialogue, interaction, and mutual biblical and theological reflection.[42]

As the Vineyard began to plant churches in major urban centers, and primarily ethnic congregations grew as a result, it was inevitable that the issues of justice, diversity, reconciliation, and immigration reform would arise. All these issues were addressed as practical ethical demands of kingdom eschatology, which held caring for the poor and breaking down barriers between peoples as an essential feature of the "works" of the kingdom of God. As previously noted, concern for the poor had been in the Vineyard DNA from its inception. The issues of justice and racial reconciliation were well noted at times in Vineyard history, and would become a growing concern in the twenty-first century, with the creation of numerous justice initiatives and conferences.[43] More will be said of this growing understanding of ethnicity and reconciliation in a concluding chapter.

From the very early days of the movement, Wimber understood that inaugurated eschatology would eventually impact all facets of church life- including justice, ethnic reconciliation and care for the marginalized of society.

The Vineyard U.S.A. developed a national initiative, Mercy Response, which focused on sending supplies, volunteers, and practical assistance to areas which had seen significant natural disasters, such as hurricanes, tornados and flooding. 2008 saw the creation of a national justice task force which focused on propagating the message of justice and assisting local Vineyard congregations to pursue justice.[44]

This group grew to become the Vineyard Justice Network, focusing on issues like:

- sex trafficking
- modern-day slavery
- immigration reform
- caring for the environment
- systemic poverty and injustice.

A growing justice issue is the concern for the environment and global climate change. Beginning with the publishing of *Saving God's Green Earth: Rediscovering the Church's Responsibility to Environmental Stewardship* in 2006, the issue of environmental stewardship and climate change was included in the justice rubric.[45] Noted Christian environmentalists like Dr Calvin DeWitt have been engaged by Vineyard leaders and invited to speak at conferences and churches.[46] Environmental stewardship was included on the agenda of the first national conference focused on justice issues in November 2013, and is likely to be a continuing concern as the movement continues to engage culture from its inaugurated eschatological framework.

Conclusion: A Unique founder, a unique movement

We have seen that John Wimber greatly influenced the identity of the Vineyard movement itself. However, it is equally clear that an essential element of Wimber's genius was precisely his willingness to investigate and absorb sources and influences dramatically different from his own, and to incorporate these influences into his thinking as he saw fit. These abilities to recognize, clarify, and evaluate theological concepts served Wimber not only in his quest to form a sustainable, healthy church organization, but he continued to rely on these gifts as he sought theological grounding for his church. Wimber's brilliance and ability to combine diverse sources is especially displayed in his blending of eschatological and pneumatological concepts to form a new theological hybrid that would become the bedrock of Vineyard identity. While it was often frustrating for many of his key leaders, his ability to hold competing ideas in tension allowed him time and patience to "see what the Father was doing" in the Vineyard. In order to understand Wimber's experiment, it is first necessary to have an understanding of the fundamental elements he chose to work with, primarily the "inaugurated eschatology" of George Eldon Ladd. Ladd's work, in turn, stands as the culmination of a century of modern investigation into the meaning of the kingdom of God in the preaching of Jesus. It is to this subject that we will now turn.

Questions for discussion:

1. If the Vineyard is just "one vegetable in God's stew", what do other churches or denominations contribute to the diversity of worship styles, approaches to ministry, or ways of doing ministry that make the overall Church (big "C") healthy or stronger? What do various theologies or practices of churches other than the Vineyard contribute that we can appreciate and be thankful for?

2. It was stated that John Wimber came from a family with no church attenders in the previous four generations. In what ways might this background influence Wimber's expectations of church, or his understanding of what the church should be? What might he see differently, be confused by, or not understand? What things might he seek to change when he began leading his own church?

3. Gunnar Payne was a model for Wimber in many ways. Why do you think Gunnar's life story had such an impact on Wimber as a young Christian? Why do you think John was so attracted to Gunnar even though they were so different in age, experiences, and occupations?

4. John Wimber moved from a position of cessationism regarding the gifts of the Spirt to one of continuationism. How might your faith and experiences change if you believed in cessationism? What about the activity and practices of the church?

5. Why do you think the exposure to Majority World students and missionaries had such an impact on Wimber while he was at Fuller Seminary? What changed in his worldview?

Section II: Eschatology in the Vineyard

This section introduces one of the main themes of the book, which is the concept of the kingdom of God in the Vineyard. As our central question is exploring the relationship between the work of the Spirit and the establishment of the kingdom of God in the Vineyard movement, this chapter plays an essential role. Before we begin the examination of the Vineyard's theology of the kingdom of God, it is necessary to understand the background of kingdom of God studies in the last century.

It is no exaggeration to state that the theme of the kingdom of God has been one of the dominant themes of recent Protestant theology. Since Albrecht Ritschl published his *Justification and Reconciliation* in 1870, which placed the kingdom of God as a central theme, scholars have recognized that no understanding of the message of Jesus can be complete unless one engages with the idea of the kingdom of God. In turn, numerous Protestant church traditions have approached the concept of the kingdom from their perspectives. The objective of these chapters is to place Vineyard eschatology within the background of two major late modern Protestant options: American Pentecostalism and Evangelicalism.

This chapter will proceed as follows. First, we will consider the history of kingdom of God studies of the late nineteenth and twentieth centuries. In connection to this study, the quest culminated in an evangelical consensus represented by the work of George Eldon Ladd, who had a primary influence on John Wimber. Thus, it is necessary to review Ladd's work in greater detail. We will then look at two contemporary Protestant traditions – Evangelicalism and Pentecostalism – to see how key elements of their eschatology fit with this consensus.

Finally, I will attempt the same process with the Vineyard by placing it in context with this broader theological conversation on eschatology. Included in this section will be more engagement with important concepts within the Old and New Testaments that are found in Vineyard eschatology. At the end of this chapter, it will become evident that not only has the Vineyard significantly engaged in the broader theological tradition on this topic, but, more significantly, has challenged various elements of the consensus from not only theological, but practical concerns. For the Vineyard movement, *living the future* meant taking the fundamental understanding of the kingdom and seeing everything else – church planting, ministry, signs and wonders, etc. – as essential elements of the kingdom life.

FOUR

The Kingdom of God in Twentieth Century Theology

In many churches today, it is quite common to hear Evangelicals and Pentecostals speak of "the kingdom of God", "the already–not yet kingdom" or even "fulfillment without consummation". It would not be an exaggeration to state that the investigation into the meaning and significance of Jesus' preaching about kingdom of God has been one of the dominant questions in Protestant theology in the last 150 years.

The contemporary understanding of the kingdom is a treasure that was not easily gained. The nineteenth-century conception of the kingdom was essentially an ethical, this-worldly expression of "the brotherhood of man under the fatherhood of God". This view of the kingdom could be considered "ethical" because it is focused on the teachings like the Sermon on the Mount that revealed a moral code of how to treat other human beings. To Western intellectuals who had recently seen the triumphs of the French and American revolutions that sought to free individuals from the tyranny of kings and monarchies, Jesus' ethical teaching seemed to provide them with religious justification for the rights of men to life, liberty, justice, the pursuit of happiness. These scholars considered the success of the American Revolution, in particular, to be an "example" of what the kingdom of God might look like, namely liberty, and how it was to be accomplished through the effort and work of men. Many of these scholars sought to strip the "historical Jesus" from the supernatural, miracle-working Jesus that was a creation of his disciples' imagination.

Near the turn of the twentieth century, this ethical conception was challenged by theologians who emphasized the *eschatological,* the "not yet", character of the kingdom message. Reaction to this eschatological over-emphasis predictably saw a growing concern with Jesus' curious proclamation that the kingdom had come in his person, the "already". The final synthesis brought together both elements, the eschatological and the imminent, in sharper focus. For each step in our brief overview, two questions will be considered. The first question will be: "What is the nature of the kingdom of God?" and the second will be: "What is the timing of the kingdom's coming?" In each of the positions noted, these crucial questions consistently come to the fore, so it is important to clarify and contrast these various positions.

In order to comprehend fully the interaction between the Vineyard's conception of the kingdom of God and its practice, a brief overview is given of the various possibilities of interpretation of the kingdom idea.[1] In order to do this, we will quickly review the major steps of the quest and representative figures that significantly contributed to the contemporary understanding of the kingdom. This discussion will conclude with a study of George Eldon Ladd. In order to appreciate Ladd's place in this story, and his substantial influence on John Wimber, some historical background is required.

Early Investigations of the Kingdom of God

Our story begins with what theologians and biblical scholars call "the first Quest for the Historical Jesus". The aim of this "Quest" was to uncover the "true Jesus" from all of the "mythological" stories (the canonical gospels) written about him. Herman Reimarus (1694–1768) was a historian who was widely credited for beginning the "lives of Jesus" movement. In *Fragments*, the collection of his writings, he posited a radical distinction between the message of Jesus, who saw himself as a political revolutionary, and thus expected the renewed Davidic kingdom to come in his mission, and the early church, who had to create an explanation of two "comings" to account for the mistaken understanding of Jesus *and* the subsequent "delay" of the *parousia*.

....

The parousia is a technical Greek expression for the royal visit of a dignitary, king or emperor.

....

40

One of the more influential of these "lives" was written in 1835 by David Friedrich Strauss (1808–1874), titled *The Life of Jesus, Critically Examined*. Strauss was one of the first scholars to claim that the miracles and supernatural events of the gospels were mythical or made up by Jesus' followers in the decades after his death. In the middle of the nineteenth century, it had become quite fashionable in German theological circles to write studies on "the life of Jesus" that basically followed Strauss. Once the "lives of Jesus" studies began, it was inevitable that the topic of the kingdom of God would come to the fore.

The modern quest on the kingdom of God began with Albrecht Ritschl's (1882–1889) massive investigation of the concept in his book, *Justification and Reconciliation*. Many commentators have disagreed about the final view of Ritschl on the kingdom. In the early revisions, the kingdom of God seems to have a more ethical nature, as he described the nature of the kingdom as "the moral organization of humanity through action inspired by love".[2] Later volumes, especially the final revision, seem to give a concept of the kingdom of God as not only ethical but spiritual in some way also. However, Ritschl does not refute his earlier work, and thus it is difficult to state Ritschl's view on the kingdom of God conclusively.

The "Quests" for the historical Jesus:
- **First Quest**: "lives of Jesus", Reimarus, Strauss, Schweitzer – late eighteenth> early twentieth centuries.
- **Second Quest**: Ernst Käsemann, Günther Bornkamm 1953 -> "Jesus Seminar": Robert W. Funk, John Dominic Crossan, 1985 >
- **Third Quest**: John P. Meier, N.T. Wright – 1990's ->

Consistent Eschatology: Weiss and Schweitzer

It was into this setting that Ritschl's son-in-law, Joachim Weiss, began his contribution to kingdom studies with a severe critique of Ritschl's work. In his *Jesus' Proclamation of the Kingdom of God* (1890)[3], written only three years after Ritschl's death, Weiss strongly challenged Ritschl for his purely ethical version of the kingdom of God, which, Weiss argued, entirely missed the eschatological aspect of the kingdom. By reducing the kingdom to an ethical idea only, Ritschl essentially misunderstood the nature of Jesus preaching the kingdom as being a *future event*. In fact, Weiss contended that there were only two possibilities: either the kingdom came fully in the life and ministry of Jesus, or, it was a purely futuristic apocalyptic event: "either the *basileia* is here or it is not here".[4]

....

The New Testament Greek word for kingdom is basileia; basileia tou theou, is translated into English as "kingdom of God" or "reign of God".

....

Since the kingdom of God obviously did not come in the life of Jesus, because human history has continued, the only option is to understand the kingdom as a completely futuristic event at the end of time. Also, according to Weiss, the nineteenth-century interpreters had understood the kingdom to be primarily a human endeavor, whereas the gospel writers teach that the kingdom is the work of God alone.[5] Jesus saw himself as the fulcrum, the very turning point of history, with the triumphant kingdom of God immediately at hand.[6] This kingdom was not of this world; neither spiritual in the lives of believers, nor continuously existing in another realm. The kingdom was to come at the final cataclysmic, apocalyptic end of history. Despite his pronouncements about the immediacy and dawning of the *parousia*, the kingdom had not come, and thus, Jesus was *mistaken both about his identity and about the nature of the kingdom itself*. Jesus was, in Weiss' view, a failed and misguided prophet who was wrong about his identity and the nature of the kingdom of God.[7]

Weiss' work brought to light an interesting problem, and three significant questions that all subsequent kingdom scholars have struggled with. The *problem* was this: "What happened to the second coming of Jesus?" This issue of the delay of the second coming would perplex and confuse scholars for decades. The problem is quite simple: in reading the gospels, and the rest of the New Testament, it seems that *both* Jesus and the early church expected his imminent return, and yet, more than 1900 years later, it seemed quite evident that Jesus had not returned. How do we account for this? *Did* the kingdom come? Was Jesus mistaken? Or were these proclamations "made up" by the gospel writers and not original to Jesus himself? After Weiss, Kingdom of God studies began to circle around three crucial questions on the kingdom.

They are:

1. *When* does the kingdom come? In the ministry of Jesus? The early church? At creation? In the future?

2. *Who brings* the kingdom, or *how does it come*? Is the kingdom entirely a work of God, or does it come by human effort? Or perhaps some of both?

3. *What* does it look like? Is the kingdom a physical realm (like the kingdom of Great Britain, or France), or is it merely spiritual? Can we *see* the kingdom? Can we determine its boundaries?

Various scholars and teachers offered different answers to these questions, but after the work of Weiss, nobody could ignore them.

Weiss was followed by Albert Schweitzer, who also highlighted the eschatological dimension. In many ways, Schweitzer was merely popularizing Weiss' views. Schweitzer, in his famous The Quest for the Historical Jesus: from Reimarus to Wrede (1906), argued for "*konsequente Eschatologie*" (consistent eschatology); that is, eschatology was not limited merely to Jesus' teachings in the parables, but was, in fact, the key to understanding the entire teachings and mission of Jesus – thus, his teaching was consistent, thoroughgoing eschatology.[8] Jesus saw himself as the eschatological prophet that was to usher in the kingdom of God.

The primary basis for understanding the *entire* message of Jesus was not through his *ethical* teachings, especially the Sermon on the Mount, as Ritschl had done, but rather through the ideas in Jewish apocalyptic writings.[9] Like Weiss, Schweitzer was devastatingly critical of the nineteenth-century "lives of Jesus" studies that tended to portray Jesus as an educated, sophisticated, liberal gentlemen of the Enlightenment.

Schweitzer speaks of the "liberal" lives of Jesus with not a little derision in *Quest,* but concedes that their futile quest laid the groundwork for the rise of the eschatological approaches. Schweitzer thought that Reimarus and Strauss overlooked the radical and completely eschatological nature of Jesus' life and ministry, so he revised Reimarus' insights regarding the nature of Jesus' teaching on the kingdom.[10] While he regarded Reimarus' work as a "masterpiece of world literature", he also spoke of the work as making a "fundamental error" by offering a political, renewed Davidic kingdom as the essential message of the preacher Jesus.[11]

Schweitzer argued that as a result of the "Quest", theologians were given two very divergent options: either they accept the "thoroughgoing skepticism" of those like Reimarus which saw very little historical validity in the story of Jesus, or they accept Schweitzer's "thoroughgoing eschatology" which understood Jesus properly placed within his Jewish apocalyptic first century context.[12]

Despite the failure of the first quest to reveal the true nature of the "historical Jesus",[13] the modern theologians had revealed an uncomfortable historical truth: the character of Jesus was less the triumphant eschatological "Son of Man" and more a flawed and pitiful hero. For it is clear that despite his pronouncements of the coming end, Jesus was mistaken about his role and the plan of history, because the expected end *did not come* in his lifetime! Even worse, he lost his own life desperately waiting for it. Schweitzer's famous statement is quite telling:

The Baptist appears, and cries 'Repent, for the Kingdom of heaven is at hand.' Soon after that comes Jesus, and, in the knowledge that He is the coming Son of Man, lays hold of the wheel of the world to set it moving on the last revolution which is to bring all ordinary history to a close. It refuses to turn, and He throws himself upon it. Then it does turn; and crushes Him. Instead of bringing in the eschatological conditions, He has destroyed them. The wheel rolls onward, and the mangled body of the one immeasurably great Man, who is strong enough to think of Himself as the spiritual ruler of mankind and to bend history to His purpose, is hanging upon it still. That is His victory and

His reign.[14]

Further, because his message was entirely eschatological, there was no sense that his teaching or ministry had any present spiritual practicality; the kingdom belonged completely to the age to come.

This Jesus of Nazareth who came forward publicly as the Messiah, who preached the ethic of the kingdom of God, who founded the Kingdom of Heaven upon earth, and died to give His work its final consecration, never had any existence. He is a figure designed by rationalism, endowed with life by liberalism, and clothed by modern theology in historical garb.[15]

For Schweitzer, the choice was clear. The historical skepticism and failure of the "lives of Jesus" projects left only the way marked by Weiss: Jesus was *the* eschatological prophet, and his life, and his message, can only be understood in the context of a thoroughgoing eschatological lens.

Realized Eschatology: C.H. Dodd

Since we now understand the background of the purely "not yet" view of the kingdom, we need to look at the totally "already" view. The interpretive bombshell dropped by Weiss and Schweitzer was bound to provoke a counter reaction. Charles Harold Dodd (1884–1973) proposed the antithesis to the consistent school by reaffirming the kingdom sayings that focused on the in-time and historical nature of the kingdom. Dodd argued that, while undoubtedly elements of Jesus' teaching did relate to the final cosmological end of history, Schweitzer had gone too far by arguing that the "realized" elements of the kingdom were creations of the early church who "edited" the gospels after the expected end did not come.[16] Dodd understood that a brief reading of the gospels makes it quite evident that Jesus thought that the kingdom was present in his person and ministry. In his view, Jesus straightforward teachings of the kingdom all supported realized eschatology; the apocalyptic perspective came primarily through the parables.[17] He reasoned therefore, that because the realized teachings were more forthright, plain, and required less subjective

45

interpretation they should be considered as the best evidence of the view most emphasized by Jesus.[18]

When Jesus said "the kingdom of God has come upon you" (RSV), [19] *ephthasen* ("is come") can only mean that the kingdom is immediate and accessible. So, the kingdom of God is historical, presently experienced by Jesus hearers, and connected with the personhood of Jesus: "In some way the kingdom of God has come with Jesus Himself".[20]

Dodd argued strongly that the "consistent eschatology" teachers had made a huge mistake. In their attempt to negotiate a compromise by asserting the "nearness" of the kingdom, they negated the plain meaning of the explicit passages which stated that the kingdom wasn't just near, but had actually come in the ministry of Jesus. The evidence of the arrival of the kingdom is found in Jesus' own words in his response to John's followers: "The blind see, the lame walk, the lepers are cleansed, the deaf hear, the dead are raised, the poor have the gospel preached to them" (Luke 7:21). Interestingly, Dodd thought that the kingdom is an act of God alone, and man can do nothing to hasten its coming, build it, or grow it.[21]

Placing the correct emphasis on the immediacy of the kingdom was a helpful correction to the purely eschatological school. However, if the message of the kingdom is historical, and present in the ministry of Jesus, Dodd still had to explain the significance of the eschatological sayings. Dodd's answer to this was to argue that the apocalyptic sayings of Jesus are primarily *symbolic*; that is, they point to an existent reality *beyond* time, space, and human comprehension.[22] So he almost agrees with Schweitzer that Jesus must be understood in the context of Jewish apocalyptic, even though Jesus dramatically revised the apocalyptic message far beyond what his hearers could comprehend. Dodd thought that he could make sense of the historical problem of the *parousia* by understanding that the apocalyptic sayings have a deep symbolic background in Jewish eschatology, such as the mysterious teachings in the book of Daniel.[23] The sayings of Jesus also point beyond the historical plane, to an absolute, eternal reality that cannot be adequately captured in human language. Thus, the eschatological sayings belong to the "absolute order" of reality, and are not expected to be fulfilled in salvation history;

that is, in the time of Jesus, the early church, or in our time.[24]

The *parables*, then, serve as commentaries of sorts on the life and ministry of Jesus; that is, they are only teaching tools of a particular time in history. They explain the present, active kingdom in the ministry of Jesus.

It is in this context that the parables of the kingdom of God must be placed. They use all the resources of dramatic illustration to help men to see that in the events before their eyes – in the miracles of Jesus, His appeal to men and its results, the blessedness that comes to those who follow Him, and the hardening of those who reject Him – God is confronting them in His kingdom, power and glory. This world has become the scene of a divine drama, in which the eternal issues are laid bare. It is the hour of decision. It is realized eschatology.[25]

Attempted Solutions to the Paradox: Rudolph Bultmann

As we have seen, at this time in kingdom studies, there were two clear and contrasting alternatives. The first option was the purely future eschatological view of the kingdom, namely the totally "not yet", and the second option was an entirely present view of the kingdom of God, the totally "already". So in many ways, Dodd's helpful correction to the purely eschatological view of the kingdom by the *consistent* School put a challenge before all the interpreters and scholars who would study the kingdom. It would seem that Schweitzer and Dodd had proved that both consistent and realized eschatology had reasonable support in the gospel texts, and yet neither attempt to dismiss the counter-example texts was particularly convincing. It became evident that either some sort of synthesis, or an entirely new approach, had to be formed.

One of the more theologically creative attempts was that of Rudolph Bultmann (1884–1976), who attempted to solve the apparent paradox of the kingdom by "demythologizing" the kingdom message, and recasting it as the existential call to commitment offered to a person by Christ.[26] Following the *konsequente* pattern, Bultmann agreed with Schweitzer that Jewish apocalyptic was the proper lens by which the modern reader could see best the message of the gospels.[27] However, Bultmann suggested a different solution to the problem of the delayed *parousia*.[28] He thought that previous interpreters had made a fundamental mistake by defining the kingdom as a *historical reality*, whether present in the ministry of Jesus (Dodd) or coming at the end of history (Weiss and Schweitzer). Because the teaching of Jesus on the kingdom belonged to the first-century world of the supernatural, of Satan and demons, of God intervening in the affairs of men, it was embedded in the pre-scientific world that the modern world had discredited. Therefore, the concept of the kingdom had to be "de-mythologized", and the essential message stripped out of the mythological trappings:

> To this extent the Kerygma is incredible to modern man. *For he is convinced that the mythical view of the world is obsolete.* We are therefore bound to ask whether, when we preach the Gospel to-day, we expect our converts to accept not only the Gospel message, but also the mythical view of the world in which it is set. If not, does the New Testament embody a truth which is quite independent of its mythical setting? If it does, theology must undertake the task of stripping the Kerygma from its mythical framework, of "demythologizing" it. [29]

In other words, Bultmann avoided the supposed paradox by simply rejecting the underlying assumptions of the gospel message (Kerygma) that there was such a thing as a "supernatural" world at all. He felt that because of the many modern advances in technology, in science, and in medicine, it was simply impossible for twentieth-century persons to believe in the world of miracles, healings, and demons found in the Bible. To rescue the message of Jesus, and make it understandable for modern persons, the theologian or teacher had to strip out, or "demythologize" those elements of the story of Jesus that would be impossible for modern persons to accept. It was somewhat simple, Bultmann thought, to strip out these mythological pieces and uncover the "core" or central message of Jesus.

However, despite the mythological elements, Bultmann suggested that the coming of the kingdom was the ultimate call by God *to the individual*; every moment, then, contained within itself *the possible eschatology moment*,[30] and thus, each person was forced to a *crisis of decision*. Every person must make the decision to accept the radical call of God, or to reject it. This was the eschatological message of Jesus. The kingdom – even though it transcended human history – demanded a response, as it was the ultimate "transcendent event, which signifies for man the ultimate Either – Or, which constrains him to decision".[31]

Quite expectantly then, in line with his mentor, Johannes Weiss, Bultmann rejected the Ritschlian *ethical kingdom achieved through the work of mankind on earth*. The coming of the kingdom was the work of God alone, and since it was existential and individualistic, the only act done by persons was the exercise of volitional will to accept the invitation of God.

> ... the kingdom of God is a power which, although it is entirely future, wholly determines the present. It determines the present because it now compels man to decision; he is determined thereby either in this direction or in that, as chosen or as rejected, in his entire present existence... The coming of the kingdom of God is therefore not really an event in the course of time, which is due to occur sometime, and toward which man can either take a definite attitude or hold himself neutral.[32]

The Building Synthesis: Cullmann, Kümmel, Jeremias

This first attempt to solve the paradox, using Bultmann's existentialist methodology, went too far for many theologians and pastors, as it pushed the concept of the kingdom of God far outside the bounds of Christian orthodoxy, and emptied the gospel of its power. However, his pastoral concern for making the claims of the gospel intelligible to modern persons did make sense. Especially in post-World War II Europe, it seemed that something more was needed to bring the insights of consistent eschatology and realized eschatology into harmony with one another. While Bultmann's demythologizing approach continued to hold some appeal among liberal scholars, a growing chorus of interpreters began to seek

49

ways to meld the various tenses of the kingdom into a unified whole.

Oscar Cullmann was one of the early voices to argue that a satisfactory account of the kingdom concept must include elements of *both the consistent and realized eschatological* views. In his wonderful *Christ and Time,* Cullmann argued that one of the mistakes of the "existential" school was its basic misunderstanding of the Jewish concept of time. Ancient Jewish writers understood time in a linear fashion; that is, they saw periods of history divided between this age, and the glorious age to come. Thinking of the kingdom in terms of an "existential" focus on the individual person standing in relation to eternity, as Bultmann had done, would obviously be a completely foreign concept to Jews in the time of Jesus, and therefore was primarily projection and needless speculation.[33]

A better answer to the problem of the delayed *parousia* was the understanding of both tenses of the kingdom, held together in tension. In his famous analogy, Cullmann likened the situation of the kingdom to a hypothetical historical conflict, where *"the decisive battle in a war may already have occurred in a relatively early stage of the war, and yet the war still continues".*[34] Many readers saw in this statement their contemporary experience of D-Day, or the invasion of Normandy, in World War II. Once the Normandy invasion was successful in June of 1944, Hitler and the Third Reich's doom was sealed. However, the actual war dragged on for another year, with many more casualties and much destruction and death, even though the eventual outcome was certain.

Cullman wrote that the Jewish, and hence, primitive Christian view of time comprised two ages: **the present age** and **the age to come.** However, the Christ event changes the decisive moment so that the age to come split into two, with the mid-point, or the Christ event, occurring in the past, yet still belonging to the age to come.[35] Thus, when the gospels speak of Jesus' victory over demons, the demons themselves bear witness to this change, as they ask Jesus: "Have you come here to torment us before the time?" (Matthew 8:29). Because this "decisive battle" has already taken place, Christians can be assured of "victory day", **despite the delay of the parousia.** Cullmann rejects Schweitzer's assertion that Jesus expected no delay in the *parousia;*[36] indeed, the primitive Church understood that it

50

was living in the time *after* the decisive victory, and yet *before the final victory*.[37]

Werner Kümmel was another scholar who supported this solution. He began his insightful work, *Promise and Fulfillment: The Eschatological Message of Jesus,* by reviewing the three main eschatological positions that had solidified by the midpoint of the twentieth century; that is, the consistent eschatology of Weiss and Schweitzer, the realized eschatology of Dodd, and the existential eschatology of the Bultmann School. While there were many similarities in the approaches of the various schools, it was evident that fundamental differences still applied. The way out of the impasse, then, was to consider the entire scope of Jesus' preaching on the kingdom.[38] Only by accounting for all the biblical data could the proper understanding be achieved that the kingdom of God had *both present and future* facets. Dodd erred by treating the parables that spoke of a future realization as merely symbolic, or made up by the primitive church. Jesus often spoke of various events that would occur *in the lifetime of his audience,* and thus, God's acting in human time was a concrete idea and "absolutely indispensable" to the understanding of the full message of Jesus.

On the other hand, while Bultmann's pastoral motivations for making the claims of the gospel intelligible to modern persons are commendable, his method of "demythologizing" is suspect. Kümmel thought that it is not so easy to detach the mythical elements from the central message of Jesus as Bultmann claimed. These different forms of teaching are intimately related, as the theme of the eschatological future breaking into the present is carried throughout his preaching.[39] Also, since Jesus spoke of the kingdom as being present *in his person and activity* – especially in Luke 10:18 – the *consistent* school had also been wrong by interpreting the kingdom message as purely future:

Now Jesus can have meant by this one thing only, that he has seen the defeat accomplished in the fight he is waging victoriously against the devils. So here too it is quite firmly established that the eschatological consummation, the kingdom of God, has already become a present reality in the ministry of Jesus. And here too the message of the approaching Kingdom of God is actually illuminated by the knowledge that through Jesus' activities the future consummation is brought into the present.[40]

Kümmel was certain, then, that a complete examination of the sources led to the conclusion that those who argued for the time of eschatological fulfillment to be either *only* future, or *only* present, were *badly mistaken*. The kingdom came and was actualized in the ministry of Jesus, for it was "the happenings manifested in Jesus' acts and words which bring about the 'presentness' of the future fulfillment". The nature of the kingdom lies in the life and death of Jesus, in his ministry on earth and in his coming in judgment at the *eschaton*:

> The fact that the true meaning of Jesus' eschatological message is to be found in its reference to God's action in Jesus himself, that the essential content of Jesus' preaching about the kingdom of God is the news of the divine authority of Jesus, who has appeared on earth and is awaited in the last days as the one who effects the divine purpose of mercy. [41]

Consequently, Kümmel forms a crucial bridge between the earlier attempts that saw the kingdom of God as *either* present *or* future *or* existentially interpreted. Over the next several decades in kingdom studies, Kümmel's thesis of the promise and fulfillment of the kingdom became the essential groundwork that subsequent authors assumed, modified or refuted, but could not ignore.[42]

Joachim Jeremias' study, *The Parables of Jesus,* was an important source for John Wimber. Jeremias had a tremendous influence on New Testament studies in general, but as an early voice in the emerging consensus his work has special import for our study.[43] Jeremias was in general agreement with the interpretative model laid down by Dodd, but he pushed towards a fuller understanding of the eschatological message within the parables.[44] Owing to the "double historical setting" of the parables, it is necessary for the interpreter to understand not only the original setting of the parable, namely its practical background in Palestine of Jesus' time, but also the historical and cultural situation of the primitive church that retold the story. In other words, Jeremias agreed with Dodd that the parables were first spoken by Jesus, and then later remembered and reworked by the primitive church in their particular concerns and historical settings. This phenomenon accounts for "editorial gloss" or explanations often given by the gospel authors that give further detail or explanation of a parable whose meaning may have been unclear in a later historical or cultural, i.e. "Gentile" situation. While this adds complexity to the interpreter's task, Jeremias still held that the original meaning of the spoken parable could be recovered, i.e. it wasn't "lost". In fact, the parables represent "a specially reliable tradition", or even a "particularly trustworthy tradition" in which we "are brought into immediate relation with Jesus".

Against the consistent school, Jeremias thought that a close study of the parables revealed that even though many of them were reworked by the early church to account for the delay of the *parousia,* **Jesus *did expect* that a span of time would elapse after his death and before his return** (Matthew 24:42-51, 25:1-13, Mark. 13:33ff, Luke 12:35-46). This is the intended meaning of the parables of the ten virgins, the doorkeeper, and the faithful servant. The early church may have expanded the meaning to account for a larger delay than what was expected; nonetheless, they did understand that the parables taught them to *expect a delay of some time.* Although it was obvious that the kingdom was *present* in the ministry of Jesus in some form, as Dodd had taught, the parables taught of a fuller realization in the future. Jesus not only spoke of the kingdom, but he *embodied* it in his person, through his actions, so that "he himself is the message" of the kingdom. To explain this phenomenon, Jeremias offered the phrase, *"eine sich realisierende Eschatologie"*, or "eschatology in the process of realization".[45]

While *The Parables of Jesus* was quite influential in parable studies and in further kingdom research, Jeremias' later work, *A Theology of the New Testament*, expanded on his view of the kingdom from his more mature scholarly perspective. Here, Jeremias examines the concept of the *basileia tou theos* (kingdom of God) in Judaism and the life of Jesus. The Jews of Jesus' day had an idea of the kingdom as both God's reign over Israel in this age, and his Lordship over all creation in the age to come when Israel will be rewarded for their faithfulness, and all the nations will acknowledge JHWH's kingship.[46] Jesus, however, turned this conception over on its head. *Now was the time of salvation*, for the kingdom had come in his person. The ultimate, eschatological victory of God is very near, so near that its presence can be felt and seen – the deaf hear, the blind receive sight, the captives are released (Luke 7:22). For those who are willing to see, it is quite obvious that *"the consummation of the world is dawning"* (italics Jeremias') and even being *fulfilled* in that day.[47] The *"basileia* is always and everywhere understood in eschatological terms; it denotes the time of salvation, the consummation of the world, the restoration of the disrupted communion between God and man".[48]

The Evangelical Consensus: George Eldon Ladd

After the harmonizing attempts by figures such as Cullmann, Kümmel and Jeremias, it was clear that a consensus was emerging that would join the consistent and realized biblical data into a unified whole. Considering the fact that the meaning of the kingdom of God and the "Jesus Quests" have been the dominant focus of much of Protestant theology over the last 200 years, we only had time to highlight a few stops on the journey. Someone could even argue that the journey continues, as the use of the term "consensus" is somewhat problematic. In recent New Testament studies, especially those of the so-called "Third Quest" and the scholars involved with the Jesus Seminar, the questions of the kingdom in the message of Jesus have re-opened. More will be said on this in the section on Vineyard eschatology, where the work of scholars like N.T. Wright will be considered as being quite in line with the eschatological theology of the Vineyard. For the purposes of this study which is focused on kingdom studies in conservative Protestant traditions like Evangelicalism, Pentecostalism, and the Vineyard movement, the apex of the twentieth century quest, exemplified by the work of George Beasley-Murray, Hermann Ridderbos, and George Eldon Ladd, does serve as a "consensus".

The emerging consensus is best represented in the works of George Eldon Ladd. George Eldon Ladd was Harvard trained, and one of the first Protestant Evangelical scholars in the twentieth century who sought to build a bridge between the mainline critical liberal scholarship and the relatively isolated island of evangelical thought.[49] The fundamentalist–modernist controversies of the early decades of the century had left a seemingly unbridgeable gulf between the followers of Ritschl, Schweitzer and Bultmann, and the evangelical and fundamentalist churches that saw higher education as primarily hostile to faith.

Ladd saw himself as having the unique gifts and passions that could bridge this gulf by showing that the methods of higher criticism and biblical scholarship were not necessarily hostile to faith. While certain elements of the liberal program were certainly out of bounds, the Evangelical church had much to benefit by understanding the methods and assumptions of higher criticism. Indeed, Ladd felt that it was his life mission to accomplish two interconnected goals: first, to show the world of liberal biblical scholarship that Evangelicals could contribute to their field on equal parity, and secondly, to show Evangelicals that what they could learn from liberal scholarship could actually *enhance their faith*, not undermine or detract from it.

This mission was indeed a difficult one, as in various times in his life Ladd felt under the crossfire from both sides. Liberal scholars at times dismissed his faith presuppositions as fatal to his critical engagement with biblical texts and sources, and more conservative evangelical critics often dismissed the entire attempt to engage in liberal scholarship as a fool's errand.

It was with this understanding in mind that Ladd attempted to bridge the world of the liberal academy and the church by producing a critical work engaging the kingdom of God that would bring the last hundred years of scholarship to its logical conclusion and, in so doing, bring the resources of faith and doctrinal commitments to the study of the kingdom which had been previously lacking. Ladd believed that the previously unsolvable riddles of the timing and nature of the kingdom could be unlocked by approaching the questions through the lens of faith.[50] The culmination of this effort was Ladd's work, *Jesus and the Kingdom: The Eschatology of Biblical Realism.*[51]

Ladd advocated for a methodology of *biblical realism,* which is an approach to critical studies that takes the biblical text as generally reliable and trustworthy, and therefore places the burden of proof on the scholar interacting with the text, rather than on the witness of the text itself.[52] Ladd wholly accepted the methods and approaches of critical scholarship, as long as the presuppositions are clearly understood and acknowledged. Unlike Bultmann, Ladd argued for a true correspondence between the text and the actual historical events in the life of Jesus.[53]

....

Ladd's biblical realism taught that the Scriptures are generally quite trustworthy, and are a reliable account of Jesus and the early church as they actually happened.

....

Ladd perceived his work as being the natural progression of the emerging consensus on the kingdom of God as being both present and future. In a brief survey of the study on the kingdom in the preceding decades, Ladd notes the strengths of both the consistent and the realized eschatological schools; their various missteps can be seen as indications of the difficulties presented by the relative texts *and limitations of the critical methodology employed by scholarship.*[54] Ladd saves his most generous praise for the mediating figures of Kummel, Cullmann and Jeremias. These figures are notable for their recognition of both the present and future elements of the kingdom, and, as such, represent a growing "consensus" of scholarly opinion on the subject.

Ladd's own view of the timing and nature of the kingdom of God changed little through his academic career. From his early short work, *Crucial Questions about the kingdom of God*, to his most mature work, *A Theology of the New Testament,* Ladd's views are remarkably consistent, suggesting that his thought was well formed early in his studies.[55] Consistent throughout was Ladd's attempt to maintain the present–future tension as being not merely a solution to a previously intractable problem, but a *crucial element of the concept itself.* In other words, the idea of "fulfillment without consummation," or even, "eschatology in process of realization", is not a desperate solution conceived by the gospel writers, the primitive church, or the modern theologians; rather, it is *intrinsic to the scriptural concept of the kingdom.*

....

Ladd understood that the present-future tension of the kingdom was not a desperate "solution" to an exegetical "problem"; but a vital characteristic of the kingdom reality.

....

The Old Testament concept of the kingdom, Ladd would argue, set the stage for the gospel presentation in ways that traditional scholarship had misread or not clearly understood.

For even here, the concept of a partial, delayed, present-but-not-complete kingdom has its roots:

> However, we have seen that both in the Old Testament and in rabbinic Judaism, God's kingdom – his reign – can have more than one meaning. God is now the King, but he must also become King. This is the key to the solution of the problem in the gospels.[56]

The kingdom of God, therefore, has a *dynamic* and *theophanic* characteristic that indicates both God's present rule, and the breadth of his rule that is to come in the new age. God is both present and active among the people of Israel, and yet is still Israel's hope of a glorious eschatological future.[57] Ladd contends that, contrary to many modern conceptions, the Old Testament picture of the kingdom is one in which the "God who will manifest himself in a mighty theophany at the end of history, has already manifested himself during the course of history".[58]

At the same time, the prophets held out an immediate hope of God's intervention in their present day. Salvation and restoration was not just some "pie in the sky" idea or future fantasy; it was concrete, historical, and anchored in their conception of the world as *God's creation* which was itself in need of redemption.[59] The prophet Joel speaks of the coming "day of the Lord" in this way:

> Blow the trumpet in Zion,
> And sound an alarm in My holy mountain!
> Let all the inhabitants of the land tremble;
> For the day of the Lord is coming,
> For it is at hand:
> A day of darkness and gloominess,
> A day of clouds and thick darkness. (Joel 2:1-2)

and

> The earth quakes before them,
> The heavens tremble;
> The sun and moon grow dark,
> And the stars diminish their brightness.
> The Lord gives voice before His army,
> For His camp is very great;
> For strong is the One who executes His word.
> For the day of the Lord is great and very terrible;
> Who can endure it? (Joel 2:10-11)

This multidimensional conception of the kingdom explains the confusion and difficulty of those who first heard Jesus' teaching of the kingdom. The conception of the kingdom as taught by the rabbis, was one of a triumphant overthrow of the political oppressor, and vindication and elevation of the Jewish people as righteous and faithful followers of Torah and Temple.[60] This confusion is revealed by the popular conception as understood by the disciples: their private conversations with Jesus betray their attempt to understand Jesus' teachings on the kingdom of God in light of their previous understandings gained from the Jewish religious establishment.[61]

Instead of a political victory over their oppressors which would lead to their vindication and exaltation, Jesus' promise of the kingdom was radically different. Ladd wrote:

> The central thesis of this book is that the kingdom of God is the redemptive reign of God dynamically active to establish his rule among men, and that this kingdom, which   will appear as an apocalyptic act at the end of the age, has already come into human history in the person and mission of Jesus to overcome evil, to deliver men from its power, and to bring them into the blessings of God's reign. The kingdom of God involves two great moments: *fulfillment within history*, and *consummation at the end of history*. It is precisely this background which provides the setting for the parables of the kingdom.[62] (Italics mine)

So, we see that for Ladd, the significant questions of the nature of timing of the kingdom are summed up in his thesis: the kingdom is the dynamic, redemptive rule of God active in history, which has two great moves – it was *inaugurated* in the mission of Jesus, and will be finally brought to completion at the end of time. Thus, the question of the delayed *parousia* is really just a misunderstanding within the early church; even they did not fully understand that there would be a significant gap between the two comings!

This brings up a question from our earlier study: if the early church was confused about the coming of the kingdom, was Jesus mistaken as well? Not in any way. Ladd argues that as the delay is a central feature of the teachings in the parables, it would be a mistake to assume that Jesus himself was confused or uncertain as to his mission, as Schweitzer had argued.[63] To the contrary, the radical conception of the kingdom and the inherent mystery explains the delay as a central feature. Further, Ladd argues that a fundamental misunderstanding from Schweitzer predisposed interpreters to consider the delay as a problem. Remembering our discussion of the "realm" or "reign" brings an important insight to this mistake of previous interpreters. Because the rule of God was considered in terms of a "realm" or a "reign", interpreters were forced, in a sense, to "pick their poison". By emphasizing the "realm", some were forced to modify their *definition* of God's rule, and those that preferred the "reign" had to redefine God's *realm* in ways that went beyond the biblical data.[64]

Ladd's offers a brilliant solution to this difficulty. He suggests that we understand the kingdom of God as the dynamic *rule or reign* of God that occurs in different *realms* in various *stages of history*. For example, while the Lord's Prayer states that in the *realm* of heaven God reigns supreme, the prayer states that in the *realm of this earth* his reign is not complete or total. The mistake of the consistent school was to assume that the realm *had to be* earthly, cosmic, and total, whereas in the kingdom prayer, Matthew 6:10, Jesus states that circumstances in the two realms are not presently the same, but he urges the disciples to pray for a time when they *will be:* "on earth as it is in heaven".[65]

Conclusion: The Mystery of the Kingdom

Thus far, we have considered three major "schools", or perspectives, on the kingdom of God. While the differences are often a matter of degree rather than hard-and-fast categories, this chart shows how the perspectives relate to one another:

	ALREADY ← TENSION → NOT-YET		
School	*Realized*	*Synthesis (Consensus)*	*Consistent*
Scholars	Dodd "Lives of Jesus" Bultmann	Kummel, Jerimias, Cullmann, Ridderbos, Ladd	Weiss, Schweitzer
Who Brings It?	God – man's help	God & Church	Entirely God
When?	Ministry of Jesus – Now in history	Fulfillment without consummation	End of time – future
What does it look like?	Spread of the Gospel/Evangelism "Fatherhood of God & Brotherhood of Man"	Process of realization (Messy!)	Cataclysmic -- apocalyptic end

So we see that, although the quest that began with Weiss' bombshell on the battleground of Jesus studies is far from over, our brief overview has shown that the positions are fairly well established. The "purely" eschatological view of the consistent school (Weiss and Schweitzer), the antithesis of realized eschatology (Dodd), and the existential interpretation of Bultmann can all be found in modern interpreters, teachers and churches.

The consensus view, especially the position of Ladd, has its proponents as well, especially in conservative scholarship. For our purposes, Ladd's influence on John Wimber is most significant, and so Ladd's views are the most important. For this reason, much of our study will focus on how Wimber understood that the promises of the Messianic kingdom were *fulfilled* in the ministry of Jesus, even as we wait for the final *consummation* of the kingdom at his return to earth. However, Wimber was not an uncritical interpreter of Ladd. He saw Ladd as a theological source, but as an eminently practical church leader; he was a careful interpreter and utilizer of *all of his* sources. Thus, it is important to understand how Wimber modified, rejected, or adopted Ladd's theology. In other words, Wimber was persistent in his quest to "eat the meat and spit out the bones".[66]

Questions for discussion:

1. John Wimber was first influenced by faith healers who he considered to be strange or bizarre. Later when he met "normal" Christians who practiced healing, it caused him to rethink some of his positions. How important are "models" of Christian practices? What kinds of models have you been exposed to, and how have they influenced your perception of faith?

2. Unlike Pentecostals, Charismatics chose to stay *in* their denominations, and still experience the gift of the Spirit and the *charismata*. What issues might some of the Charismatics experience if they sought to incorporate the gifts into their established church practices?

3. We discussed the *"constitutional"* view of the gifts compared to the *"situational"*. How might these different approaches affect how a person or a church might experience the gifts like healing, prophecy, evangelism, etc.?

4. The issue of the "delay of the *parousia"* became super important in kingdom of God studies. What have you heard taught about "the second coming", the "rapture", or the return of Christ? Has the "delay" ever been a question or problem for you?

5. The kingdom questions of *when it comes, who brings it,* and *what does it look like* will be a major focus of our study. What answers have you heard to these questions, and what do you think are the best answers?

FIVE

Contemporary Protestant Eschatologies

After John Wimber took the helm of the Vineyard movement, he was quite eager to create a church movement from the raw materials he had gathered from sources like Gunnar Payne, the Friends Church, Yorba Linda Calvary Chapel, and his time at the Fuller Institute of Church Growth. His exposure to the teachings on the kingdom of God by G.E. Ladd had given him a base by which he could begin to fill in material from his church leadership experience. After Wimber encountered Ladd's work, he became convinced that Ladd's notion of the consummated, but not fulfilled, kingdom of God was not just the dominant subject in Jesus teaching, but was a blueprint for how the church should do its ministry. However, even though there was a theological consensus in the academy, this same theological consensus had not yet worked its way through to the churches. Therefore, in the late 1970s and early 1980s, there were few, if any, churches that actually *applied* Ladd's theology to their practices. It was a *theory* only, with no practical models as to how to incorporate the theory into action. Even though Wimber largely embraced Ladd's work, we will see that Wimber extended Ladd's model to include such things as charismatic experience and serving the poor.

This is not to say, however, that Wimber did not have *other* eschatological models available to him within the American Evangelical Protestant church. Certainly his time at Fuller Seminary, and especially his time at the Institute of Church Growth, exposed him to numerous theological approaches to the kingdom of God and to eschatology. Because they are still quite common in the church today, it is very important to understand two of these dominant models, and suggest reasons why Wimber found these models inadequate. First, it's important to understand *dispensationalism*, which was the dominant eschatological system of most Evangelical churches at this time.[1] While Wimber noted in a sermon series in 1982 that he at one time embraced the dispensationalist teaching and owned the Scofield Bible, as he became more convinced of Ladd's theology, he subsequently rejected dispensationalism. For Vineyardites, it is crucially important to understand *why*.[2] The second model, which was exemplified by classical and contemporary Pentecostal churches that tended to combine a "soft dispensationalism" with a *restorationist* eschatology, was rejected by Wimber as well. There were three principal features of these models that Wimber came to reject. First, both classic dispensationalism and Pentecostal restorationism divided church history into artificial "ages" or epochs which were not consistent with Wimber's understanding of the Bible. Secondly, they both embraced an apocalyptic schema that included such features as the "rapture theology" which held that Jesus would return at some point in the future in a secret, sudden manner for a select group of believers, and that many of the peoples of the earth would not witness or be included in this "snatching away".

Finally, Wimber came to reject another significant tenet of classic dispensationalism as well: the cessation of the *charismata*. At the close of this section, it will become quite clear that neither classic dispensationalism, nor the restorationist Pentecostal version of the theology, was capable of being blended with the Laddian paradigm that Wimber had embraced. It simply cannot be done. Inaugurated eschatology is completely incompatible with both dispensationalism and restorationism. This conclusion will be substantiated in the next section of this chapter where we will study the growth and development of the Vineyard's eschatology.

Evangelical Eschatologies: The Influence of Dispensationalism and "Rapture Theology"

The first model was an Evangelical dispensationalism that was quite prevalent, even dominant, in the American Protestant church in the latter half of the twentieth century. This eschatological approach had its beginnings much earlier, in the American academies and seminaries of the late nineteenth century. Dispensationalism was championed by notable teachers such as John Nelson Darby (1800–1882), C.I. Scofield (1843–1921), and Charles Ryrie (1925–). By the mid-twentieth century, primarily through the popularity of the Scofield Reference Bible, dispensationalism had become the primary eschatological approach in North American Evangelical Protestant theology.[3]

According to its original proponents, the whole of salvation history can be neatly divided into separate eras, or *dispensations*, which are differentiated from each other by the way God interacts with humankind. Darrell Bock and Craig Blaising state that classical dispensationalism, as exemplified by the Scofield Bible, entailed seven dispensations.[4] A dispensation "refers to a distinctive way in which God manages or arranges the relationship of human beings to Himself".[5] The classical model, which would have been most well-known when Wimber was developing his eschatology, was largely built upon the Scofield system. According to Scofield, the seven stages are:

1. Innocence (Creation to Fall)
2. Conscience (Fall to the Flood)
3. Human Government (Flood to Babel)
4. Promise (Abraham to Sinai)
5. Mosiac Law (Sinai to Calvary)
6. Grace (Calvary to Second Coming)
7. Kingdom (Second Coming to the end of the Millennium)

Dispensationalism and Cessationism

The earliest teachers of dispensationalism leaned heavily on the reformers as a historical theological resource. Dispensationalists discovered that the Protestant reformers' suspicion of Catholic "superstition" led them to promote *cessationism*. Cessationism is the belief that miracles and the *charismata* functioned *only* to authenticate the ministry of Jesus and the apostles, and once the Bible was written (the "closing" of the biblical canon) these miraculous acts were no longer needed, for the church had the completed Holy Scripture at her disposal.[6] So, miracles like healing, demonic deliverance, nature miracles, speaking

65

in tongues and prophecy were no longer needed; therefore, they "ceased". In other words, the Holy Spirit no longer did this kind of work. Dispensationalists saw this proposition as fitting neatly into their system: the miraculous gifts of the Spirit could be relegated to an earlier dispensation, not the church age. By default then, whatever miracles that were supposedly claimed in the church age had to be counterfeit or misguided.[7]

For Wimber it was this marriage of cessationism and dispensationalism that first caused him to question other beliefs of the system.[8] While noting that as a young Christian he was enamored with the popular-level works of the 1970s that focused on the rapture, such as Hal Lindsey's *The Late Great Planet Earth,* once he began to experience the works of the Spirit like healing, prophecy, and tongues, he realized the fundamental incompatibility between the kingdom theology he had absorbed from Ladd and the dispensationalist model.[9]

A second major concern for Wimber was the clear division between Israel and the church, so that in reading scripture, the dispensationalist always had to ask if the particular text in focus applied to Israel, or the church. For Wimber, this was nonsense, and it broke Ladd's understanding of the present kingdom being comprised of both ethnic Jews and Gentiles.[10] In his short book published in 1958, *The Gospel of the Kingdom: Scriptural Studies in the kingdom of God,* Ladd had explicitly rejected the separation of Israel and the Church. Based on Paul's illustration of the olive tree and the grafted-in branches in Romans 11, He argued: "It is impossible to think of two peoples of God through whom God is carrying out two different redemptive purposes without doing violence to Romans 11".[11]

Ladd continues:

The work of God's Spirit in the formation of the Church and the future divine visitation of Israel by which the natural branches are re-grafted into the olive tree ought not to be seen as two separate and unrelated purposes but as two stages of the single redemptive purpose of God through His kingdom. There is a single olive tree, and there is one kingdom of God.[12]

To complicate the matter further, the dispensationalist schema had the unfortunate effect of rendering much of Jesus' teaching on the kingdom as *irrelevant for the Church*. So, the very notion of the kingdom of God as "fulfillment without consummation" in the church age would be rendered nonsensical in the dispensationalist view, for these kingdom teachings were *restricted to the millennium*.[13] It made no sense to Wimber that Jesus would spend so much time teaching on something *that couldn't possibly apply* to his listeners, the disciples, or the churches that would soon be gathered in his name.

A third major problem Wimber had with dispensationalism was the so-called "rapture theology" that had become so popular in the Evangelical church of his day. Charged by writers such as Lindsey, who is widely credited for popularizing dispensationalism, "rapture talk" had moved into near-hysterical heights in the late 1970s. According to this teaching, at the end of time there will be a secret return of Christ in which he will "snatch away" believers while all other peoples on earth will be "left behind". This view is largely based on an interpretation of I Thessalonians 4:16-17, which reads, "For the Lord himself will come down from heaven, with a loud command, with the voice of the archangel and with the trumpet call of God, and the dead in Christ will rise first. After that, we who are still alive and are left will be *caught up together* with them in the clouds to meet the Lord in the air. And so we will be with the Lord forever".

The implication is that the words, "caught up together", imply that this coming will be secret, and meant only for a few, and that these few would be "taken away" from the earth by Christ. Christ would then return again in a visible, cosmic manner at a later date which would usher in the last days. The timing of the rapture could come at the beginning, the middle, or the end of the millennium.

When he examined the supposed biblical support for the rapture, Wimber again questioned the biblical validity of the entire dispensationalist system. While cautiously accepting that the Jews returning to the ancestral lands and the establishment of the State of Israel in the twentieth century likely had some eschatological import, Wimber firmly rejected any form of "date setting" or eschatological mathematics that was so popular in his day.[14] More significantly, he simply could not accept the idea of a secret "rapture" supposedly taught by such texts as I Thessalonians 4:17. Wimber had a number of questions. For example, how could an event signified by the "voice of the Archangel", and "trumpet blast" describe a "secret" event? Wimber once stated, "I never could find in the scriptures where Jesus came *twice*, in a secret event – if you are a Dispensationalist you have to believe this".[15] He firmly believed that the "rapture theology" came from a personal interpretation of the text, not from the text itself.[16] That is to say, the scriptures speak of only two comings of Christ: one at his birth, and the other when he returns for the final judgment at the end of time.

It's important to understand that many evangelical commentators have questioned the idea of a "rapture" as well. First, it is not at all clear that the translation of the Greek phrase σὺν αὐτοῖς ἁρπαγησόμεθα is really "caught up together" or "catching away". Quite helpful here is Ben Witherington III, who argues that *apantesis* does not have the idea of "catching up" at all, but rather refers to Hellenistic custom of a greeting committee which meets a visiting dignitary outside of the city, and then escorts him into the city. F.F. Bruce sees *apantesis* as the process of escorting a dignitary on an official visit, *parousia*, on the last stage of his journey. Leon Morris and J. Moffatt also note the cultural and historical use of *apantesis*, and strongly question the translation of "caught up together". These commentators suggest that a better understanding of this passage would be something like this: when Christ returns a second time, those saints alive in that day will meet him in the air, and then return with him to earth as people would welcome a conquering hero or king – which he most definitely is![17]

For many reasons, Wimber rejected the dispensationalist eschatology which was so popular within Evangelicalism in the 1970s. His experiences at Fuller Seminary, which began to challenge his cessationist hermeneutic, his exposure to Ladd's work on the kingdom, and his personal experience with the *charismata* all rendered the dispensationalist framework suspect.

However, many of these experiences presented another option to Wimber: the eschatology of Pentecostalism, which he encountered by both meeting leading Pentecostal teachers, and reading many books written by Pentecostals on the subjects of healing, prophecy, and tongues. While the Pentecostal eschatologies that Wimber encountered had considerable similarities with Evangelical dispensationalism, there were numerous unique features as well. Wimber's engagement with these Pentecostal eschatologies is the subject of our next discussion.

Pentecostal Eschatologies: an End-Time Restoration of the Gifts?

By the time John Wimber began to develop the establishing for the Vineyard movement, his personal view on Pentecostalism had undergone a significant transformation. As discussed earlier, in his early years in the faith, Wimber considered Pentecostals to be unsophisticated charlatans who were overly obsessed with tongues-speaking to the exclusion of the main teachings of scripture. In *Power Healing*, Wimber wrote that his early idea of Pentecostal healers was that they often appeared "foolish, weird, or bizarre".[18] However, after he personally encountered Pentecostal students at Fuller Seminary and began to meet Pentecostal pastors, teachers, and laity in his travels with the Church Growth Institute, his perception began to change. As he began to accept the gifts of the Spirit and embraced the practice of healing, he began a furious study of Pentecostal theology, history, and personalities. His aim was to learn all he could from those who had gone before him, in order to develop healing in his churches. What he discovered was that he was not so much dismayed by the *idea* of divine healing itself, but by the individuals that were often held up as "divine healers". Therefore, it was the *models, the styles, and the personalities* that he found disagreeable, not the *practice* of healing itself.[19]

When it came to the eschatology of Pentecostalism, however, Wimber once again found it difficult to meld Ladd's ideas with Pentecostal eschatology. While the obstacle of cessationism did not exist in Pentecostal eschatology, there were numerous other factors that caused Wimber to reject the Pentecostal approach of his day.

69

The first element was the Pentecostal focus on the *end-time restoration of the spiritual gifts.* Since the birth of Pentecostalism in the Azusa street outpouring, Pentecostals had seen their movement as being divinely ordained in the "last days" to achieve the evangelism of the world. Thus, early self-descriptors including significant terms such as "The Full Gospel," "The Pentecostal Movement," "The Apostolic Faith," and "The Latter Rain Movement", all pointed to the idea that the supernatural gifts which were so prevalent in the apostolic age, and recorded by Luke in The Acts of the Apostles, had been *lost or neglected* in church history, but now were being *restored to the church* for the purposes of preparing for the second coming of Jesus.[20]

In contrast to the dominant fundamentalist eschatology of the time that was pessimistic, and looked at current political events for confirmation of their belief that world events would get worse and worse until the rapture,[21] the Pentecostal restorationist paradigm, at least at first, had a fairly positive historical outlook. This makes sense in light of the Pentecostal belief that tongues-speaking would be the missiological key that would open all peoples to the gospel.[22] The Pentecostal view of church history was that the original vitality and life in the Spirit evident in the early church **gradually faded after the time of Constantine**. The following centuries of church history were a time of gradual decline, with growing ecclesial corruption and compromise with worldly systems. The Reformation began the restoration leading to the final return of the apostolic faith immediately before the return of Christ.[23] Thus, as Pentecostals experienced the revival of tongues-speaking, physical healing, and other manifestations of the baptism of the Holy Spirit, they connected these events to the time of the "latter rain"; that is, a period of time prophesied by the scriptures when the Holy Spirit would restore the charismatic gifts to the Church.

The term "latter rain" was taken from the biblical text of Deuteronomy 11, which speaks of God sending the "early rain" and the "latter rain" to sustain the crops of the Hebrews. The term occurs seven times in the scriptures for example, Joel 2:23 (KJV) and Acts 2. Early Pentecostals did not quite understand the atmospheric cycle of the Ancient Near East, and somewhat misapplied the idea by proclaiming that the first Pentecost recorded in Acts was the "Early Rain", with their experience being the "Latter Rain" of the Spirit before the imminent coming of Christ. The Near Eastern climate of the Bible actually described the exact opposite: a "wet" season between the early and latter rain. Pentecostals did not understand this, so they understood the interim as a "dry" season – that is, a relative *absence* of the Spirit's presence. So we can see why their view has been called *restorationism*. [24] As the church preached the "Full Gospel",[25] many would be converted and purified, which would thus lead to a restored and full bride ahead of the second coming of Christ.[26]

When Wimber first began to shed his cessationism and accept the continuationist view, he undertook a historical study of the gifts of the Spirit in the church. What he discovered, contrary to the Pentecostal restorationist model, was that the *charisms* were operational throughout church history to one degree or another. His study of the early church fathers, the Montanists, healings in the Catholic Church, the beginnings of the Quakers, Shakers, Pietists, and Moravians, all revealed a story that had been largely ignored by mainstream Protestantism and Evangelicalism. Particularly useful for Wimber were Jonathan Edward's writings on the manifestations of the Spirit in New England during the First Great Awakening.[27] While Wimber appreciated and gleaned a good deal from his study of Pentecostalism, he had many reservations as well. In reflecting back on his early exposure to Pentecostalism, Wimber wrote:

Back in the 1970s, before I had any inkling of leading our movement, I had already been introduced to the rapid growth of the Pentecostal church (primarily in the Third World). This introduction occurred in the midst of my association with Fuller Evangelistic Association and the School of World Mission....at the time, I had resisted the Pentecostal experience, because I was only aware of the Pentecostal extremes (and their usually negative examples). In the ensuing years I have become aware of mainstream Pentecostalism that has produced so much fruit for the kingdom.[28]

71

However, it was not merely the truncated and narrow view of history implicit in the Pentecostal eschatology, but also their *over-realized eschatology* in the practices of healing that troubled him. Wimber's own study of scripture and experience led him to reject certain aspects of Pentecostal practice and theology, such as the ideas of tongues as *evidence* of the baptism of the Holy Spirit, and the Pentecostal emphasis on healing being *guaranteed* in the atonement of Christ.[29] Most importantly, he saw that there was a conflict between the restorationist view of history and Ladd's teaching on the kingdom. In other words, Wimber understood that, since the ministry of Jesus, and after the resurrection and Pentecost, all subsequent history was "the last days".

Wimber later wrote:

A fundamental and usually unspoken assumption of the view of these same leaders is the idea that we are now the unique recipients of the latter day work of the Spirit and that the Holy Spirit took a "leave of absence" from the church for the past nineteen centuries. This a-historical view misrepresents church history, in my opinion. The church under the administration of the Spirit has continued to grow and mature during the past nineteen centuries, albeit through ebbs and flows. I don't see any long parenthesis in which the Holy Spirit was absent from the church as I read church history.

I believe Peter's sermon on Pentecost marks this age as distinctively the Age of the Spirit from start to finish...We have been in the last days since Pentecost, and this is still the time of the outpouring of the Spirit as the Administrator of the church. I think that the scattered remnants of church history we have access to today demonstrate sufficiently that church history is replete with repeated outpourings of the Spirit.[30]

In Wimber's view, the kingdom of God had come in the ministry of Jesus, but the Pentecostal restorationist paradigm tended to ignore this crucial fact, instead focusing primarily on the Acts of the Apostles as *the* paradigm for church ministry. Pentecostals had in effect given pride of

72

place to the *early church and the apostles*, whereas his reading of the gospels led him to believe that it was the *ministry of Jesus* that was the primary model for all believers, including the early church.[31] These theological concerns, combined with the lack of what he considered to be usable models of ministry, caused Wimber to look beyond Pentecostalism as he constructed the early eschatological vision for the Vineyard Movement.[32]

As we have seen from this brief survey, Wimber evaluated several eschatological models as he began to mold his understanding of Ladd's theory of the kingdom of God with his (Wimber's) growing experience and convictions. It is quite evident that, while he respected many elements of both the current Evangelical and Pentecostal belief systems, neither gave him what he needed to construct a Vineyard eschatology. The ecclesial model he wanted to create and multiply simply did not exist at the time: a church that was firmly grounded in the kingdom message, combining the best of several traditions. From Evangelicalism, Wimber would borrow the commitment to the renewed life, personal witness, cultural engagement, and faithful to the scriptures; to this he would add elements of the Pentecostal faith's expectation of the Spirit's work in the life of the church. This new eschatological focus provided him with a practical model he could develop in the Vineyard. Understanding how he did this is crucially important for anyone attempting to understand the Vineyard movement.

SIX

The Beginnings of Wimber's Eschatology

As we saw from the previous chapter, while both the Evangelical church and Pentecostal theology were most likely aware of the "fulfillment without consummation" consensus in theology, this theological system had not yet filtered down into church practice. In the case of the Evangelical church, a pre-existing commitment to dispensationalist theology and accompanying *cessationism* tended to tilt practice towards the "not yet" side of the dynamic tension. In other words, they had little expectation of the miraculous work of the Spirit because they believed the miraculous had largely ceased! In the case of Pentecostal theology, the influence of *restorationism* and prior theological commitments to subsequence and second blessing doctrines, combined with leftover theological remnants from influences such as the Latter Day Rain tended to collapse the eschatological tension towards the "already" side of the equation.

For Wimber then, as he engaged with the works of G.E. Ladd and James Kallas (and to a lesser extent, Charles Kraft), he realized that the gospels themselves held the blueprint he was seeking. *The ministry of Jesus provided him with a model that combined the already–not yet kingdom concept with practical ministry.* In his early years of ministry at Yorba Linda Friends Church, he had absorbed the idea that Jesus' teaching on repentance and the new birth was the heart of his message. However, the practical aspects of his ministry such as healing the sick or freeing the demonized, were not to be imitated, just like his so-called "nature miracles", i.e. turning water into wine, multiplying bread, or calming the sea, could not be imitated. As discussed previously, the theological model of the Friends church, like the broader Evangelical church, tended to see the nature miracles *and* the healing miracles of Jesus as expressions of his "divine prerogative" or divinity, and thus obviously were not models to be emulated by the post-Acts church. This is an important question to ponder: "Did Jesus have the capacity or ability to do the miracles he did because he was the Christ, the Son of God, or was it because *as the Son of God*, he was uniquely endowed with the Spirit?"

Scholars have offered many opinions on this question. Certainly, Orthodox Christianity must believe that Jesus was divine, and there were certainly elements of his divinity that he retained in the incarnation. However, a close examination of his ministry reveals that his baptism with and dependence on the Spirit empowered much of his ministry. Further, what he passed on to the disciples and the church was not his divine nature –humankind *still* has a fallen human nature – but the possibility of the Spirit's empowerment to make that human nature a "new person" or "spiritual person" (2 Corinthians. 5:17).

In contrast to the Evangelical view, and siding with the Pentecostal tradition, Wimber began to understand that a distinct separation could be made between those miracles that were unique, distinct, and not to be repeated, such as the virgin birth, transfiguration, or resurrection, and those miracles that Jesus not only performed, but more significantly, trained and exhorted his disciples to perform.

This new understanding of the gospels was monumental for Wimber. A fuller application of the kingdom concept was so paradigm-shattering that when he finally put the concepts together, he ecstatically exclaimed to his wife, Carol, "THIS IS IT! We *proclaim the words* of the kingdom and *do the works* of the kingdom".[1] Further, as he read Kallas' books, Wimber saw that an essential feature of the kingdom was *conflict*: the kingdom of God was moving aggressively against the kingdom of Satan, and so, every act in the kingdom was an act of warfare and aggression.[2] Wimber began to re-read the gospels with new eyes, not merely mining the story of Jesus for potential evangelistic material as he previously had done, but now appreciating the essential element of *conflict* that he previously had missed. Further insights came as he read the kingdom story back in the Old Testament, especially the Exodus narrative, and discovered the conflict theme reaching deep into the kingdom narrative.[3]

While Wimber and the early Vineyard leaders around him set the idea of **inaugurated eschatology** as the distinctive theological framework of the Vineyard, the early focus on church planting, church renewal, and structural development left little time for formal theological reflection. Wimber was fortunate to have trained scholars join him at various seasons of the movement's growth; all these contributed to the theological breadth of the movement.[4] While the theological form of inaugurated eschatology was firmly entrenched as the primary ideology of the Vineyard, subsequent Vineyard thinkers developed and extended the theological paradigm as diverse issues confronted the growing movement. Indeed, this dynamism of theological reflection interacting with ministerial concerns continues to this day.[5]

The Gospels and Ministry of Jesus

The first and most prominent theological source for John Wimber was undoubtedly the scriptures, particularly his reading of the gospels. In the gospels Wimber saw not just a historical description of the life of Jesus, or source material for understanding Trinitarian theology. As the consummate practitioner, Wimber understood the gospel records were also a textbook, or perhaps more specifically, a *manual for ministry.* Whereas classical Pentecostalism took Acts to be their model for church practice, and understood the primitive church as their launching point, because of his eschatology, Wimber understood the early church to be little different from the contemporary church age; that is, after the resurrection and sending of the Spirit, the entire church age was in "the last days". Hence, since the apostles in Acts were primarily the disciples of Jesus, it made sense to Wimber to consider the apostles as "contemporaries" or *fellow students*, who had learned their models of ministry and their practices from Jesus.[6] Thus the gospels were the primarily sources for understanding the model of ministry that should be emulated by the whole Church throughout history.[7] The message of Jesus was that the kingdom of God, and hence, the *eschaton*, had in some way entered into human history in the person and ministry of Jesus. When he announced that the kingdom of God had come, he was effectively stating that *his rule* had come to earth.

76

In his reading of the gospels, Wimber noted a frequent two-fold pattern: there was first a *proclamation* of the kingdom followed by a *demonstration* of the power or presence of the kingdom.[8] In his typical no-nonsense expressions, this became known in the Vineyard as "Word 'n Works". That is, proclaiming the *word* of the kingdom alongside doing the *works* of the kingdom.[9] Wimber writes of one moment when his thinking on this subject became clearer:

> John 14:12 caused me to suddenly drop in my tracks: 'If you have faith in me, you will do the same things that I am doing'. (CEV) I had been taught the traditional cessationist view of supernatural works and had accepted the fact that this verse did not mean what it says—that we should be able to minister like Jesus. Signs and wonders had stopped at the end of the apostolic age, so I thought. Yet at that instant, the text exploded before my eyes. Jesus did all kinds of things that I had never even attempted, like healing the sick, casting out demons, and cleansing lepers. I had taught and preached the Gospel but had never healed any kind of sickness or disease. What I didn't discover until that day was that being a Christian with an obedient walk also included the risks of believing and doing those things that Jesus believed and did. That day I wrote in the margin of my Bible, "I must learn to believe everything that Jesus believed and learn to do everything Jesus did".[10]

While the gospels served to give Wimber a blueprint for the practice he would infuse into the Vineyard, it wasn't until he began to merge this understanding with the inaugurated eschatology of Ladd that a fuller eschatological framework came into view. As he read Ladd, Kallas and Ridderbos, a more robust theological framework began to emerge that greatly excited him. So while he consulted essential secondary sources, the ministry of Jesus was his primary source. In inaugurated eschatology, or "fulfillment without consummation", Wimber saw a lens through which he could properly understand the ministry of Jesus, including his teaching and miraculous ministries. Therefore, the secondary sources gave him a structure to explain, process, and teach the primary source. While Wimber was a voracious reader, and synthesized many elements from countless sources, he credits Ladd and Kallas for giving him a theological foundation for ministry in the early stages of his theological development.[11]

Wimber's Appropriation of G.E. Ladd and James Kallas

As dissatisfied as he was with the eschatological frameworks of Pentecostalism and dispensational evangelicalism, eschatology was not Wimber's first concern in the early years of his ministry, as more practical concerns consumed his time. However, once he became familiar with the works of Ladd, he began to reflect on the relationship between eschatology and practical ministry. Wimber began to see that the **fulfillment without consummation** was more than just the current academic consensus; it explained both the teaching and the ministry of Jesus. If it was so that the ministry of Jesus inaugurated the end of the age, then the entire dispensationalist framework, and its attendant cessationism, *was wrong*. Of further importance was the very nature of the kingdom itself – the ministry of Jesus and the early church was evidence of the presence of the kingdom.

As Ladd wrote:

...this age, which extends from creation to the day of the Lord, which in the Gospels is designated in terms of the *Parousia* of Christ, resurrection and judgment, is the age of human existence in weakness and mortality, of evil, sin and death. The Age to Come will see the realization of what the reign of God means, and will be the age of resurrection into eternal life in the kingdom of God.[12]

Following Ladd, Wimber understood the reality of this kingdom as the *rule or reign* of God, rather than in terms of a physical territory or spatial *realm*.[13] This rulership was demonstrated by Jesus' command over demons, physical healings, natural processes and even death itself, as evidenced by the resurrection.[14] The ministry of Jesus could then be seen as an invasion of sorts; that is, one rule usurping another–the rule of Jesus came against the existing rule of Satan, demons, and death. Thus, the state of earth was one of spiritual *warfare*. As Ladd expressed it, "the theology of the kingdom of God is essentially one of **conflict and conquest** over the kingdom of Satan".[15] Wimber embraced this invasion/warfare metaphor for understanding the nature of the kingdom, but extended it as well, as the church through the ages was to engage in this conflict, using the very means and methods of Jesus.[16] This conflict, and the already–not yet nature of the kingdom itself, gave Wimber further explanatory reach for his eschatology. Seeing the coming of the kingdom as God's *rule* solved the issues related to a cosmic coming that would usher in a new *realm*. Wimber conceived the realm of the Kingdom as the reach or impact of God's rule. Hence, when the Kingdom advanced on earth by renewed people, renewed communities – even renewed cities and states – the realm expanded. However, owing to the warfare between the Kingdoms of God and Satan, territory or realms could also be *lost or weakened*.[17] Rather than collapse to either pole of a consistent or realized eschatology, the already–not yet warfare conception explained both the future, cosmic, apocalyptic elements of the kingdom, as emphasized by the *consistent* school, and the present, here-and-now realities preferred by followers of Dodd's *realized* eschatology. In practical ministry terms, this dynamic rule explained why Jesus commanded his followers to pray for the sick, and yet, not all who are prayed for were healed.[18] Furthermore, rather than delay the blessings of the kingdom to a future, idyllic age, as in classic dispensationalism, inaugurated eschatology gave the blessings of the kingdom to those *living in the present church age*, which Wimber was beginning to experience in his ministry through healings, deliverances, and conversions. The Vineyard would be forever marked as a church committed to living the future reality of the kingdom in the present.

This dynamic rule also helped Wimber to explain the relationship between the church and the kingdom. The kingdom gave birth to the church, but the church was the agent of the kingdom. Thus the church is the primary representative and instrument of the kingdom, as it performs the work and establishes the rule of the kingdom. The church age will end, but the rule of the kingdom will have no end.[19]

Wimber also saw that this new understanding better explained the problem of the delay of the *parousia* that had so vexed theologians from the consistent, realized, and existential programs. The kingdom *had indeed* come in the ministry of Jesus, but only partially, and in a supernatural essence. This misunderstanding held not only for the gospel witnesses, but for contemporary theology as well. Consider the parables that taught delay or growth of the kingdom. Far from being confused, mislead, or in error, as Schweitzer and Dodd had thought, they could

....

Inaugurated Eschatology allowed Ladd, and Wimber, to avoid the problem of a 'secret" Rapture accompanied by loud trumpets and the voice of the Archangel!!

....

now be read as setting the two-stage coming of the supernatural kingdom: a first coming that inaugurated the kingdom, if only partially, and a second, final, cosmic coming that would finally bring the full reality of the kingdom into existence on Earth. Thus Wimber, with Ladd, saw only two comings, *and had no need for a secret "rapture" to solve the issues of the delayed coming of the kingdom.* Also, if the kingdom had come partially, but in a way that the Jews and contemporary theologians (and even dispensationalists!) did not expect or recognize, then there was no need to explain the promises of the *parousia* as having a *different impact on the Jews and the Gentile nations.*[20]

In contrast with the ethical concept of the kingdom, Wimber now understood that while the ethics of the kingdom could be embraced by the "already", ethical concerns did not completely encompass the range of activity and responsibility of those under the rulership of the kingdom. The ethical implications of the Sermon on the Mount were not unimportant, but they were only the start. Other "works", such as healing, praying for the sick, and delivering the oppressed should be pursued *along with* the ethical demands of holiness and righteousness.[21]

In reading the gospels, Wimber rediscovered a theme which had been summarily dismissed in the academic tradition since Bultmann[22] – the warfare motif that pitted the ministry of Jesus against the power and rule of Satan and demons.[23] He found a worthy ally in the Lutheran theologian James Kallas. In Kallas' works, *The Real Satan, The Significance of the Synoptic Miracles,* and *Jesus and the Power of Satan,*[24] Wimber found an academically strong theological examination of the "kingdoms at war" motif with practical consequences. Kallas moved against much of the tradition by asserting that the worldview of the Jewish Inter- testamental period and the New Testament was shot through with the reality of Satan, demons, fallen angels, and their influence on the world of men.[25] The reality of Satan and demons served as a theodicy for the Jews under the persecution of Antiochus Epiphanes and the subsequent oppression of Rome.[26] The writings of Jewish Apocalyptic attempted to describe how Satan fell from a servant of the Most High to the principal enemy of God who wrought vengeance and destruction on God's chosen people through human servants like Antiochus.[27] Thus, the Jews of the Second Temple period had a relatively robust understanding of Satan and demonology, and their priests were quite familiar with the concept of demonic influence on persons and the removal of that influence.[28] The ministry of Jesus can be seen as a *frontal attack on the powers of Satan which had usurped the good creation of God*; the ministry of Jesus was the **counter-attack**, or invasion of the rightful ruler to throw out the rebellious forces which had plagued mankind. Kallas writes: "The New Testament takes seriously the conviction that this world is enslaved under Satan who causes all suffering and woe, and Jesus is the one sent by God to destroy the devil and usher in the kingdom of God".[29] Wimber also saw this taught explicitly in Matthew 11:11-15, when Jesus states that even as the kingdom of God has been "forcibly advancing, and violent people are attacking it" (New Living Translation),[30] the "ones" here cannot be "men" or humans, but *servants of Satan*. The *kingdom* advances aggressively against its enemy and, in turn, suffers violence itself as the enemy fights back.[31] Kallas comments on this text: "Which violent ones? The overall context makes it clear that Jesus is referring to the devil and the entrenched powers of evil. The original words of John the Baptist, 'The kingdom of God is at hand' *were the declaration of war against Satan*".[32]

Kallas makes another connection that Wimber certainly resonated with:

> The miracles are not merely proofs of the identity of Jesus, nor are they mere signs designed to attract attention to his words and startle men into paying attention….Instead, the words and works of Jesus are of the same order. The miracles have precisely the same message as the words of Jesus. The message of Jesus concentrated on the announcement of the kingdom of God…and the miracles showed what the kingdom of God would be like. The parables and preaching were verbal announcements: the miracles were physical anticipations. [33]

It is quite simple to discern how Wimber was able to draw on these elements of Kallas' studies and combine them with his growing conception of eschatology founded on Ladd's work. To the idea of the already–not yet kingdom, Wimber now began to speak of an inaugurated, *enacted* eschatology; that is, as Kallas notes above, Jesus inaugurated the kingdom not merely in some esoteric, existential form, but in a concrete, demonstrable fashion by *words and works*.

Considering the congruence between Wimber and Kallas' view on the kingdom and the nature of the miracles, the divergences show the degree to which Wimber was a selective and careful expositor of his sources. A significance example of this turns on Kallas' view of the nature of the kingdom. In order to understand this, and to illustrate where Wimber would have been uncomfortable with Kallas, Kallas' views on the ministry of the *disciples* must be brought into focus. In *The Real Satan,* Kallas writes of the "failed" mission of the disciples as recorded in Luke 10: "The disciples go out, and they return. There is no end to Satan's empire. The foray has been unsuccessful…the efforts of the disciples were not enough. The kingdom of God did not come".[34] Furthermore, this setback was a surprise to Jesus: "Jesus expected to be transported on high and to return in triumph as a result of the ministry of the disciples".[35] It is at this point, that Jesus begins to rethink his strategy, and is forced to confront the reality of his own death and suffering as the final blow that will defeat the kingdom of Satan.[36]

Wimber's take on this episode is quite different. First, rather than seeing this record as one of *failure*, Wimber read it as a training session that *went spectacularly well*. Indeed, the post-mission response of the disciples was one of *amazement and joy*, not of defeat and loss, as Kallas seems to indicate.[37] This passage was paramount to Wimber because it sets a pattern: Jesus gave power and authority first to the twelve, then to the 70, and, at Pentecost, to the entire church.

Wimber saw that the episode of the sending of the 12 and the 70 as "training missions" that established a pattern for church pastors to follow.

For Wimber, living the future meant that *all* were called into this eschatological kingdom, to do the works and preach the word, not just a select few. Furthermore, Luke 10 is really a live training demonstration, albeit with a limited scope and time frame, as any capable trainer would do.[38] Far from being a failure, it was a successful, *initial move of a much larger campaign that would ultimately conquer the forces of evil*.[39] Secondly, while this first commission was paramount, it set a pattern expected to be continued throughout the ages. The **practice** of the eschatological, enacted kingdom of God was to be continued until the final *parousia.* Wimber's understanding of Ladd's already–not yet dynamic, which took the "growth" parables seriously, allowed him to accept as victorious what Kallas declared to be either a "failed" mission or at best, a "limited, local" success.[40]

Wimber credited numerous scholars who influenced him as he was forming his eschatology. While at Fuller, he became friends with Dr Charles Kraft, who gave him a credible witness to the possibility of power ministry while Wimber was beginning to question cessationism.[41] After encountering Ladd, Wimber read Ladd's sources, including Jeremias and Cullman.[42] By the late 1980s, Wimber's eschatology was firmly set. He was insistent that the already–not yet, inaugurated, enacted, eschatological kingdom of God would become the theological foundation of the Vineyard movement, and sought to infuse this understanding into every aspect of the movement. The degree to which this desire was successful is yet to be determined. First, however, the focus of this study must move to the next stage of theological growth in the Vineyard, as this kingdom vision was expanded, deepened, and extended by other scholars.

Questions for discussion:

1. What might be some of the implications of holding the Pentecostal restorationist view of church history?

2. The Pentecostals saw their experience of the Spirit to be the last herald that would usher in the second coming of Christ. What are some issues or problems that might arise from this view?

3. Wimber understood with Ladd that, since the resurrection, we are all in the "last days". How might this view change our view of church history?

4. If Wimber was right in that the gospels could be read as a "training manual" of sorts, how does this change our view of the gospels? How have you heard the gospels taught in the past? What are the primary *lessons* Christians can take from the gospels?

5. How do the different explanations of realm, rule, and reign change your understanding of the kingdom?

6. The issue of *conflict* between the kingdom of God and the kingdom of Satan became a primary theme for Wimber. How have you seen this work out practically in your church and life?

85

SEVEN

Towards a Vineyard Eschatology: the Growth of an Inaugurated, Enacted Eschatology

As the Vineyard movement grew in numbers and influence, John Wimber managed to gather a significant number of scholars to his fledgling movement. These scholars assisted Wimber in articulating his developing eschatology. At first, these scholars primarily solidified the enacted eschatology message, as well as adding theological substance and legitimization to Wimber's teaching. In the second decade of the Vineyard, the movement came under significant theological challenge from other Evangelical church pastors. While at first Wimber chose not to respond to these challenges, in the 1990s he changed his mind and enlisted several prominent academics who had come into the Vineyard to serve as "apologists" in order to refute these new challenges. Finally, in the last decade, a set of thinkers have emerged across the growing worldwide movement that are beginning to refine, extend, and strengthen Vineyard theology.

The Work of Dr. Derek Morphew

The message had been clarified and defended well, but not greatly *expanded* until a South African scholar, Derek Morphew, burst upon the North American Vineyard landscape.[1] Dr Morphew (Ph.D., New Testament, University of Cape Town), had come to know about the Vineyard through Wimber's ministry travels to South Africa in the early 1980s. Morphew had become an adherent to Ladd's inaugurated eschatology, and when he met Wimber and heard his articulation of Ladd combined with practical ministry, he understood immediately that this was the robust theological paradigm that he had been seeking to develop.

87

A close friendship with Wimber ensued, and in 1997 Wimber and Bob Fulton asked Morphew to take over the leadership of the Vineyard Bible Institute (VBI).[2] Morphew began a Vineyard church in Cape Town, South Africa, and began to apply his theological mind to developing teaching materials based on Wimber's theology. Morphew's book *Breakthrough: Discovering the Kingdom* has most likely become one of the most read and influential work on Vineyard theology to date, trailing only Wimber's books in influence.[3] In addition, Morphew contributed over a dozen monographs in the VBI catalog, ranging from studies on canonical scriptures, to theological studies, theology of social and political ethics, and even an exposition of contemporary Gnosticism.[4] The scope and influence of his writing, leadership, and mentoring makes Morphew the most significant expositor of inaugurated eschatology in the Vineyard today.

In *Breakthrough*, Morphew first discusses the Old Testament conception of the kingdom, which he finds is first articulated in the Exodus narrative, and reinforced through the Davidic reign. With Ladd, Morphew argues that two major themes emerge in the Old Testament regarding the kingdom: "The Lord is king, and the Lord will become King".[5] The first statement is the message of the pre-prophetic writings that record the Exodus, the conquest of Canaan, and the Davidic monarchy. The prophetic books and post-exilic writings reflect the promise that at "the day of the Lord", the Lord will ***become*** king. [6] In the Exodus story, the kingdom of God is seen in a powerful conflict with the kingdom of darkness, exemplified through Pharaoh and the gods of Egypt (Exodus 12:12). Morphew states: "The message of the Exodus is of two kingdoms in collision: the power of God against the power of darkness, the power of Yahweh against the power of Egypt. To say, 'kingdom of God' is therefore to say something about power, battle, conquest, and victory".[7]

Thus, Morphew has taken the influence of Kallas and Wimber, and pushed the kingdom ideal further back into the scriptural narrative than even Ladd had.[8] The liberation of the Hebrews from Pharaoh was not merely a triumph of oppressed peoples over their oppressor, but a spiritual battle between Yahweh, Israel's king, and the gods of Egypt. This picture of the kingdom is representative of Israel's subsequent history: Yahweh is king, and will fight for his people. The conquest of Canaan, and the golden age of David's monarchy reveal this relationship. The Davidic monarchy is a particularly notable image of the reign of God. The wars of David that established the kingdom were wars of Yahweh against the Canaanite gods; the establishment of David, and then Solomon, as the "anointed" ones were symbolic of God's reign over Israel.

The reign of Solomon was characterized by kingdom prosperity, *shalom*, and celebration. However, after the divided kingdom, the prophets paint another picture of the kingdom – the nations and kings of the earth still had power, but one day, they too would be subject to Yahweh's reign, and the Lord would become king over all the nations of the earth in the apocalyptic "Day of the Lord" at the culmination of human history.[9]

The New Testament, according to Morphew, introduces four tenses in which the kingdom is "coming", as Jesus speaks of a kingdom that *will come, has come, is coming immediately, and will be delayed.*[10] Of these, the first two have received the bulk of focus by modern kingdom studies. However, Morphew argues that by overlooking the last two tenses, or merging their meaning into the first two, much of modern scholarship has fallen into the same trap that confused Jesus' early audience. Matthew 21-25 most clearly teaches that the coming of the kingdom will be *delayed.* The parables of the virgins and the talents reveal a delayed coming; that is, a period of time before the bridegroom or the master returns.[11] It is the lack of taking this sense seriously, Morphew argues, that explains the problem of the "delay of the *parousia*" that has vexed modern kingdom scholarship. These parables make it clear that Jesus himself *knew of and taught the disciples* of a delay between his first and second comings – hence there was no "problem", other than a lack of understanding regarding the *length* of the delay. He argues:

Because of the texts about the kingdom being imminent and those about the kingdom being present, there are any number of commentators and biblical scholars who are quite convinced that these texts cannot be original to Jesus. A whole "theology of the delay" has developed in some circles, arguing that Jesus and the disciples believed in the imminence of the kingdom, but when time went by and the end did not materialise, the disciples had to find an explanation. This caused them to read back into the teaching of Jesus' statements about a delay.[12]

In contrast to some liberal scholars who doubt the authenticity of these parables, Morphew confidently asserts that there is no reason to question their validity, given the multiple attestations in Matthew and Luke, and multiple parables containing the central idea.[13]

In a similar fashion, the "immediately" or "near" sayings have often been reduced to the present tense "has come" or "arrived" statements of the kingdom. Morphew argues that this is a mistake, as the "immediately" texts offer an important nuance that displays *the progressive revealing and growth* of the kingdom, as in the parables of the seed and the leaven. Furthermore, understanding this nuance removes the concern that Jesus was mistaken regarding the kingdom; rather it adds depth to both the mission of the disciples (Matthew 10:23) and the growth of the kingdom.[14] All of these facets convey the mysterious nature of the kingdom, which "breaks through, from the future into the present, in successive interventions of God".[15]

This already - not yet nature of the kingdom is displayed in multiple dimensions; followers of Jesus have become already–not yet *people* (as in 2 Corinthians 5:2-17),[16] who are new creatures, and yet "groan and are burdened". Building on Ladd, the idea of only two ages, "this present age" (after the first coming) and "the age to come" (after the final *parousia*) not only settles matters of eschatology, but also refutes dispensationalism's distinction between the church and Israel, and deals a death blow to cessationism.[17] Morphew finds much in the most recent "Third Quest for the historical Jesus" that reinforces his inaugurated eschatology, but also asserts that missteps in the Quest can be adequately re-addressed from the framework he has proposed.[18] Dr Morphew now speaks of an "inaugurated, *enacted* eschatological kingdom of God, "thus putting equal emphasis on the continuing *action* of the kingdom that was inaugurated

90

in the mission of Jesus, and yet is profoundly *eschatological* as it brings the powers of the future kingdom of God into the present history of man. Dr Morphew continues to write and teach in the Vineyard, and will likely be an influential voice in the continuing development of Vineyard theology.[19]

Conclusion

It is quite evident that the eschatology of the Vineyard movement is a fusion of elements that surfaced in twentieth-century theological study, matured in the subsequent paths of investigation, and solidified in the evangelical consensus exemplified by Ladd. John Wimber seized upon Ladd's work when he realized it provided a prototype for the vision of the kingdom of God that he discovered in the scriptures. After he infused this rich concept into the Vineyard movement, subsequent Vineyard teachers buttressed and refined this vision, which naturally led others to extend the model into the inaugurated, enacted eschatological construct that is both well-formed, and yet maturing. A unique eschatology is, however, not the only component of the Vineyard's theological basis, for it is the *combination of eschatology and Pneumatology*, the church experience of *living the future* that makes the Vineyard movement distinctive and interesting. It is now time to turn to the important discussion of the work of the Spirit in Vineyard Pneumatology.

Section III: The Work of the Spirit in the Vineyard Movement

By 1982, John Wimber had several components of his theological framework in place. He had shed cessationism, begun to pray eagerly for the sick, and had a sturdy foundation of inaugurated eschatology. However, as he gained more experience in praying for the sick, he was faced with the realization that what he *lacked* was a theology of healing. He began to engage with other theological traditions in his quest to learn more about healing and other charismatic phenomena. In other words, while his eschatology constructed from Ladd and Kallas gave him the basic framework he needed, there were numerous gaps that needed to be filled in his *Pneumatology*.

As he engaged with diverse authors from Pentecostal, Charismatic, Liturgical, and Catholic traditions, it became quite evident that each tradition operated out of an explicit or implicit Pneumatology that affected their approach to the *charismata*. As he examined these pneumatologies, he understood that first a Pneumatology for the Vineyard would have to be compatible with his understanding of eschatology, and secondly, that while numerous pneumatological options presented themselves, none of the available options were built "from the ground up", as it were, on the model of inaugurated eschatology that he had embraced. Once again, what Wimber needed was a new prototype: a Pneumatology that was not merely *compatible* with inaugurated eschatology, but one that strengthened, extended, and grew out of his eschatology.

Wimber's quest for a pneumatology came at an opportune time, as the twentieth century had seen a resurgence of pneumatological interest and investigation. The birth of Pentecostalism, while it produced little "systematic" theology at first, had provided the Church with a vital experience of the Spirit that could not be ignored. When the "Charismatic" movement of the 1960s arose, Catholic, Reformed, and Wesleyan scholars all began to turn their attention to the previously "neglected" Holy Spirit. At the same time, Pentecostal scholarship began to mature, and "homegrown" Pentecostal scholars began to contribute to scholarship from their unique hermeneutical horizons. Predictably, ecumenical dialogue began to flourish, as a virtuous cycle began: Pentecostal practitioners challenged the mainstream academy, Pentecostals themselves were encouraged to deeper theological reflection, and the mainstream and the Pentecostal academy were mutually enriched.

The Pentecostal movement contributed three major issues that those in ecumenical dialogue – and later, John Wimber – were forced to consider. The first issue was the distinctive Pentecostal doctrine of the baptism of the Holy Spirit as an experience *separated from* and *distinct from* conversion. In classical Pentecostal traditions, this would become known as the doctrine of *subsequence.* Secondly, Pentecostals argued that this experience was evidenced by speaking in the gifts of tongues; this would become known as the *initial evidence* doctrine. Finally, Pentecostals developed a robust theology of the divine healing of the body, borrowed from their Holiness tradition, that stated that healing was *guaranteed in the Atonement*. These three distinctive doctrines would both confound and attract theologians from Catholic, Reformed, and Evangelical traditions. Much of the ecumenical dialogue was dominated by discussion of these issues, especially the doctrines of subsequence and initial evidence.

It is clear that Wimber had a great deal of raw material at hand with which to build his Pneumatology; the important question then became: *"What materials* should he utilize?"

This chapter will focus on this question. First, we will consider the late twentieth century "Turn to the Spirit" which brought Pneumatology sharply into focus in Christian theology. From the perspective of formal theological reflection, this stage began with the arrival of the Charismatic movement in 1960, built considerable strength in the Catholic Church in Vatican II, and drew scholars from numerous Protestant traditions through the 1970s and 1980s. As we discovered in the development of his eschatology, while Wimber was quite aware of these developments in the larger church, his primary sources were from the Evangelical, Charismatic, and Pentecostal streams. Therefore it is important to understand these pneumatologies. Once again, it will be obvious that Wimber was both a generous interpreter and a wise borrower, for he selectively harvested from these traditions those shoots which he saw could be grafted into his eschatology. Finally, I will describe this distinct Pneumatology that evolved as Wimber's understanding and experience grew, and became normative in the Vineyard movement.

EIGHT

Contemporary Protestant Pneumatology

While Pentecostalism as a movement had existed since the Azusa street revival of 1906, and formal Pentecostal denominations like the Assemblies of God had existed since 1912, Pentecostals were often not welcomed by Evangelical or Protestant churches, nor recognized as having much to contribute to scholarship.[1] Much of this had to do with the absence of the Pentecostal *experience* within the wider church. With the advent of the Charismatic movement in the mainline churches in 1960, however, this began to change. The Charismatic movement spread through numerous Protestant denominations, and entered the Catholic Church in America in 1966. Even Vatican II became known as the conference of the Spirit, and the subsequent Catholic academic engagement gave the Pentecostal experience further legitimacy and traction. Protestant scholars began to engage in pneumatological reflection, and notable theologians and scholars brought focus on the continuing work of the Spirit throughout the 1970s. In turn, Pentecostalism itself began to accept and reward theological scholarship; therefore, conversation partners between the various traditions found each other, and valuable ecumenical dialogue revolving around issues in Pneumatology began to flourish. It is remarkable that in a scant three decades, Pneumatology had gone from a side concern in systematic theology, to a major focus and distinctive place.

This remarkable turn to Pneumatology engaged many more traditions and scholars than noted in this brief overview; but it is enough to show how the rise of Pentecostalism and the growth of the Charismatic movement brought increasing focus to the Holy Spirit in the late twentieth century. This synergy of focus provided many opportunities for scholars and practitioners to reflect on their unique beliefs and practices, what they held in common, and where they differed. However, we are going to focus on the pneumatological options available to John Wimber as he began his

97

personal reflection on the work of the Spirit.

Evangelical Cessationism

The steady growth of Pentecostalism and the emergence of the Charismatic movement forced the Evangelical church in America to take stock of its view of the Holy Spirit. While the Trinitarian personhood of the Spirit was rarely in question, Evangelicals, like the Catholics and Episcopalians before them, were forced to consider the issues of baptism in the Holy Spirit and the role of the gifts in the life of the Church. If we remember that by 1982 John Wimber was striving to include the ministry of the Holy Spirit into his kingdom theology, it is important to know those evangelical teachers and scholars who were influential in the 1960s and 1970s, as these would have the most influence on Wimber and his associates. Wimber saw himself as an Evangelical, and held many established Evangelical pastors and theologians in high esteem, so it is important to understand the range of perspectives that he could draw from. The specific issues focused on in this chapter – those of the baptism of the Holy Spirit, and the operation of the *charismata* in the life of the Church, especially speaking in tongues and the phenomenon of divine healing – were often addressed by Evangelicals, but, as expected, from a variety of perspectives.

For the dispensationalist Evangelicals, there was little controversy: the gifts had belonged to an earlier dispensation, had their role confined to the ministry of the apostles and the church, and were thus no longer needed.[2] This conviction also solved the issue of the baptism of the Holy Spirit; as well as the gifts of tongues and healing. Most Evangelicals held that the baptism of the Holy Spirit was none other than the reception of the Holy Spirit in the believer at conversion, and thus was the inheritance and mark of all who had confessed faith in Jesus.[3] The Reverend Billy Graham is representative of this claim when he stated: "In my own study of the Scriptures through the years I have become convinced that there is only one baptism with the Holy Spirit in the life of the believer, and that takes place at the moment of conversion".[4]

For the cessationist, however, this claim could be expanded

considerably. Not only is the giving of the Spirit a one-time experience at conversion, *Pentecost itself* was a one-time experience for the church! Richard Gaffin contended in 1979:

> The baptism with the Holy Spirit at Pentecost is a unique event of epochal significance in the history of redemption. Therefore it is no more capable of being repeated or serving as a model for individual Christian experience than are the death, resurrection and ascension of Christ, with which it is so integrally conjoined as part of a single complex of events.[5]

By placing the experience of Pentecost within the *historia salutis*, and not with the *ordo salutis*, cessationists like Gaffin bracketed the entire renewal experience of the Pentecostals and Charismatics as being decidedly out of bounds in the current age.[6] When theologians speak of the *ordo salutis* (Latin for 'order of salvation') they mean events in the life of the Christian *person* such as calling, conversion, repentance, regeneration, sanctification, and so on. Different theological systems have different events and order of events. The *historia salutis* (Latin for 'history of salvation') are those events by which God brings salvation to people, like creation, the fall, the Exodus story, the birth, life, and death of Christ, etc. By placing Pentecost in the *history of salvation* like creation or the birth of Christ, by default it becomes a non-repeatable event. Gaffin would say that because Pentecost is the precise act of the establishment of the church as the people of God; there is no need for it to be repeated.

Put differently, since this process required the powerful work of the Spirit, once the church *was established* and the ministry and authority of the apostles *was confirmed*, there was no further need of the "dispensational, *once-for-all*" Pentecost experience. Gaffin here is restating much of the argument in Benjamin B. Warfield's *Counterfeit Miracles,* where he developed the extensive argument that the miraculous acts of the Spirit in Acts were primarily to "authenticate the Apostles as the authoritative founders of the church" and as such, "the extraordinary gifts belonged to the extraordinary office and showed themselves only in connection with its activities".[7] Warfield's position was a harsh academic reaction to the birth of Pentecostalism. It became the standard decree against both Pentecostals and the possibility of the *charismata* in the church, and by the later twentieth century had become nearly universally established in Evangelical seminaries, bible schools, and pulpits.[8] Warfield also popularized the so-called "cluster theory" of biblical miracles which proposed that miracles were generally found in four different periods in salvation history: the Exodus story, the ministry of Elijah and Elisha, the Exile, and the ministry of Christ and the apostles.[9]

....

For many years John Wimber believed in the so-called "cluster theory" of biblical miracles which taught that miracles were relatively rare in salvation history, and confined to Exodus story, the ministry of Elijah and Elisha, the Exile, and the ministry of Christ and the apostles.

....

Evangelical cessationists of the 1970s were then forced into the difficult situation of accounting for not only the *growth* of Pentecostalism and the Charismatic movement, but also, the *accompanying signs and wonders* that became the hallmarks of both movements. In a sense, Warfield had a far easier task in debunking Pentecostalism, as it was just beginning, and its growth was generally limited to the less educated and lower classes of people. With the spread of the Charismatic renewal in the Catholic and established churches, even among the educated and scholarly, personal attacks against flamboyant Pentecostal "faith healers" were not enough. Gaffin attempts to draw a line between the so-called "word gifts" of tongues and prophecy, which have unequivocally ceased, and "healing gifts" which may continue as they do not raise issues of revelation and the sufficiency of scripture.[10] The famed evangelist Billy Graham posits a different suggestion:

Several theologians to whom I have talked recently, both in Europe and America, hold the view that the Holy Spirit is gradually being withdrawn from the world as we enter what may be the climactic moments of the end of the present age.[11]

Graham wants to argue, from a dispensationalist perspective, that the miraculous gifts, if they *are still operative*, will gradually become *rarer*.

....

Even the renowned evangelical Dr. Billy Graham doubted that the Pentecostalism or the Charismatic movement would have a lasting impact on the world. His dispensationalist background made it hard for him to believe that the miraculous works of the Spirit were continuing in his day.

....

Graham also seeks to "redefine" to some degree the operation of some of the gifts. For example, the gift of prophecy is really the process of illumination that allows evangelists and preachers to *exegete and present the Gospel properly*. Foretelling the future "no longer exists" nor is it necessary, for, owing to the completeness of the scriptural canon, "God no longer directly reveals new truths".[12]

He continues:

It is the work of the Holy Spirit to illumine the minds of those called to the prophetic office so they understand the word of God and apply it with a depth impossible to those who do not have the gift of prophecy...the New Testament prophets had ministries more like that of Evangelists. They proclaimed the word of God and called upon people to repent of their sins...[13]

John R.W. Stott was one of the leading evangelical scholars of the 1970s and 1980s. With Graham, he argued against the Pentecostal "second blessing":

The baptism of the Spirit is identical with the 'gift' of the Spirit, that is one of the *distinctive* blessings of the new covenant, and, because it is an *initial* blessing, is also a universal blessing for all members of the

101

covenant. It is part and partial of belonging to the new age.[14]

But Stott took a more conciliatory tone towards the operation of the gifts of the Spirit:

What then should be our response to miraculous claims today? It should neither be a stubborn incredulity ("but miracles don't happen today'") nor an uncritical gullibility ("of course! Miracles happen all the time!"), but rather a spirit of open-minded inquiry: "I don't expect miracles as commonplace today, because the special revelation they were given to authenticate is complete; but of course, God is sovereign and God is free, and there may well be particular situations in which he pleases to perform them.[15]

Interestingly, Stott argued for a hermeneutical position that gives preference to the "didactic" passages of scripture (e.g. the teaching in Paul's letters), over the "descriptive" passages (e.g. narratives like Acts). For this reason he cautioned against the use of Acts in the *establishment of doctrine*. This move is not unusual among cessationists; Gaffin makes a similar claim as well. Stott also contends for a "richer" experience of the Spirit and concludes his study by encouraging believers to "seek ever more of the Holy Spirit's fullness, by repentance, faith, and obedience, and also to keep sowing to the Spirit so that his fruit may grow and ripen in our character".[16] Thus, Stott seems to offer a "soft cessationism" that is not nearly as restrictive as Gaffin's, but nonetheless *does not* see the operation of the *charismata* as *normative* in the church today. Significantly, the influence of the Charismatic renewal movement caused Evangelicals to reconsider their own lack of a robust experiential faith, and to recognize this gap in many Evangelical churches as well.[17]

For these cessationist Evangelicals, the work of the Spirit consisted primarily as:

- convicting the world of sin (John 16:8)
- teaching believers about Christ (Luke 12:12; John 14:26)
- giving believers hope and joy (Romans 14:17; 15:13)

- being the seal of faith or "down payment" in Christ (Ephesians 1:13; 2 Corinthians 1:21; 2 Corinthians 5:5)
- giving the fruits of the Spirit (Galatians 5:22).

Quite positively, numerous Evangelical scholars encouraged and exhorted Christians to pursue the "fruit of the Spirit,"[18] viewed the work of the Spirit in the life of the individual Christian as crucial,[19] saw the Spirit as being active in the world,[20] and understood the presence of the Spirit to be eschatological in character,[21] even though they were cautious or skeptical towards the more dramatic Pentecostal and Charismatic *experiences*, i.e. claims of divine healing, prophecy, or the ecstatic speaking in tongues. It is no exaggeration, however, to claim that for a vast majority of Evangelical scholars in the late twentieth century, Pneumatology did not occupy a central place.[22]

Evangelical Continuationism

Despite this lack of emphasis on the work of the Holy Spirit in Evangelicalism, there were several scholars who eagerly embraced the principles of the Pentecostal and Charismatic renewal. James Dunn's influential and respectful *Baptism in the Holy Spirit* served as a theological introduction to the claims of Pentecostalism for many Evangelicals. Dunn's treatment was not merely a critique of Pentecostal doctrine; he also found much of Protestantism guilty of neglecting the Spirit, even subordinating the third person of the Trinity to the scriptures:

In scholastic Protestantism the Spirit became in effect *subordinate* to the Bible...Protestants fastened on to the objectivity of the Bible. Though the Spirit was regarded as the principal participant in the work of salvation, he was still hardly experienced apart from the Bible.[23]

In the following paragraph Dunn continues:

It is a sad commentary on the poverty of our own immediate experience of the Spirit that when we come across language in which the NT writers refer directly to the gift of the Spirit and to their experience of it, either we automatically refer it to the sacraments and can only give it meaning when we do so (1 Corinthians 6:11; 12:13), or else we discount the experience described as too subjective and mystical in favor of a faith which is essentially an affirmation of biblical propositions, or else we in effect *psychologize the Spirit out of existence*.[24]

In subsequent articles and monographs, Dunn developed many of these themes he hinted at in *Baptism;* he became even more convinced that a Christianity that lacked or neglected a dramatic, evidential presence of the Holy Spirit had *deviated from the model of the New Testament church*.[25]

Perhaps the most notable advocate of the Charismatic renewal experience was Dr. Martyn Lloyd-Jones, who wrote *Joy Unspeakable* to contend not only for a powerful, vibrant baptism of the Holy Spirit; but to strongly urge believers to "seek earnestly...the greater gifts" (1 Corinthians 12:31). Dr. Lloyd-Jones held a more Pentecostal view of baptism, as he stated a central principle: "All I am trying to establish is this – that you can be regenerate *without being baptized with the Holy Spirit*".[26] His concern was that in combining the two experiences: baptism often becomes both non-experiential and unconscious, which is a very different experience from that described in the book of Acts. The effect of the baptism of the Spirit is empowerment for service:

> And so we are trying to show that the central, main object of the baptism with Holy Spirit is to enable us with the power to be witnesses to the Lord Jesus Christ, to his person, and to his work.[27]

The exercise of the gifts accompanies the baptism for "we need some supernatural authentication of our message".[28] However, he equally cautions against positions like the Pentecostal "initial evidence":

> It seems to me that the teaching of the Scripture itself, plus the evidence of the history of the church, establishes the fact that the baptism with the Spirit *is not always accompanied* by particular gifts... There are

104

people today, as there have been now for a number of years, who say that the baptism with the Spirit is always accompanied by certain particular gifts. It seems to me that the answer of the Scripture is that that is not the case, that you may have a baptism with the Spirit, and a mighty baptism with the Spirit at that, with *none of the gifts of tongues, miracles, or various other gifts.*[29] (Italics mine)

Through much of his preaching and ministry, Lloyd-Jones continued to advocate for a deeper experience with the Spirit and the operation of the gifts within the church, even as he challenged some firmly-held doctrines of classical Pentecostalism. There seems to be some inconsistencies and paradoxes in Lloyd-Jones' teaching, which may be either a factor of his changing views, or related to the nature of his two main works on the subject being essentially collected works of sermons completed at a much later period of time. [30]

While there is little doubt that more examples of Evangelical continuationists could be referenced, especially among Protestant evangelical churches impacted by the Charismatic renewal, these examples serve to illustrate that before Wimber, *Evangelicalism was not uniformly dispensationalist and cessationist.* There was a range of perspectives, from hard cessationists like Gaffin, to those who were more open to the gifts like Lloyd-Jones, and many like Graham and Stott who could be placed somewhere in the middle.[31] Like those in the Charismatic renewal, however, most Evangelical continuationists questioned and rejected several distinctives of Pentecostal theology even as they pursued a more obvious *experience* of the Spirit. As John Wimber would later come to many of these same conclusions, it is essential to have a firm understanding of the Pentecostal doctrines Wimber would contend against and ultimately discard.

Pentecostal Restorationist Pneumatology

When considering the association of Pneumatology and eschatology in classical Pentecostalism, it is vital to keep in mind that its Wesleyan-holiness roots had a vibrant understanding of a baptism in the Holy Spirit. Pentecostals certainly did not "invent" this distinctive doctrine, but they expanded the idea far beyond previous conceptions.[32] In the middle nineteenth century, many churches became influenced by "Wesleyan holiness tradition", which placed a great deal of emphasis on the process of sanctification in the life of the believer. John Wesley had laid the roots of these ideas in his work, *A Plain Account of Christian Perfection,* in 1767. It is quite interesting to note that, at the same time, German liberal scholarship was enthralled with the "lives of Jesus" idea that eviscerated the Bible of any real meaning. In many parts of the church there was an *opposite movement* which placed emphasis on the continuing sanctification of the believer *after* conversion. Modern-day churches like the Christian and Missionary Alliance, Nazarene churches, and most Pentecostal churches are all progenies of the Holiness movement.

The Nineteenth Century Holiness movement taught that believers could experience a "second work of grace" after conversion that would empower them to live a holy life free from the tendency to sin, which they called "entire sanctification".

A major concept of this movement was the idea of "Christian Perfection" or "Entire Sanctification". This was the idea that through discipleship, prayer, and reliance on the power of God, a Christian could become "sanctified", or almost entirely avoid *willful* sin altogether. This was, of course, quite a controversial claim, and has been modified and debated within holiness churches to this day. While there is a great deal that could be said about this, for the purposes of our study a detailed examination of this movement is not necessary. By the latter half of the nineteenth century, the language of "the baptism of the Holy Spirit" began to supersede that of "entire sanctification" in many churches and teachers. In some cases, the baptism was an instantaneous transformation, as in the work of Phoebe Palmer; others believed the baptism to be a one-time experience that eventually culminated in a holy life.[33] Some held that the baptism was the *sign* of "entire sanctification" and still others understood it as an empowerment for service.[34] Even tongues was known in the tradition; thus, when early Pentecostals experienced tongues they felt they were strongly within both the Acts church model and their own tradition.[35] Most importantly, we must keep in mind that for *all* of these Holiness and Pentecostal groups, the baptism of the Holy Spirit came *after,* sometimes well after, conversion. It was separated not just in time, but more importantly, in kind and in purpose. Pentecostals would later describe it as a "second work" of grace, *separate and distinct from conversion.*

In many ways, Pentecostals took existing theological and experiential ideas and applied them to new conclusions: the baptism in the Holy Spirit, and the accompanying signs, were irrefutable evidence that they were *living in the last days before the triumphant return of Christ.* They often spoke of their experience as a *restoration* of a faith that had been lost through the centuries owing to apostasy, complacency, or human arrogance.[36] Quite relevant to this conclusion was the idea that other forms of Christianity had *left* the apostolic faith, and thus the resurgence of the signs, especially tongues, functioned as a warning to these apostate groups.[37] For most early Pentecostals the baptism became one of the "four-fold" or "five-fold" cardinal doctrines.[38] A full engagement with the deep breadth of Pentecostal Pneumatology would be impossible in a short digression; thus I will focus on three major themes that would be taken up by John Wimber as he developed his Pneumatology: the nature of Spirit baptism, the initial evidence doctrine, and the theology of the gift of healing.

Early Pentecostals had a restorationist eschatology as they saw that they had been called by God as a renewal force to restore the life and vitality of the early church that had been lost in history.

Early Pentecostals were faced with much the same conundrum as their holiness forbearers; that is, their scripture methodology taught them that the baptism was a *second work of grace subsequent to conversion,* but what advantage does this bring in the life of the Christian? In the holiness movement, the "advantage" of Spirit baptism was obvious: it made possible either the movement towards holiness or Christian perfection itself. In Pentecostalism, the concept burgeoned into the concept of *empowerment for service or mission.* This conception of Spirit baptism has become the dominant theme of Pentecostalism; a self-identifier shared by Pentecostals worldwide. Frank Macchia states that Spirit baptism has imprinted itself as the "crown jewel" of doctrines on the Pentecostal psyche; thus it is a concept worthy of being defended, and even expanded, in the face of criticism and neglect.[39]

One of the first studies of the doctrine by a non-Pentecostal was James Dunn's book in 1970, Baptism in the Holy Spirit: a Re-examination of the New Testament Teaching on the Gift of the Spirit in relation to Pentecostalism today.[40] Dunn was suspicious of the Pentecostal doctrines of second blessing and subsequence, and his critique is directed towards some aspects of Pentecostal theology. However, as noted above, he also charges the wider church with missing many of the blessings of the Pentecostal experience that is described and expected in the New Testament. Because Dunn's view would later prove to be formative for John Wimber, it is worth quoting his thesis:

> For the writers of the New Testament, the baptism in or gift of the Spirit was part of the event of becoming a Christian, together with the effective presentation of the Gospel, belief in Jesus as Lord, and water-baptism in the name of the Lord Jesus; that it was the chief element in conversion-initiation so that only those who had received the Spirit could be called Christians; that the reception of the Spirit was a very definite and often dramatic experience.[41]

Dunn presses his case against the Pentecostal second blessing by contending that in Acts, "it is only by receiving the Spirit that one becomes a Christian". This would become the major objection from Evangelicals against the "Second Blessing" view of the Holy Spirit Baptism. It would seem that, if the Pentecostals are correct, there are "two classes" of

Christians: those who have undergone the second blessing, and thus *have the Spirit,* and those who have not undergone the second blessing, who *would not have the Spirit.* However, Dunn (and many others) countered the second blessing doctrine with verses like Ephesians 1:13-14: "When *you believed, you were marked in him with a seal, the promised Holy Spirit,* who is a deposit guaranteeing our inheritance until the redemption of those who are God's possession—to the praise of his glory." (NIV)

If the Spirit is given *when you believed* then there seems little room for a "second blessing" or reception of the Spirit *after* (sometimes long after!) conversion. We will see that Wimber would strongly react against this view as well. However, Dunn also contends against a "sacramentalist" view that *conflates* water baptism and reception of the Spirit, for "water baptism is clearly distinct from and even antithetical to Spirit-baptism, and is best understood as the expression of the faith which receives the Spirit".[42] This would be the view that John Wimber would later hold and instill in the Vineyard movement against the classic Pentecostal position. It is also interesting to note that Dunn's claim that "scholastic Protestantism had subordinated the Spirit to the Bible", would be a theme that Wimber would later adopt as he developed his "empowered evangelical" ideas. While Dunn is critical of the second blessing doctrine, he nonetheless acknowledges that there is much in the Pentecostal faith experience of the Spirit that the Protestant church should respect.[43]

In perhaps the most robust defense of the Pentecostal doctrine, Howard Ervin directly challenged James Dunn's critique. Ervin clarifies some misconceptions about the doctrine of Spirit-baptism, and offers a strong rebuttal of Dunn's "conversion-initiation hypothesis", which stated that the baptism in the Holy Spirit is *always* initiatory, and although it may yield empowerment for service, the baptism itself cannot be separated from the complex of conversion-initiation.[44] In response, Ervin charges that much of Dunn's exegesis reflects his *a priori* concerns; thus, many of the main planks in his structure are conjecture or arguments from silence.[45] Ervin states that in the New Testament, the "gift" of the Spirit is *always a distinct event separate from conversion,* and explicitly *for empowerment for mission.* Ervin admirably clarifies the position he defends in the question of whether Luke considers the Ephesian "disciples" in Acts 19 to be "Christians" proper (as the Pentecostal position would affirm) or whether he thought of them as "sub-Christians", i.e. disciples of John and Jesus who had not heard a completed presentation of the Gospel (as Dunn had suggested):[46]

> No responsible Pentecostal theologian would argue *simpliciter* that they were Christians who had not received the Holy Spirit. Implicit in the Pentecostal position is the understanding that, if they were Christians, then they had experienced the regenerating work of the Holy Spirit through repentance and faith but had not been baptized in the Spirit for power-in-mission.[47]

The distinction Ervin makes is crucial for the Pentecostal position, for it attempts to evade the "two classes of Christians" charge by agreeing that *all believers* did indeed "possess" the Spirit. This blunted Dunn's contention that to be a Christian is to *possess the Spirit.* Ervin still pushed for something greater, namely *empowerment,* which is given *in the* Pentecostal experience.[48] Ervin charges that even conversion-initiation proposals like Dunn's have "consistently ignored the clear charismatic dimension of Spirit-baptism that distinguishes 'the gift of the Holy Spirit' from conversion-initiation".[49]

Harold Hunter offered a similar defense of the classical Pentecostal position in his *Spirit-Baptism: A Pentecostal Alternative.*[50] Hunter concedes that there has been a great deal of ambiguity and confusion in classical Pentecostalism in defining exactly *what of* the Spirit is received at conversion. Hunter notes that some groups influenced by the Keswick tradition (for example, the Assemblies of God) come closer to the Evangelical/Reformed position; yet the common element among all strains of Pentecostals is the belief that "Spirit-baptism is to be understood as a work of the Spirit *which is distinct from and (usually) subsequent to his work of regeneration, adoption, and justification".*[51]

Furthermore, an obvious and strong case can be made that nearly all

Protestant Christians understand the Spirit to work throughout the *ordo salutus;* that is to say, that the entire process of justification, regeneration, and sanctification have distinct and notable *works of the Spirit.*[52] Hence, arguing for a distinct "second blessing" for empowerment is not *categorically* (emphasis mine) different from how Christians understand other elements of the *ordo salutus.*[53] He is adamant, however, that a close examination of the biblical texts reveals that "the charismatic work of the Spirit does not always become operative immediately in the life of the believer", citing such texts as Acts 8:14, 9:17; Galatians 4:6 and Ephesians 1:13, in evidence that both Luke and Paul support this claim.[54]

As he believes the biblical data is conclusively on his side, Hunter concludes that the thorniest issue is that of the "two classes" of Christians. In reality, this is an unavoidable consequence of any theological system that entails spiritual progress; thus, the classical Pentecostal position is merely caught in a biblical paradox not unlike many of its historical theological predecessors.[55]

For classical Pentecostals then, the point of the baptism became explicit: coupled with the latter days eschatology, and the emphasis on the imminent return of Christ, it *empowered* believers to carry the Pentecostal message to all people so as to evangelize them before the return of Christ.[56]

Tongues as initial evidence

The "second blessing" position, predictably, forced yet another issue: How can we be certain that we have undergone the baptism, and thus are equipped suitably for service? How can we be assured that *others* are equipped for service? Acts once again provided an answer: Pentecostals saw the *gifts of tongues* as authenticating the baptism of the Holy Spirit in passages like Acts 2, 10:46, and 19:6. Divine healing also provided an immediate sign of the Spirit's empowerment, but it would be the gift of tongues that would eventually become intimately associated with Pentecostalism in America.[57] This mark of Pentecostalism begs the question: "Why was tongues elevated over other gifts like healing and prophecy?" At least part of this question was the immediate nature of tongues – there was no ambiguity, or progress of time needed as in the case with healing or prophecy. Perhaps another response may be related

111

to the early Pentecostal hope that tongues was *xenolalia*, or the speaking of an existing human language unknown to the tongues-speaker. Their hope was that this would be the key to successful missions and the complete conversion of the world which, again, would fit into their eschatological paradigm.

....

Early Pentecostals often thought that some speaking of tongues was actually human languages like Chinese, Japanese, or an African language, and would allow the tongues-speaker to preach the gospel without "knowing" or having to learn the language.

....

Charles Parham should be credited for first making this claim which would become the trademark of a distinctive Pentecostal theology. Parham argued that "the speaking in other tongues as an inseparable part of the Baptism in the Holy Spirit distinguishes it from all previous works; and that no one has received the Baptism in the Holy Spirit who has not a Bible evidence to show for it".[58] According to J. Roswell Flower, while tongues had been well known previously, Parham and his students took a momentous step in asserting that speaking in tongues was *the* biblical evidence of the baptism in the Holy Spirit, and this assertion "made the Pentecostal Movement of the Twentieth Century".[59]

Contemporary Pentecostal scholars have provided several defenses for this preference. Ervin notes the "objective criteria" of the phenomena of tongues and prophesying, and explains theadvantages of his position over the conversion-initiation paradigm:

In Acts the reception of the gift of the Spirit is not simply a subjective, intuitive awareness of the Spirit's presence, for tongues and prophesying (Acts 2:4; 10:45, 46; 19:6) are *objective (and the Pentecostal would add, normative) witnesses to the reception of the gift of the Spirit.* They are not, however, evidence of the new birth.[60]

Frank Macchia offers a "sacramental" view of tongues with Spirit-

Baptism that is sympathetic to the early Pentecostal attempt to distinguish itself from the Holiness movement. The early Pentecostal tongues-speech not only set the Pentecostal experience apart from their Holiness forebears, but practicing tongues was seen "as a form of inspired speech which causes one to transcend the limits of one's human speech and thought in order to become an *oracle of the Spirit*".[61]

Understood in the context of the Azusa outpouring, tongues took on an eschatological significance key to Pentecostal self-understanding:

> Seymour and others of the Azusa Street Mission were unique in attaching tongues as *xenolalia* to the intercultural witness of the poor and disenfranchised. But both sought to describe the new outbreaks of *glossolalia* as a breakthrough in the most characteristic sign of the Spirit's presence to empower the people of God in the latter days, namely, inspired speech. Tongues as cryptic and miraculous speech functioned as *the final breakthrough in the Spirit's witness to, or praise of, God in the latter days.*[62]

Once again, their restorationist eschatology caused Pentecostals to interpret the gift of tongues as yet another sign of the coming end of the age. It is clear that the initial evidence doctrine was foundational to early Pentecostal self-understanding, because it served as a marker to distinguish their experience of the baptism of the Holy Spirit from their Holiness forefathers. In the following decades, speaking in tongues would often be considered as *the* distinctive Pentecostal practice by those *outside* the movement as well. Within classical Pentecostalism, however, the early conception was more complex, as the movement developed a wide range of perspectives and theological diversity quite early in its history. The baptism of the Holy Spirit was not a simple metaphor; as the definitive evidential phenomenon of their restorationist eschatology, it had to contain *more of* the primitive church experience than just tongues-speaking.

For Pentecostals convinced they were living in the "last days" or the "latter rain", the doctrine of divine healing would become nearly as important as speaking in tongues.

The Pentecostal Doctrine of Divine Healing

If early Pentecostals strained to find evidences of speaking in tongues in the history of the church, they had little difficulty finding historical justification for their practice of divine healing, as the Holiness tradition provided all the support they would require. Divine healing of the body was taught and practiced by many of the leading figures of the Holiness tradition in America including Charles Cullis, a Boston physician who, by opening a "healing house" in 1864 in Boston, essentially launched the healing movement in the Holiness tradition.[63] A.J. Gordon, strongly influenced by Cullis, began teaching on the subject and published an extremely popular book, *The Ministry of Healing,* in 1882. The founder of the Christian and Missionary Alliance, A.B. Simpson also vigorously promoted the doctrine. These leaders and countless others proved to be highly influential for Charles Fox Parham and William Seymour.[64] The "four-fold" formula of the full gospel in Holiness churches included "healing of the body as in the atonement"; it was this audacious claim that would not only be adopted by Pentecostals like Parham and Seymour, but would also became nearly as controversial as speaking in tongues. Holiness preachers like Simpson and Gordon made what they considered a logical deduction: if it was true that "He forgives all your sins and heals all your sicknesses" (Psalms 103:3), "By his stripes we are healed" (Isaiah 53:5), and "He Himself took our infirmities and carried away our diseases" (Matthew 8:17), then *sin and sickness, forgiveness and healing were intrinsically linked.*[65] The Holiness quest for "entire sanctification" could then be married with a complete faith for healing of *all physical infirmities.* Just as sin, or the effects of sin, was removed in the atonement, *so also was sickness and disease overcome in the atonement.*

114

Based on their interpretation of Isaiah 53:5, early Pentecostals believed that healing, like salvation, was "guaranteed" in the Death and Resurrection of Christ.

This legacy was carried into the embryonic Pentecostal movement by Charles Parham. At his Bethel Bible school in Topeka, Kansas, Parham taught divine healing as being guaranteed in the atonement.[66] Seymour also taught "a sanctified body is one that is cleansed from all sickness and disease. The Lord gives you power over sickness and disease".[67] As Pentecostalism exploded across North America, the emphasis on healing, and the controversial claim attached to it, became trademarks of the faith, eventually becoming codified into the statements of faith of many Pentecostal denominations.[68]

After the beginnings of Pentecostalism, and the emergence of the Charismatic movement, Pneumatology had moved from a place of inattention, to a primary focus of late twentieth century systematic theology. Truly, this was a case where experience in the church forced theology to re-examine whether a currently accepted doctrine, cessationism, was supported by scriptural and historical evidence. In many cases, theologians concluded that the modern cessationist framework was in error. This still left open, however, how a *theoretical* commitment to a vibrant work of the Spirit could be *guided and practiced in the churches*. Classical Pentecostalism offered several answers to this question, as did the various flavors of the Charismatic renewal.[69] What remains to be understood, is how John Wimber developed his understanding that would form the basis of Vineyard theology regarding the work of the Spirit.

NINE

The Baptism of the Holy Spirit in Vineyard Theology

As John Wimber turned away from his skepticism about tongues, healing, and prophecy being possible in the present-day church, he came to the realization that being open to these new experiences was not enough. His scriptural study convinced him that Christians were *commanded* to *engage* in these activities; they were not merely "options" to be considered. He came to the further recognition that whatever form or methodology of practice he would adopt, it must integrate with both his scriptural study and his understanding of the already–not yet kingdom of God. As he became convinced of the reality of divine healing, he embarked on a journey to learn all he could, in order to infuse the theology and the practice into the churches he was leading. He immediately discovered that, while the practices of healing in the Pentecostal and Charismatic movements gave him much insight and reinforced his theological commitment against cessationism, they gave him little in the form of models that he could incorporate into his churches.

Thus, as he began to consider the issues of the baptism of the Holy Spirit, the operation of the *charismata,* and divine healing, he found that he could *borrow* some elements from the Pentecostal and Charismatic traditions, but, in essence, he would have to build a theology of the work of the Spirit *from the ground up*. It had to evolve from his understanding of inaugurated eschatology.

....

John Wimber knew he had to develop his theology of the work of the Spirit in a way that would strengthen and extend his theology of the kingdom of God.

....

Once again, he turned to the gospels in an attempt to understand how Jesus integrated these concepts. Recalling that Wimber considered the primitive church in Acts to be "contemporaries" or fellow students of Jesus also living in the "last age", it is understandable that he became more focused on *what the primitive church had learned from* Jesus, rather than taking his model *from the* primitive church itself. So once again, the gospels became his primary manual for developing a ministry of healing, to which he added the writings of the apostles as expanding upon the teaching and practices they had received from Christ.

The purpose of this chapter is to track how Wimber incorporated his theology of the kingdom of God with his theology of the work of the Spirit in the individual and the church. The concepts discussed in the previous sections of baptism in the Holy Spirit, tongues, and healing will be discussed, but this will lead to a greater engagement with the operation of the *charismata* in the body of Christ, and the Spirit as the "first fruits" of the already–not yet kingdom, and the dynamic force of the kingdom. At the conclusion, it will be clear that for Wimber, the Spirit was not simply the "seal" of the individual's final redemption; rather, the powerful presence of the Spirit in healing, in prophecy, and signs and wonders is evidence *here and now* of God's ultimate eschatological triumph *in the future*. The presence and power of the Spirit, then, is the force which guarantees the eschatological consummation that was fulfilled in the ministry of Jesus.

We are going to focus on several questions as we study how Wimber developed his theology on the work of the Spirit:

1. How does the Spirit manifest itself in the life of a believer?
2. How should the gifts (*charismata*) operate in the Church?
3. What about those who seem especially gifted at healing?
4. Finally, what can we say about the relationship between the Spirit and the kingdom?

In order to answer these questions, we will proceed in the following manner. First, we will explore the issues of Wimber's conception of the

Holy Spirit's full work in the life of the individual believer, which will include issues relating to the baptism of the Holy Spirit, sanctification, the speaking of tongues, and the practice of divine healing. In this section we will discover that Wimber adopted many Pentecostal *practices*, even while he rejected the classical Pentecostal *theological justification for these practices*; therefore *theologically* he had much in common with classical Evangelical views. Then we will move on to determine Wimber's understanding of the work of the Spirit in the believing community, i.e. the community comprised of Spirit-empowered persons. Here we will discover that Wimber sought to infuse his churches with a full operation of the *charismata* and solid scriptural and theological instruction, once again employing the *word and works* cultural identifier. Finally, we will investigate the expansive issue of how Wimber understood the work of the Spirit to function as the driving component in the enacted, inaugurated eschatological kingdom of God.

So far, two major groups of options have emerged in regard to the baptism of the Holy Spirit. In classical Pentecostalism, the baptism is separate from, and distinct in function from the act of conversion. Protestant scholars like James Dunn and many Charismatics rejected this claim, and perceived the biblical pattern to be *unsupportive* of the Pentecostal view. We shall see that as John Wimber examined the scriptures and reflected on his experience, he developed an alternative to these positions that cannot be merged with either of them.

In order to understand the various positions on the baptism of the Holy Spirit, we are going to focus on four questions:

1. What is the baptism of the Holy Spirit?
2. When does this baptism occur?
3. How do we know we have had this baptism?
4. How do the gifts relate to the baptism?

The Nature of the Baptism of the Holy Spirit

First, it should be noted that Wimber's own perspective on these issues changed considerably in his lifetime. By his own account he explored, considered, and held a variety of positions on this issue before he settled on his mature view.[1] In an early teaching in the 1980s, he avoids precise definitions, but reveals the kernel of his mature perspective on Spirit baptism. In his pastoral experience, he had trouble distinguishing "salvation" and "Holy Spirit baptism", and argued that they were "all just one work, sovereignly initiated by God, but with many separate events".[2] However, since his own personal experience was such that there was a significant gap between his conversion and his later experiences of the power of the Spirit, including the *charismata*, this simple formulation was not a sufficient explanation for either Wimber or his congregants. Owing to his success at evangelism, teaching, and preaching, he *could not accept that previously he had been "deficient" somehow in his experience of the Spirit.* As an attempt to resolve this tension, he suggested that perhaps "there is a distinction between having received or having been filled with the Holy Spirit, and having been *immersed in* the Holy Spirit".[3]

To his amazement, he realized that in the case of Jesus, his baptism with the Holy Spirit occurred synonymously with his water baptism and the beginning of his ministry.[4] This realization sent Wimber back to the scriptures for more reflection.[5] By the 1990s, Wimber had settled on what would be his mature view on the subject. In his book on the essentials of the Christian life, *Power Points*, he concluded:

How do we experience Spirit baptism? It comes at conversion. Scripture teaches, "No one can say 'Jesus is Lord' except by the Holy Spirit" (1 Corinthians 12:3) and "If anyone does not have the Spirit of Christ, he does not belong to Christ" (Romans 8:9). Conversion and Holy Spirit baptism are simultaneous experiences. The born-again experience is the consummate charismatic experience.[6]

However, merely being converted does not automatically guarantee the experience of power so treasured by Pentecostals, for there is an additional *filling* of the Spirit which is optional to the believer, and *may occur to greater or lesser degrees*. What is needed is an avoidance of a too-precise delineation of the various aspects of the baptism, for in the scriptures, the metaphor is fluid, elastic, polyvalent, and even differs in content among the biblical authors themselves.[7] This is yet another example of Wimber's ability to hold divergent views in tension.

The experience of Cornelius in Acts 10 was a particularly helpful example for Wimber, because the Spirit falls on the household *while Peter is still preaching*; they are not even "converted" yet![8] It was fascinating to him that the Gentile members of Cornelius' household in Acts 10 had the *same experience as the Jewish believers in Acts 2*. This data convinced Wimber that "our scenarios and ideas about the Spirit and conversion *are not adequate to embrace all the scripture evidence*", for "sometimes our theologies are neat and nice...yet our ideas about how God works are not adequate to cover all the text. Here is evidence of the Spirit working in a slightly different way than the patterns we have seen already in Acts 2, 4, 8, and 19".[9] The obvious conclusion for Wimber was that there *was no clear-cut "pattern" in scripture*, and thus neither classical Pentecostals *nor* scholars like Dunn had it quite right, for each attempted to force a pattern into the biblical data that couldn't be substantiated by the text. In *Power Points* he states, "There is in scripture *no discernable pattern or formula* for how the Spirit falls on us. But this should not be a surprise to us, because Jesus said: 'The wind blows wherever it pleases.' "[10] He elaborates on this:

> It is a simple fact: God has a work of conversion; God has a work of empowerment. It can occur simultaneously, it can occur sequentially, it can occur with a long intermission in between the two, or it can occur in a short period of time, but the bottom line is that it needs to occur. It is the infilling empowering of the church and we need that in order to accommodate the work of God. Conversion is truly a baptism in the Holy Spirit. There is no reason that we cannot use baptism to refer to subsequent fillings of the Spirit as well, and I do.[11]

Thus:

> The major experiences of the Spirit should not be tied down to a tight, second blessing idea, but should be seen as an actualization of what we have already received in initial charismatic experience which is

121

conversion.[12]

Wimber agrees with Dunn and Stott that there is *no such thing* as a Christian without the Spirit. Dunn argued that the Pentecostal witness issued the challenge that the primitive church *experience* is lacking in the contemporary church. Of course, Wimber would agree that the experience of signs and wonders should be *expected and normative* in the church today. Wimber, like Stott, expected multiple, powerful "infillings" of the Spirit as normative and an essential element in the life of the believer.[13] While he rejected a stringent Pentecostal "second blessing" or "subsequence" doctrine, he nonetheless agreed that Holy Spirit empowerment was essential for an empowered Christian life, and that the gifts of the Spirit should be in evidence after conversion. However, the Pentecostal *initial evidence* doctrine of tongues would be a matter of difference between Wimber and classical Pentecostals.

Speaking in tongues and the initial evidence doctrine

At this point in our discussion, it should be obvious that Wimber would expect the baptism of the Holy Spirit to be accompanied by evidence; this is the essence of his "power evangelism" and "word and works" idioms. That he took a divergent path from classical Pentecostalism should be no surprise either. Instead of positing speaking in tongues as *the* initial evidence of Spirit baptism, Wimber understood that *all charismatic phenomena* were "evidences" of a sort; but crucial to his model is the essential characteristic of the *charismata* as *gifts of the sovereign Lord.* The Spirit may choose to dispense the *gifts* as *He* chooses. Looking at the biblical pattern, Wimber saw that sometimes people spoke in tongues when overcome by the Holy Spirit, but in other occasions, this was not the case. Further, he observed that the *charismata* were in their very essence *gifts,* and, as such, they could be *accepted* or *rejected.* Wimber likened this to any other human experience of gift-giving; that is, we may offer a gift to another, but it would be their choice whether to accept or reject the gift. In the same way, Wimber reasoned, the Holy Spirit offers the gifts of the Spirit at conversion; the onus is on the believer who may accept or reject the gift(s).

....

Wimber thought that since the charismata were gifts, like any other gift they could be accepted or rejected. In other words, the Holy Spirit may offer the operation of his power to all believers, but it is up to the individual believer to "accept" this gift...or not.

....

In the cases where the believer was not adequately taught to *expect and accept* the gifts, the believer *would not be aware* of the offer of the gifts, and so it makes sense that the gifts would not become active.[14] This solves the problem of both the "evidence" and the possible "delay" in expression of the gifts in the experiences of many, including Wimber himself. In the Pentecostal formulation noted above, if the doctrine of initial evidence holds, the gifts *must follow from an "authentic" baptism, for they are the empirical evidence of that baptism.* That is to say, they are not optional, they are directly consequential and they are the *empirical verification* of the baptism. Instead, Wimber understood the gifts *not* as "necessary outcomes", but as possibilities or potentialities that *could* (and should!) follow from the baptism of the Holy Spirit.

The gifts, then, function as tools or "enablements" that allow the believer to participate powerfully in the mission of the Spirit. If this is so, then it would be reasonable that a Christian could obey the call to mission without utilizing the tool given to accomplish the mission. This is how Wimber understood his own experience before he became aware of the *charismata*. To illustrate, Wimber thought of the *charismata* as *power tools*. A carpenter can use both hand or power tools to build a house, but utilizing the power tools allows her to construct the house with less effort. In the same way, the *charismata* could powerfully assist the believer in the task of evangelism, but there was nothing stopping any believer from evangelizing *without* the operation of signs and wonders. This is the essential claim of Wimber's *Power Evangelism* book.

Regarding the gifts of tongues specifically, Wimber embraced the expression of the gift, but understood its public expression to be limited to a form of prophetic speech; in other words, public speaking of tongues must be accompanied by a subsequent interpretation of the *glossolalia*, following the instructions of Paul in 1 Corinthians 14.[15]

Divine healing and the atonement

We have seen that for Holiness Pentecostals, the atonement and divine healing were inseparably linked. Commenting on Isaiah 53:4, R.A. Torrey would be representative of this position:

> It is often said that this verse teaches that the atoning death of Jesus Christ avails for our sickness as well as for our sins; or, in other words, that 'physical healing is in the atonement'. I think that is a fair inference from these verses when looked at in their context.[16]

As Wimber began to pursue the ministry of healing, he was forced to confront this theory. Were the people he prayed for "guaranteed" complete healing, in the same way they were guaranteed salvation when they professed faith in Jesus? For Wimber, the issue had obvious practical consequences, as he had clearly seen that not everyone he prayed for was healed, like his dear friend, the Anglican vicar David Watson.[17] His study of the scriptures revealed that the apostle Paul had similar experiences – at least four occasions were recorded when illnesses were not "cured":

- Epaphroditus in Philippians 2:19-30.
- Timothy in 1 Timothy 5:23: "Stop drinking only water, and use a little wine because of your stomach and your frequent illnesses."
- Trophimus in 2 Timothy 4: "Erastus stayed in Corinth, and I left Trophimus sick in Miletus."
- Paul himself! 2 Corinthians 12:7-10: "Therefore, in order to keep me from becoming conceited, I was given a thorn in my flesh, a messenger of Satan, to torment me. Three times I pleaded with the Lord to take it away from me. But he said to

me, 'My grace is sufficient for you, for my power is made perfect in weakness'."

It seemed to him that Epaphroditus, Timothy, Trophimus, and Paul were apparently not healed. Wimber assumed that in all these cases, based on what we know of Paul's ministry, they would have received healing prayer, yet they were not healed![18] Another favorite text on this issue was 2 Kings 13:21. This amazing story tells the story of a man being buried, and when a band of raiders appeared, the Israelites, who were burying him, quickly threw his body in Elisha's tomb. When the dead man's body touched Elisha's bones, the man came to life and stood on his feet right in front of the astonished men. If divine healing was guaranteed in the atonement, and therefore merely a matter of faith, then Wimber would ask: "*Whose faith* brought about this healing? The *dead* man's or *dead Elisha's bones?*" It would seem that much in divine healing is a mystery, and to force a model or pattern on the biblical evidence when there clearly is *not* a definite pattern, is a mistake.

For Wimber this meant that healing could not be compared to salvation in this way; he suggested that healing could happen *because of* the atonement, or *through* the atonement, but it is not a covenantal promise of God (as the forgiveness of sins is promised), and hence *was not "in" the atonement*.[19] Healing was possible because of the inauguration of the kingdom and the sending of the Spirit; thus, central to Wimber's theology of healing was his theology of the kingdom. To teach, as some did, that God was bound to respond to healing prayer not only presumed on the sovereignty of God, it also broke the eschatological tension of the already–not yet:

The fact that we are living between the first and second comings of Christ, what George Ladd calls living between the 'already and the not yet', *provides the interpretive key* for understanding why the physical healing that Christ secured for us in and through the atonement is *not always* experienced today. His sovereignty, lordship, and kingdom are what bring healing...and if in this age it does not come, then we still have the assurance from the atonement that it will come in the age to come. The examples of Epaphroditus, Timothy, Trophimus, and Paul-and David Watson-are humbling reminders that the fullness of our salvation is yet to be revealed at Christ's return. [20]

This robust "theology of failure"[21] allowed Wimber to pursue divine healing eagerly, and even practice, mentor, and teach the practice, without having to explain or cast blame when the hoped-for healing did not come.[22] Further, as Wimber had a "situational" view of the gifts, rather than a "constitutional" view, he was not interested in finding those Christians who "possessed" the gift of healing; instead, in keeping with his overall understanding of the *charismata*, he was primarily interested in teaching all who desired to learn how they may receive, experience, and *practice* the gift of healing.[23] Living the future meant releasing an army of heal-*ers*, who could continue to pray obediently for the sick, *despite* setbacks and the inevitable experience of seeing the "failure" of their healing prayers.

Sanctification, assurance, and transformation in the Spirit

True to his evangelical roots, Wimber incorporated the common evangelical understandings of the work of the Spirit into his developing theology. Thus his acceptance of the charismatic experience did not replace his earlier understanding of the Spirit's work; rather he re-imaged these experiences as further expressions of the powerful indwelling Spirit. In teaching on healing, for example, Wimber was fond of saying that conversion was the greatest healing miracle of all.[24] In discussing the gifts of the Spirit mentioned in Galatians 5, Wimber understood these as further individual empowerments not merely for the betterment of the individual believer, but as additional "tools" or characteristics that were both a result of the empowering Spirit, and potentialities that were given by the Spirit for mission.[25] The presence of the Spirit as the eschatological down payment is evidenced by his work in the believer, not only in operation of the gifts, but also as *the agent of transformation* into the character of Jesus. This transformation and empowerment is not an automatic blessing given at conversion, however, for the maturity of character and increase in

126

empowerment is dependent on both the activity of the Spirit, *and* the cooperation of the individual.[26]

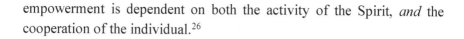

The presence of the Spirit in the life of the Christian is not just to produce signs and wonders, but is primarily given to transform us into the character of Jesus..

If conversion was the greatest miracle, perhaps the penultimate healing expression in the ministry of Jesus was the healing of a person afflicted by demonic spirits.[27] Wimber's understanding of the kingdom from Kallas emphasized Jesus' bringing the kingdom in forcible attack on the kingdom of Satan. This view was brought into fresh understanding as he began to pray for healing, and encountered those who exhibited symptoms of demonic influence.[28] The eschatological significance of the powers of the future manifesting themselves in the present in the ministry of Jesus explained the confusion of the demons in Mark 1:23-24:

> Now there was a man in their synagogue with an unclean spirit. And he cried out, saying, "Let us alone! What have we to do with You, Jesus of Nazareth? Did You come to destroy us? I know who You are—the Holy One of God!"

The presence of demonic influence reveals the already–not yet dynamic of the kingdom of God, for when the kingdom comes in fullness, the enemies of God will be completely defeated. In the meantime, believers are called to war against "the world, the flesh, and the Devil".

In *Power Healing,* Wimber wrote: "Like Jesus himself, we have a job to do: proclaim the kingdom of God and *demonstrate* it through healing the sick and casting out demons (John 20:21)".[29] In his writing, sermons, and teaching, Wimber replayed this message many times, encouraging his listeners that this, also, was an occasion where "everybody gets to play". Praying for the demonically influenced was not restricted to the realm of highly trained or educated specialists, or those who held the office of deliverance; it was in the hands of all believers empowered by the Spirit. His overarching goal, once again, was to allow the Spirit to work in individuals by empowering both individuals and communities to move in the gifts and experience the life-giving power of the Spirit for the good of the community.

The Work of the Spirit in the Christian Community

If the life of the Spirit should be characterized by an empowered communion with the Holy Spirit, what should the community comprised by people of the Spirit look like? As a technician, sociologist, and researcher, Wimber had studied and consulted with many thousands of churches. As he began to lead the Vineyard movement, he took what he learned from his studies of ecclesiology and infused what he considered to be the best principles into the DNA of the Vineyard. His principal concern was to develop a community of people who were marked by the presence of the powerful Spirit. In the early years of the Vineyard he tirelessly repeated this message, and when he taught on the gifts and practice of the Spirit, he maintained a primary focus on the *communal experience* of the gifts of the Spirit.

Wimber eventually came to the realization that the presence of the Spirit in the life of the Christian is not just to produce signs and wonders, but is primarily given to transform the body (the entire church) into the character of Jesus – together.

This means that:

- relieving suffering, releasing people held in demonic bondage, being led by the Spirit's guiding through prophecy, are *all-important and part of the full Christian life*.
- all of the gifts are given *to the church in order to bring maturity to the body and make us all more like Jesus*.
- the gifts and practice of the Spirit, then, should have a primary focus on the *communal experience, not the individual*.

Perhaps the most radical departure from the individualistic nature of the Pentecostal "initial evidence" doctrine was his argument that while the private expression of tongues was indeed legitimate, any tongues spoken in public, by definition, would *require interpretation by the community*, thus elevating tongues-speech closer to the manifestation of prophecy. Corporate tongues-speaking differs from prophecy, however, in that in the biblical pattern, tongues always connoted a message *from the community towards God:*

> According to the examples in Scripture, tongues plus interpretation always constitute a message from our spirits to God, exalting him for who he is and what he has done. In contrast, prophecy is always a message to the church from God. We can be immediately edified by either one.[30]

Likewise the gift of prophetic speech in the community must happen in an arena of communal participation. Wimber was extremely suspicious of the parade of self-proclaimed "prophets" that flocked to his meetings in the early years. His initial suspicion was basically similar to his previous wariness towards the entire charismatic experience. He had seen very few trustworthy examples of prophets who had the character and maturity he admired, or who operated within a church or accountability structure as in the New Testament pattern.[31]

Wimber would later admit that in his previous ministry, he "didn't take prophecy too seriously".[32] When he was introduced to men who did have the character and accountability structures in place, he eagerly sought to infuse the practice of prophecy into the Vineyard.[33] For a period of time, he encouraged "popular" Pentecostal-influenced prophets to speak and minister at Vineyard churches and conferences. This phase passed out of the Vineyard story for a number of reasons: Wimber and other Vineyard leaders grew increasingly disenchanted with the style of the prophets; numerous, publicized prophecies failed to come true; and the prophets themselves experienced moral failings that damaged their credibility.[34]

For Wimber, it was the gradual realization that by promoting certain captivating prophets onto the center stage, the biblical pattern of *communal* processing and discernment was cast aside, as was his desire to "equip the saints". Wimber's account of this is illustrated in his address to the movement at a pastor's conference in 1996, "The Movement I would build". In this address, he stated: "During the prophetic era and on into the new renewal, our people quit starting small groups, they quit prophesying, they quit healing the sick...because they were waiting for the Big Bang, the Big Revival, the Big Thing...I thought: "My God! We've made an audience out of them! And they were an army! In effect we told them, 'You can't do anything, you aren't talented enough. You're not gifted enough'...we did it not so much by precept, but by example...and it went against everything I believe in, in terms of freeing the church to minister". [35]

Most disconcerting to him was that he had repeated an error from decades past; by elevating certain men with a prophetic gifting he had once again turned his churches members into an *audience*, who relied on the "experts" to participate in the prophetic gift, when his stated desire at the beginning was just the opposite, namely to stir up the gift of prophecy among all the people in the movement.[36] In the post-Kansas city era, Wimber strove to re-ignite the communal practices which he felt had been neglected in previous years. The leitmotif of "everybody gets to play" in relation to the prophetic ministry was reinforced in teachings, conferences, and sermons.

While Wimber was known on popular levels for healing physical infirmities, his healing model is communal, holistic and comprehensive, believing that the biblical and Hebraic understanding of man was of a whole unity of physical, emotional, spiritual and psychological aspects. Common sense and observation would indicate that disease often affected several of these elements: physical issues often caused emotional distress, and untreated emotional and psychological issues, in turn, could create physical issues. If this is so, Wimber reasoned, then healing would have to be multifaceted as well. His healing model emphasized this collective, participatory, holistic approach to healing and transformation and was demonstrated in MC 510, in healing seminars, and throughout his ministry.[37]

His desire to release the ministry of healing in the whole church surfaced a problem that surfaced within many churches that practiced healing, especially those that understood the gifts from a constitutional perspective. Specifically, what are we to make of those who, like Wimber himself, seemed to *personally* have an extraordinary "gift" of healing? That is to say, if the *charisms* were situational, why did certain individuals, like Lonnie Frisbee and John Wimber have so much more "success" than "average" believers ministering in healing? This was not merely a theoretical objection, as it struck at Wimber's deeply-held conviction of "equipping the saints for ministry".[38] Wimber reasoned that, in some cases, there *is* a progression; that is, a person can first minister simply as all Christians are commanded to. In other words, they fulfill the *role* of an obedient believer.

Sometimes, certain people will have more effectiveness or power in a particular *gift*. If this person continues to develop and practice their gifts, it may develop into a *ministry*. Thus, this pattern of progression, from role, to gift, to ministry, should be operating everywhere in the church among all believers practicing all the gifts.[39] Therefore, while not everyone may have the *ministry* of praying for the sick, *all* should obediently fulfill the *role* of healing, as the situational view of the gifts logically entailed that the sovereign Spirit may choose to act at *any* moment through *any* obedient practitioner.[40] These two factors, his situational view of the gifts and the belief that *all members* of the body should move in the operation of these gifts, undergirded Wimber's belief that people can *learn* and *practice* gifts like healing and prophecy:

> The church needs to leave room for people to learn to do the works of the Father, a place where people can experiment. A place to succeed and fail. A safe place should be provided within the local church for the believer to learn to prophesy, to heal the sick, to minister in evangelism. The Apostles had a safe place with Jesus. First, they watched him minister. Then they assisted. Next they ministered while he watched. Finally, they ministered on their own. It took time for them to learn.[41]

Then, as it would be expected, the work of the Spirit in the community mirrors that of his role in the life of the individual, because the Spirit convicts, guides, restores, reassures and blesses individuals and communities in the same manner. The empowered community is comprised of empowered individuals that value love and shared experience; thus the work of the Spirit that strengthens, comforts, and encourages can be more explicitly validated in the shared communal experience, as Paul encouraged in 1 Corinthians 12:7, "But the manifestation of the Spirit is given to each one for the profit of all".

The Spirit as *Prolepsis*: the Driving Force of the Kingdom of God

It should be quite obvious by now that for John Wimber there was an intimate connection between his conception of the kingdom of God and his expectation of the Spirit's work; indeed the idiom of "doing the works of the kingdom" implies this connection. Perhaps this connection is most clear in Wimber's perspective on healing of the demonically afflicted, for he undoubtedly understood the implications of Jesus' saying: "If I cast out demons by the finger of God, then the kingdom of God is upon you". Wimber taught and experienced this reality; he *enacted* the practical implications of Ladd's notion of the powers of the future breaking into the present. It was not just a theory; it was *living the future reality of the kingdom now in the present.*

In his ministry of healing, Wimber experienced the first fruits (*prolepsis*) of the Spirit's ultimate eschatological triumph.[42] The healings in the present, whether complete, partial, or delayed, were blessings of God surely, but they contained within themselves the very essence of the already–not yet kingdom, for even those fully healed now would most likely still suffer physical death. Hence, the first fruits of divine healing were real, and of the same essence as the final eschatological experience of the fullness of the kingdom, but they were nonetheless pointers to that ultimate transformation as well.

The dynamic *tension* of the Spirit's presence is also seen in two other elements of Wimber's theology of healing. His rejection of the Pentecostal doctrine of "healing as guaranteed in the atonement" was based on his understanding of the "not-yettedness"[43] of the kingdom. He further

132

contended that not everyone would be healed in this age, a fact that was illustrated in scripture and in his experience, for expecting such would presume on the sovereignty of the Spirit. This theology of failure is what allowed Wimber to continue the ministry of healing in face of painful setbacks, like the death of his dear friend David Watson.[44] This difficult embrace of the present–future tension allowed Wimber to both eagerly seek and expect healing, and yet not diminish the reality of suffering in his own life, in his family and among those who were not miraculously healed.

A word about suffering and the already–not yet:

The practical implications of a "theology of failure" in regard to healing also extends to the biblical concept of suffering and the relationship between suffering and maturity in Christ. At least two dangers exist for those churches which practice healing yet lack this mature understanding:

1. The danger of the "winners club", where only the "whole, healed and healthy" feel welcome, but the chronically sick or disabled are treated like a "project" and not valued as fellow members of the body.
2. Misunderstanding or not appreciating the lessons we can learn from suffering as bringing us to maturity in Christ.

The apostle Paul said this about his own suffering:
> "I want to know Christ and the power of His resurrection and the fellowship of sharing in His sufferings, becoming like Him in his death, and so, somehow, to attain to the resurrection from the dead." (Philippians 3:10, 11).

In *Everybody Gets to Play*, John Wimber wrote:

> First, some mistakenly believe that all Christians are protected from calamity, hardship, pain and loss. Because God is with them, they reason, their lives will turn out according to their

expectations. Secondly, some believe that Christians never struggle. And if they do, it is because they're not exercising the quality of faith they ought to for those circumstances. People with this belief system see themselves as sinning if they have periods of disillusionment and despair.

In an article 'Why Christians Must Suffer" in *Equipping the Saints,* (Winter 1988) Wimber wrote:

> The Goal of the Christian life is that we might "become mature, attaining to the whole measure of the fullness of Christ" (Ephesians 4:13). The goal of the Christian life is maturity in Christ, to become more like Jesus...One of the means he uses to gain his lofty goal is obedience in suffering. If we understand that the goal of the Christian life is maturity, then our ***response to suffering either in our own lives or in the lives of our brothers and sisters is faith***.

The danger of an over-realized eschatology that collapses to the "already" side of the equation is missing the *primary goal* of the believer to become more Christlike. God is most interested *not in* our happiness, our health, or success, but in our *conforming to the image of His Son.* Living the future means accepting the biblical truth that God can, and often does, use *both healing and suffering* to make us more like Jesus.

The present reality of the Spirit in the life of a Christian in the "usual" ways of comfort, peace, and presence was also a foretaste of the comfort believers were to receive as they were transformed from the "natural body" into the "spiritual body" (1 Corinthians 15:44).

....

Wimber saw the presence and power of the Holy Spirit in his churches, working acts of physical healing and other miracles, as being both an essential element of church life in this age, and as the "first fruits" (*prolepsis*) of the age to come.

....

134

As Gordon Fee states: "For Paul, the Spirit was an essential eschatological reality. For him and for the Judaism he represented, the outpouring of the Spirit and the resurrection of the dead were the key elements to their eschatological hopes".[45] It was a future glory that had yet to be fulfilled, certainly, but the present experience of the Spirit assured the future eschatological reality when "God will be all in all".

Living the future brings an essential "sameness" in essence between the Spirit's powerful sealing in this age, and the fullness of his presence in the age to come. This speaks of the "guarantee of our inheritance" that is more than just a "down payment" or "first installment" – it is the beginning of an experience that will be continued in eternity (Ephesians 1:14).[46] When Wimber first experienced the Spirit breaking into his fellowship on that day in May 1982, his search of the scriptures led him to accept the experience *because of his understanding of eschatology*. He now saw with new eyes that the reality of the powerful Spirit "completed," in a sense, the theology of the kingdom he had adopted. Wimber's friend, the Charismatic Lutheran pastor Larry Christensen stated it like this:

> The biblical terms seal, guarantee, or earnest or first fruits…all denote the Spirit as both experiential and eschatological- as a present and a future reality; in the life of faith we experience him now, and in the life of the coming kingdom we shall experience him even more fully.[47]

This tension was also in force in Wimber's appropriation of Kallas' work. The battle between kingdoms in the ministry of Jesus, *were but the first skirmishes of the battle to be continued throughout the church age.* The church was called into war, yet even as their ultimate victory was ensured by the death, resurrection, and triumph of Christ, in the present age there would be struggles, losses, and casualties. Wimber was hurt by the suffering and death of dear friends, and by the moral and ethical failings of pastors and leaders in his care. Wimber was fond of saying that "The Christian disciple is called to be a warrior, yet too many of us desire to be conscientious objectors".[48]

Conclusion

For John Wimber, the fundamental questions relating to the baptism of the Holy Spirit and the operation of the *charismata* were intrinsically linked to his eschatology. His eschatology anchored his understanding of the work of the Spirit as he searched the scriptures to understand the proper function of the gifts of the Spirit. He discovered anew in the ministry of Jesus the connection between the message of the kingdom and the works of the kingdom: the blessings of healing and deliverance were evidences of God's mercy, but they also functioned as signs to a wonderful future when all will be healed and free from corruption. In this way, Wimber pushed beyond the kingdom idea he had received from Ladd, as the activity of the Spirit in the present supplied the power to the "already" side of the equation. His embrace of the warfare motif not only gave him an understanding of the *works* of Jesus, but also *practical insight* as his healing ministry grew in depth and he began to understand healing holistically. His quest to find a theological model fused with practical application was once again fulfilled as he studied the ministry of Jesus; thus "word and works" were held together by his fusion of eschatology and Pneumatology.

It is clear that for Wimber and the other leaders and founders of the Vineyard, practical ministry and theology had a mutually beneficial relationship, but an obvious question remains: What might we learn from a study of the religious *experience* of Vineyard adherents? What factors are common to Vineyard practitioners in their history of more than thirty years? How might this study of experience enlighten our understanding of Vineyard theology and identity? In short, what does *living the future actually look like in Vineyard Churches?* These questions are the subject of our next chapter as we investigate Vineyard charismatic experience.

Questions:

1. For an evangelical cessationist, what might be the "proof" of conversion or reception of the Spirit? And for an evangelical continuationist?

2. Pentecostals saw their experience of receiving the gift of tongues *after* conversion to be mirrored in the experience of the Ephesian believers in Acts 19. What was your reception of the Spirit like? Did it come when you professed faith in Jesus, or afterwards?

3. A concern of Pentecostal critics has been that the subsequence doctrine created "two classes" of believers: those "with the Spirit" and those without. Is this a real problem? Have you ever heard this taught or discussed?

4. Pentecostals in the Holiness tradition taught that divine healing was "guaranteed in the Atonement", based on verses like: "He forgives all your sins and heals all your sicknesses" (Psalm 103:3), "By his stripes we are healed" (Isaiah 53:5) and "He Himself took our infirmities and carried away our diseases" (Mathew 8:17). What might some of the implications be on the practice of healing for those who hold this view? Can you think of other biblical exceptions to this view?

5. What might be the practical implications of praying for healing under the "already–not-yet" kingdom view?

6. In what ways does "living the future" include both the "already" and the "not yet" of the kingdom of God?

Section IV: Vineyard Charismatic Experience

In order to fully understand charismatic experience in the Vineyard, it is important to understand how the Vinyardites recognize their experience *as* charismatic experience. Several basic observations immediately emerge as we begin our study. By examining Vineyard experience, we can see that there is an *expectation* that *God is both capable and willing to act in the world*, and he is *able to act* in a way that can be *interpreted and comprehended by humans*. What may sound even more crazy to some is the idea that it is *possible to receive communication from,* or interact with, the Holy Spirit.

Vineyardites believe that the Holy Spirit acts in a way that can be understood in plain human language. When a person "hears" this communication from God, it is often described by the phrase, "hearing God's voice". What is more astounding is the belief that one person can "hear" revelation intended for another person; or even, a "group" may collectively experience and "feel" the presence and activity of the Spirit together.

We may now turn to a closer examination of these experiences. The Vineyardites often relate an awareness of the "presence" of God – often spoken of in terms of the *Spirit of God* – which they recognize by a heightening of the senses, physical manifestations such as trembling, shaking, the awareness of a noticeable increase in body temperature or atmosphere, or "heaviness" (as if the room had somehow undergone an increase in gravitational pull). Psychical responses often include a sense of peace, comfort or an awareness of "something being in the room". This awareness of spiritual peace, confidence, or hope is characterized by Wimber and others as knowing the presence of God in a heightened and dynamic way. Vineyard persons note that through experience and practice, they can attempt to evaluate the *validity or source* of these charismatic experiences. They recognize the possibility of deception, illusion, or

139

emotional manipulation, and seek to identify or eliminate non-constructive influences; they are open to both *verification* and *falsification*. We shall see that a particularly fascinating form of evidence surfaces in many instances where "prophetic" words have startling accuracy or contain great detail that is meaningful to a person requesting prayer, which Wimber referred to as "words of knowledge", or divine communication about one person given to another.

To understand Vineyard Charismatic experience, we will consider examples from three periods of Vineyard history: the early years after Wimber first established the genetic code, the growing years through the "Toronto Blessing" era, and the post-Wimber Vineyard. I will select first-hand accounts of charismatic experience from a variety of authors associated with the Vineyard, describing phenomena that occurred in Vineyard contexts. In this section, we will be focusing on three main questions:

1. How should we think about "evidence" of the gifts (*charismata*)?
2. Can there be such a thing as "Idolatry" in charismatic experience?
3. What do our experiences tell us about our theology?

TEN

Charismatic experience in the Vineyard Movement

Charismatic experience in the Beginnings (1978-1989)

As he repeatedly noted, John Wimber's introduction to divine healing had an inauspicious beginning. He describes the event of his young son, Sean, who had inadvertently wandered into a bee hive near the Wimber household, and subsequently was stung many times. Despite his suspicion and lack of experience with healing, John Wimber nonetheless began to pray for his son:

> I began to pray for Sean's healing, but I did not know how to pray. I was desperately in need of words when I broke out into a language I did not understand. My "tongues" were accented by intermittent salvos of "heal him, Jesus, heal him". The longer I prayed, the more confidence and power welled up within me. I could feel faith for healing (although at that time I did not know what to call it) being released. As I prayed I could see Sean's welts go away. Within five minutes Sean was sleeping peacefully, and I was slightly confused about what happened. When he awakened a few hours later, Sean had only one small red bump on his body. He was healed.[1]

Wimber's report of this early incident is remarkably absent of the detail that would characterize his later, "clinical" descriptions of healing; however, this merely serves to illustrate the significance of Wimber's careful chronicling of these phenomena in later years. He makes little mention of his own physical state, the attitude or participation of his wife, Carol, or physical responses of Sean's body other than the disappearing welts. The only notable feature, other than the healing itself, was Wimber speaking in tongues; a gift which he had previously discounted, and would continue to deny as an authentic expression of the Spirit for many years after this event. While "faith for healing" is mentioned, it is not said how he knew or recognized this, or even if it was an emotional, mental, imaginative, or other awareness. Carol Wimber's account in *The Way it Was,* adds some detail; she notes that John "placed his hands" on Sean, while she merely observed the event "listening and watching".[2]

What is noteworthy is the lack of expectation or confidence that would characterize Wimber's later experiences; instead his account reveals desperation and self-doubt. Even after Wimber became convinced of the *plausibility* and theological validity of divine healing, his experience was still marked by questioning, self-doubt, and a lack of expectation. These emotional states are yet evident during the nearly year-long pursuit of healing in 1977 with no success:

> But after ten months of unsuccessful prayer, I had my greatest defeat...on this occasion several men and I prayed for another man. We prayed for two hours, praying every prayer we knew, desperate to see the man healed. Finally, in despair, we stopped. I was so disconcerted that I threw myself on the floor and began weeping. 'It's not fair!' I screamed. 'You tell us to teach what your book says, but you don't back up your act. Here we are; we're doing the best we can do- and nothing happens....oh God, it's not fair!'[3]

However, this event was closely following by one that would change Wimber's subsequent healing ministry; as the very next day he went to the home of one of his parishioners to pray for a sick wife at her husband's request:

> His wife looked terrible. Her face was red and swollen with fever. 'Oh no,' I groaned inwardly 'this looks like a hard one.' I walked over and laid hands on her, prayed a faithless prayer, and then I turned around and began explaining to the husband why some people do not get healed - a talk I had perfected during the past ten months.[4]

Despite his lack of faith and expectation, to Wimber's amazement, the fever immediately left the woman. She was healed, got out of her bed, and began to make breakfast for her husband. Wimber was incredulous, not believing what he was seeing. "I could not believe it. She was well! My despair from the previous night was instantly transformed into joy and exaltation...the healing ministry was born in me...I drove off knowing that I was embarking on a new journey of faith." As in the first experience, Wimber was not attentive to great detail in this account. He notes her physical appearance, his own lack of faith, and the physical act of touching her, but does not state his exact words, other physical responses, or other phenomena such as tongues-speaking. The prayer was essentially a "two-person" communication, with Wimber alone praying to God; neither the woman nor her husband participated in the prayer.

Carol Wimber's retelling of a ministry trip to South Africa in 1981 reads, in her own words, "like a chapter out of Acts". She details dramatic events such as healing of blindness, non-functional legs, cancers, kidney diseases, coronary issues, and spinal conditions. The ministry times were often accompanied by physical manifestations such as trembling, violent shaking, falling down, laughing, crying and speaking in tongues. Carol Wimber relates that in one case, with a "group of thirty people praying intensely in the Spirit", a woman was healed of blindness.[5]

As his experience and desire to see more healing increased, Wimber sought to develop a model that could be easily taught and reproduced in churches, so that as many people as possible could be equipped for prayer and healing ministry. He eventually developed the "five step healing model" made famous in *Power Healing*. In short, Wimber urged his practitioners to move through a progression of steps that entailed an interview, a diagnostic decision, a prayer selection, the prayer engagement, and post-prayer directions. [6] Wimber's desire to equip as many Christians as possible in the healing ministry, rather than being a healing *minister* only, was fortunate in that there are countless examples of charismatic healing or prophetic experiences. Many of these accounts reveal striking similarities, and the richest accounts are those that entail many participants interacting in a single ministry incident. Quite often, various kinds of charismatic sensations occurred in a single event; that is, the receiver or intercessor *may both* experience physical reactions such as trembling or shaking, speaking in tongues, prophecy, sensual or physiological responses such as fluttering eyelids, deep breathing, sweating, an increase of perceived bodily or atmospheric temperature, or an awareness of psychological states such as calmness, peace, joy, anger, shame, anxiety or fear.[7]

Wimber used this model in the academic setting of MC 510 as well as in church and conference settings. Rather than perform the role of the intercessor, Wimber would often employ other trained practitioners to be intercessors, while he would play the role of an observer and interpreter, explaining and describing the experience to the audience.[8] As MC 510 and the Vineyard grew in popularity, numerous scholars and pastors observed and chronicled these events. By the time Wimber was teaching MC 510 at Fuller Seminary, his healing technique was quite developed. Dr. John White, a psychiatrist from Vancouver, Canada, recorded his detailed observations of a MC 510 class, richly detailing facets of the prayer ministry led by Wimber. White observed that in these classes, there was often so much occurring at once that it was difficult to carefully observe all that was happening.

Typically, Wimber would transition from the lecture to the "clinic time" by inviting the Holy Spirit "to come" via audible prayer, and then asking all those in attendance who sought prayer to come forward. Several trained members of his church would begin the "five step prayer model" with an individual, while Wimber would seat himself in the audience, and quietly narrate and explain the unfolding events to those who were watching. Wimber would draw the audience's attention to various physical responses such as trembling, shaking, or swaying, fluttering eyelids, and even on one occasion, a violent shaking resembling that of a grand mal or epileptic seizure.[9] Following his visit to the Fuller classroom, Dr. White visited the Anaheim Vineyard and witnessed much of the same types of reactions on a much larger scale. These early accounts of the baptism and ministry of the Holy Spirit are often broad overviews of particular experiences, but, as Dr White noted, their limitations surface owing to the sheer amount of simultaneous activity. The many filmed episodes of

144

Wimber performing prayer ministry reveal features quite similar to Dr White's account.[10]

Wimber and the other Vineyard leaders intentionally programmed their church services to make room for the practice of prophetic ministry and this often followed a general pattern. Towards the conclusion of the meeting, Wimber would often instruct the church musicians to continue playing quiet or contemplative songs. An announcement would be made that those who were seeking personal prayer should come to the front of the auditorium. When the individual came forward for prayer, an intercessor or group of intercessors would question them as to what they needed prayer for (i.e. the *interview* stage of the five step model). The intercessors often physically touched the person, and then began to pray out loud requesting that God meet the need or answer their prayer. During this time, the intercessory "team" would often decide who should pray audibly, and who should be "listening for the voice of God". Prophetic revelation would take the form of thoughts, words, sensations, phrases, scripture verses, lines from worship songs, and "images" or "pictures" in the mind. [11] Once the intercessor "received" the revelation, he offered it to the person requesting prayer for consideration (i.e. the prayer selection and engagement phases). This often took the form of a question such as: "Does this mean anything to you…?"

Observing these interactions shows that this process is more or less normative and that most prophetic encounters follow a similar pattern of expectation, prayer engagement, and response.[12] The actual effect of the words or sensations can have a much greater variety. At times, the "words" or prophecy have more direct and immediate impact on the individual, who may respond with confirming words or physical responses such as emotional expressions (crying, trembling, or even falling down). The effectiveness of the process is somewhat uncertain, and retains a sense of mystery.[13]

Even while saying this, it was Wimber's claim that through a repeated process of prayer, feedback, and verification, a minister could *increase in their ability* to understand charismatic experience and thus their prophetic ability could be "improved"; that is to say, the revelation that is given from the Spirit, and then offered to the requester is more accurate, has more effect on them, or is more effective in bringing them to a closer relationship with God. Wimber also spoke of the occurrence of delayed or unreported effect whereby, although there was no immediate confirmation of healing or effectiveness of the prayer, reports sometimes came later or through other channels, which confirmed the validity of a prayer experience. Fortunately, Wimber wrote of numerous accounts of miraculous *charismata* of prophetic speech, healing, and deliverance from spirits; these precise reports often provide great detail and are easy to investigate.

A story that Wimber often retold was one of his most unusual experiences of prophecy. On a plane flight to New York, Wimber gave a casual glance to the passenger next to him, and to his amazement, he "saw" words written on the man's face:

> I saw something that startled me. Written across his face in very clear and distinct letters I thought I saw the word 'adultery'. I blinked, rubbed my eyes, and looked again. It was still there. 'Adultery'. I was seeing it not with my eyes, but in my mind's eye…it was the Spirit of God communicating to me. The fact that it was a spiritual phenomenon made it no less real.[14]

Wimber relates that immediately afterwards he received two more distinct communications from the Spirit: a woman's name and a conviction that if the man did not leave this relationship, God was going to take his life. Wimber asked the man if the female name meant anything to him, and the two went to the plane lounge to talk. According to Wimber, the man confessed that he was indeed in an adulterous relationship with a woman of that name. When Wimber told him that "God" had given him this message, the man's psychological defenses immediately broke down, he began to weep, prayed to accept Christ, and even confessed to his wife when he was back in his seat. In the Vineyard culture, this story has become an oft-quoted example of prophetic communication from God, and is seen as a modern-day example of the exhortation of 1 Corinthians

14:24-25:

> "But if all prophesy, and an unbeliever or an uninformed person comes in, he is convinced by all, he is convicted by all. And thus the secrets of his heart are revealed; and so, falling down on his face, he will worship God and report that God is truly among you."

For many Vineyardites, their experience follows 1 Corinthians 14, as prophetic communication is usually directed *towards another*, and often contains a "supernatural" message, such as details about past experiences, names, locations, or even images that the intercessor *could not possibly have known* through their personal knowledge or awareness.[15] In these cases where the knowledge could not possibly be known by the intercessor (Wimber had never met the man before, but "knew" the name of the woman involved), it serves as a form of *evidence* for Wimber that the prophetic message was authentically from God.[16] In this example Wimber received this message from the Spirit that was intended *for* another person. The other distinctive element of this case is the setting: it was not in a church or ministry situation; it occurred in everyday life. Wimber coined the phrase, "naturally supernatural", for this "openness" to charismatic experience; that is, an expectation that in everyday routines and relationships one could expect the in-breaking of the kingdom, and the power of God to be manifested.[17] Psychological manifestations of deep emotion (crying, shame, sorrow, fear) were present in this account as well.

Another form of prophetic expression that is frequent in the Vineyard tradition is the experience of images, pictures, or vignettes that occur via "visions" either in the mind, or "visibly", that have a prophetic message or significance. The iconic example of this comes once again from Wimber's early years, this time in relation to divine healing. Wimber recounts that shortly after this first "successful" healing, as he drove away from the house, he had a stunning experience:

> Suddenly in my mind's eye there appeared to be a cloud bank superimposed across the sky. But I had never seen a cloud bank like this one, so I pulled my car over to the side of the road to take a closer

look. Then I realized it was not a cloud bank, it was a honeycomb with honey dripping out on the people below. The people were in a variety of postures. Some were reverent; they were weeping and holding their hand out to catch the honey and taste it, even inviting others to take some of their honey. Others acted irritated, wiping the honey off themselves complaining about the mess. I was awestruck. I prayed, 'Lord, what is it?' He said 'it's my mercy John. For some people it's a blessing but for others it's a hindrance. There's plenty for everyone, don't ever beg me for healing again.[18]

Along with the "vision" of the honeycomb, there was an accompanying "message" that provided the explanation of the vision. This pattern of combined forms of the *charismata* would become commonplace, and often accompany healing events.

Perhaps the most difficult form of *charismata* for the modern mind is that of the experience with "demons" or evil supernatural forces, including the prayer of exorcism performed in the healing context.[19] Wimber's adoption of charismatic experience, and his commitment to reproducing the ministry of Jesus, inevitably led him to develop a theology and practice of deliverance, as confrontation with demons was a repeated element in the ministry of Jesus. Wimber's detailed account of an early experience is worth citing in full:

Although she was only 18 years old and weighed only 100 pounds, she was thrashing about so violently that the truck was rocking. Strange, growling, animal-like sounds were coming from her—not her normal voice at all. I was to meet a demon. The girl, or rather something in the girl, spoke. "I know you," were the first words to assault me packaged in a hoarse, eerie voice—"and you don't know what you're doing." I thought: 'You're right'. The demon then said through Melinda, 'You can't do anything with her. She's mine." ...During this time, I smelled putrid odors from the girl and saw her eyes roll back and her profuse perspiration. I heard blasphemy and saw wild physical activity that required more strength than a slight girl operating under her own power could possibly possess. I was appalled and very afraid, but I refused to give up the fight.[20]

Among the intriguing aspects of this story are the physical responses (thrashing about violently, physical strength that belied her stature, animal-like sounds, a hoarse, unexpected voice coming from the girl, putrid odors, etc.), and the *four-way* interaction, with the participants being the intercessor (Wimber), the teenage girl, the Holy Spirit, and a demonic presence that had *intelligence,* communicative ability, and even "knew" Wimber, or at least accurately "perceived" Wimber's psychological state. The fact that the demonic activity apparently ceased at some point (Wimber said: "when the demon left..."), determines a beginning and end of this encounter. These basic elements of physical, psychological, and cognitive states and interactions are replete in Vineyard accounts of deliverance.[21]

Charismatic experience in the Prophetic and Toronto Blessing Eras (1989-1996)

The experience of charismatic phenomena increased in variety and intensity during the "prophetic" and "Toronto Blessing" eras of the Vineyard movement.[22] In the circumstances of the "Kansas City Prophets", private, interpersonal occurrences became overshadowed by public, televised, and media-saturated pronouncements by prophetic celebrities. During the Toronto era, the experiences we examined in Wimber's analytical, reserved, "clinic time" crafted in MC 510 gave way to an explosion of remarkable phenomena that were evident in gatherings of thousands of people, with global media attention. In these cases, it was not only the range of observations that changed, or their public nature, but the observed phenomena themselves were often of a more bizarre nature.

Examples of prophecy were often evident in the popular ministers of Kansas City Fellowship such as Paul Cain, John Paul Jackson, and Bob Jones.[23] Paul Cain was a Pentecostal minister popular in the healing revivals of the mid-twentieth century, who had retired from public ministry.[24] He began to minister again publicly in collaboration with Mike

Bickle. Dr Jack Deere's account of the first time he saw Paul Cain minister is typical of his style of prophetic ministry:

> Paul had just finished giving a wonderful message and was beginning to pray for the people in the audience. There were about 250 people there that morning. He asked the diabetics to stand. As he started to pray for the diabetics, he looked at a gray-haired lady on his right. He stared at her for a moment, having never met her (or anyone else in the audience for that matter); and then he said, "You do not have diabetes; you have low blood sugar. Lord heals you of that low blood sugar now...your allergies torment you so badly that sometimes they keep you awake all night. The Lord heals those allergies, now. That problem with the valve on your heart—it goes now in the name of Jesus. And so does that growth on your pancreas. The Devil has scheduled you for a nervous breakdown. The Lord interrupts that plan now. You will not have the breakdown".[25]

Deere writes that this prophecy was amazingly accurate; he was able to interview this woman and her husband personally and confirmed both the existence of the medical conditions Cain specified, and their sudden disappearance after Cain's proclamation.[26] On another occasion, Cain revealed in detailed accuracy the medical and psychological states of a woman and her husband, including arthritis, neck and back pain, and psychological issues related to personal rejections and relational insults. Cain even pronounced the maiden name of the woman that he could not possibly have known. Deere writes that he was able to interview this couple personally and confirm the accuracy of Cain's words.[27] John Wimber detailed a number of Cain's public prophecies that were quite similar; that is, they were pronounced by Cain in public services, contained a great amount of detail, and were often stunningly accurate in regard to names, medical conditions, pronouncements of emotional or physical healings, etc.[28]

Similar accounts of prophecy were related about John Paul Jackson and Bob Jones.[29] Owing to the detailed nature of the public pronouncements, they were open to scrutiny and examination in a way that the smaller-scale "clinic time" events were not. Upon closer scrutiny, a number of the prophetic claims were found to be *inaccurate,* and thus the authenticity of the ministers themselves was called into question.[30] Obvious prophetic inaccuracies present a problem; the "evidence" can be logically deduced from actual events, because the events *did not happen as the "prophets" had predicted.*

In much the same way, the experiences of the Toronto era were comparable to the classic Vineyard ones, yet there were differences as well. Certainly Wimber and the Vineyard had experienced large-scale, public, charismatic experiences such as the events of the Mother's Day service that birthed the Vineyard.[31] The Vineyard had considerably less experience with the unique phenomena that surfaced in the Toronto meetings such as individuals expressing "animal noises," uncontrollable laughter, and the extreme versions of being "slain" or "drunk" in the Spirit.[32]

Guy Chevreau was a Baptist pastor who visited the Toronto Airport Vineyard in the winter of 1994, during the very early stages of the outpouring. He became a chronicler of the course of the renewal:

> It is an understatement to say that I was personally unfamiliar with the kinds of physical manifestations we saw at the Airport meetings – uncontrollable laughter and inconsolable weeping; violent shaking and falling down; people waving their arms around, in windmill-like motions, or vigorous judo-like chopping with their forearms.[33]

The forms of spiritual activity in these gatherings included physical responses such as extreme shaking, violent movement of the arms, hands, or legs, being "slain in the Spirit" or falling, where a person would collapse to the ground and enter a trance-like state. Chevreau described an early personal experience as:

> I went 'down' yielding to the feelings of weakness and heaviness. With

151

no cognitive or emotive content, I lay there thinking '...did I get pushed?' The third time...Randy prayed very gently, very quietly for me, and I went over, feeling too tired to stand any longer. As I lay there, I started weeping. Wailing, if the truth be told, for something like forty minutes. While there were no conscious, cognitive pictures, or images, memories or impressions, a long-standing bitterness and resentment lifted in the process.[34]

Thus, for him there was significant spiritual meaning in the experience, as a "long-standing bitterness" was "lifted" from his conscience. The physiological response of crying in a prone state was not unknown in Vineyard charismatic experience, but the prolonged duration (forty minutes) of this experience became something of a hallmark in the Toronto outpouring, with meeting often lasting far into the night. This "resting in the Spirit" became so prevalent, that the church began to utilize "catchers" standing behind the persons requesting ministry to assist them in being lowered to the ground so they would not be injured falling backwards.[35] During this resting "trance-like" or meditative state, participants would often exhibit a range of physical manifestations such as trembling, jerking, feeling heat, fluttering eyelids, and increased pulse and breathing rates.[36] Participants stated that these experiences would last from a few minutes to many hours. A common physiological description of this experience was likened to intoxication by this Vineyard pastor in his visit to Toronto:

All but one of our team experienced immediate fainting and deep laughter. For well over an hour we laughed with all of our might. Later when I recovered, I felt as if I were drunk. I needed assistance to gather my things and head back to our hotel. I felt tremendous peace and a lack of fear for the future".[37]

The same pastor described a meeting several nights later in his own church this way:

I stood and began to call people forward. Many collapsed under the anointing of God before they even reached the front. When the dust settled, over 100 people were doing 'carpet time', and the Holy Spirit wasn't finished. We finally concluded the morning meeting at 3:30 in the afternoon after seeing massive laughter, joy, peace, deliverance, and such.[38]

This report connects the physical reactions with spiritual sensations such as joy and peace. Also consistently noted was a heightened spiritual state that often included physical healing, acts of deliverance from spirits, and emotional healing. Chevreau cataloged the common connection between physical and spiritual manifestations as uncontrollable laughter, drunkenness' in the Spirit, intense weeping, falling to the floor, physical convulsions or 'jerks', pogoing and bouncing, shouting and roaring. Visions, prophetic words and announcements, often accompanied with physical demonstrations.[39]

Chevreau catalogs dozens of experiences that share many of these elements in over fifty pages of text.[40] These accounts of divine healings, prophetic announcements, unusual physical manifestations, and deliverance from Spirits are continued in Chevreau's follow up work, *Share the Fire.*[41]

Charismatic experience in the Post-Wimber Vineyard

While the most extreme manifestations faded from the Vineyard after the Toronto-influenced churches left the movement, the emphasis on signs and wonders in a more traditional form was re-established. After Wimber's death in 1997, it was commonly questioned whether the Vineyard would be able to maintain its identity as a signs and wonders movement after the death of its founder, the controversy of the Toronto blessing era, and the division caused by a number of Toronto-influenced churches leaving the movement, including Mike Bickle's Kansas City Metro Vineyard, and Randy Clark's St. Louis Vineyard, both prominent churches in the practice of signs and wonders.[42] While many in the movement underwent a prolonged period of grieving for the loss of John Wimber, his son Chris Wimber, and the relationships lost due to the separation of fellowship in many churches, the movement identified a new leader and continued to seek its identity in these new circumstances.

Gary Best was a Vineyard church planter and pastor in Canada who had first encountered Wimber's teachings in 1984. After Wimber's death, Best published *Naturally Supernatural: Joining God in His Work* as a summation of teaching material that he (Best) had presented about signs and wonders ministry.[43] While this work narrates experiences over his entire ministry, it was published after Wimber's death and became an influential account of Vineyard experience. Best records a number of charismatic experiences that share many features with early Vineyard accounts. On one occasion Gary and his wife prayed for the bad back of a man who was not a professing Christian:

Almost immediately as we began to pray…his back began to twitch, then jerk. Soon he began to shake as the power of God's Spirit came upon him. He was very aware of the power that was touching his body as we prayed in the name of Jesus. Within a few minutes, his back was completely free of pain through its entire range of motion.[44]

This account is reminiscent of the early "clinical" accounts: simple, not overly "hyped" or extraordinary, but with physical reactions that Best considered were evidence of the presence of the Holy Spirit. In another event, Best describes a fascinating sequence of events at a youth-oriented service. First, a female intercessor "had a picture" of a man's left hand with two crushed knuckles. This picture was an "impression" or vision in her mind. Best then spoke to the crowd to determine if there was a person with crushed knuckles on their left hand. A young man hostile to the faith came forward to receive prayer ministry. After a prolonged prayer period, Physiological symptoms were evident on the man:

His body temperature started to rise until his whole body was perspiring. This confused him because no one else seemed to be affected by the obvious overheating in the room. Next he began to feel a tingling in his body, a slight current that grew more and more intense until he began to fear that he was being electrocuted. This current moved through his body and down his arms. Finally it shot into his hand – the one with the injured knuckles….He heard a distinct cracking sound, and then to his amazement, his knuckles reformed perfectly so he could move his hand freely…The young woman who had originally seen the picture began to speak directly to him and said, "When you were six years old you were sexually abused". She proceeded to identify the man who had abused him. She then related to him a number of details of his earlier life. He went white as a sheet. This could only be God speaking to him.[45]

This experience detailed by Best contains a number of elements: a group of intercessors praying for a single person, the combination of numerous prophetic "words" or messages from the Spirit received in prayer and offered to him, physical reactions such as the perspiring, perception of heat, electric "shocks', and the physical healing itself. Best includes a number of accounts of physical healings that contained many of these same elements.[46] This account certainly reveals something fascinating, as a person skeptical towards Christianity moved into a place where he understood this event *as a* religious experience.

Alexander Venter is a South African Vineyard pastor who was a research assistant for John Wimber at the Anaheim Vineyard in the 1980s. Venter went on to write several books on Vineyard subjects with material gleaned from his time with Wimber.[47] For over twenty years he has been a pastor of a Vineyard church in Johannesburg, South Africa. As a close associate of Wimber, he is a figure like Best, who straddles the time of Wimber's mature charismatic ministry and the contemporary post-Wimber Vineyard. His book, *Doing Healing*, contains not only elements of the sophisticated "clinical" investigations of healing similar to Wimber's early writings, but also numerous accounts of charismatic phenomena and pastoral experiences like other, more popular, accounts we have inspected. In this way, it functions like a companion volume to *Power Healing*, written some twenty years later.

Venter's work has the greatest theological depth of any of the works on healing written in the Vineyard. The themes of the kingdom of God, and the function of healing in the already–not yet are discussed. In addition, the concepts of authority, worldview, expectation of healing, mystery, and God's sovereignty are well-supported in *Doing Healing*.[48] Particularly interesting are Venter's reflections on worldview and healing, as he is a white South African pastoring in Johannesburg, a city with large suburban areas of poverty and a radical wealth gap between rich and poor. Thus, his understanding of healing deeply intertwines with concerns of social concern, poverty, racism, and institutional injustice. Much like Wimber's journey, Venter began his healing experience in a personal crisis. He developed a robust approach to healing that has essentially become the "codified" Vineyard healing model.[49]

Venter writes that revelation from God can come in the form of thoughts and words, ideas or pictures in the mind, memories, intuition, emotions, and physical senses of taste, touch, smell, and sight.[50] All of this potential communication from God may happen in a healing situation; thus, it is essential for the practitioner to "practice hearing God", and understand the meaning of these types of prophecy. Venter is in firm agreement with Wimber that a Christian can "learn" or develop their healing ministry; that is to say, it is both a work of God's grace and human collaboration. The very experience of a particular instance of healing will most likely contain elements of successive knowledge or insight gained by the intercessor. The *goal* of the healing event is not merely the resolution of the illness, but *wholeness* for the individual. Therefore, as we have seen before, the "presenting issue" – Wimber's term – may not be the actual *cause or root* that needs healing; it may be the physical, outward manifestation of a deeper emotional, psychological or spiritual problem.[51]

In specific relation to our attentiveness towards *corporate or communal experience*, he emphatically endorses the effectiveness of *teams* of intercessors, as various members take turns initiating prayer, sensing the work of the Spirit, and cooperatively engaging in the process of healing.[52] As physical manifestations may occur in both the person and the intercessor(s), these collaborative healing experiences can be discussed, evaluated and sensed even within the healing prayer session;

however, Venter cautions against developing a strict explanation of precisely *what* a particular manifestation might indicate. Thus, his suggestions are cautious and limited.

While he lists a number of experiences as *possible* manifestations of the Spirit, he is reluctant to claim adamantly that a particular manifestation –shaking or trembling, for example – *must be* an indicator of the Spirit's presence.[53] Venter's book on healing is of such substantial depth and pastoral insight that it is not surprising that it has held such wide influence in the Vineyard since its publication. We will conclude this stage of our study by examining the work of a contemporary American Vineyard pastor, Robby Dawkins, whose report may lack the theological sophistication of Venter's account but who, nonetheless, is highly influential as a teacher and practitioner of the charismatic ministry.

Dawkins is a pastor in Illinois, who ministers in churches and conferences across the United States and many other countries. He is currently high in demand as a conference speaker, and probably has the most well-known and respected healing "ministry" in the Vineyard and other third-wave churches. Dawkins published an account of his miraculous ministry experiences.[54] He writes of his own change of perspective and introduction to signs and wonders, which occurred at a meeting led by a woman whom Dawkins considered to be a fraud. While the woman prayed for him, Dawkins "tipped backwards in the air", fell to the ground, and entered the trance-like state of "resting in the Spirit" for over three hours, during which time he had an extraordinary vision. This vision consisted of Dawkins re-enacting the "dry bones" vision of Ezekiel 37, with himself as the principal actor, not the prophet Ezekiel. God "spoke" to Dawkins, telling him that he was among those "dry bones" who needed to be revived, and he became aware of his "dry" condition.[55] After his strength returned, he attempted to stand and speak with his wife, but could not speak coherently and could barely keep his balance or equilibrium. This experience created a passion for evangelism, and a fearlessness that allowed him to minister in crime-infested neighborhoods in his town. He states that this experience "was the beginning of a journey toward understanding what it means to be a carrier of His presence".[56]

Dawkins relates numerous examples of *charismata* that are quite familiar to this study. He relates countless instances of divine healing in response to prayer, physical responses to prayer including the feelings of electricity, heat, or pressure, and prophetic manifestations such as knowledge of persons and circumstances that are unknown to the intercessors through natural means.[57] In many of these cases, after the prayer the individual often feels peace, a sense of relief, belonging, or an increased sense of being accepted and loved by God.[58] Dawkins speaks often of receiving an "impression" from the Spirit that he understands as a prophetic communication from God. Interestingly, these communications are not restricted to mental processes, for Dawkins contends that at times *his own physical body* can be the receiver of the communication. On one occasion, while praying for a woman involved in witchcraft, Dawkins notes:

> Right about then, I felt this slight pain between my shoulder blades. I sensed that it wasn't a natural pain, but a sympathy pain- like a prophetic manifestation in my body of something that was going on with her...I asked her 'By any chance, do you have a bad back pain?" "Yes," she said. I got another impression from the Spirit and asked her, "Was it from a car accident two years ago?" She said "Yeah, it was two and a half years ago- I was in a bad car accident...I've been through three surgeries but they can't fix it."[59]

Dawkins states that this woman's back was healed in response to prayer. Other possible forms of prophetic revelation could include such things as "popping" words, scriptures, images, or symbols into an intercessors' conscious thought processes while they are praying.[60] Since publishing this work, Dawkins continues to minister and travel widely in Vineyard, Pentecostal, and charismatic circles.

From this detailed analysis, it is quite evident that there are a number of characteristics of charismatic experience that have been present throughout the Vineyard history, from the beginning era when John Wimber was first introduced to signs and wonders ministry, through the various growth stages of the movement, to the contemporary practice of ministers like Alexander Venter and Robby Dawkins. Despite the extraordinary amount of data available to our study, several questions remain unanswered. For example, in these experiences the possibility of deception and falsification of data creates a constant tension; therefore, Vineyard practitioners are extremely attuned to evidence and verification of these subjective experiences. [61]

ELEVEN
Evidence in Charismatic Experience

One of the major criticisms of charismatic healing is that there is little hard "evidence" for the miracles. Skeptics claim that supposed "miraculous healings" simply don't stand up to solid, objective evaluation. Some claim that the miracles were really the results of medical or practical treatments and, therefore, are not really "divine" in origin. In some cases, the scope of the miracles were overstated, or involved relatively minor conditions like mild headaches that can be just as easily "cured" through rest or drinking fluids. Some of the harshest critiques of modern-day miracles even suggest that both practitioners and supposed "healed" persons are foolishly deceived, or worse, are attempting to deceive other Christians into believing something that is not real.

What are we to make of these kinds of accusations? Do all healings, when scrutinized by the objective lens of medicine or logic, really lose their supernatural validity? Are Vineyard persons who practice divine healing deceived? Are they attempting to deceive others? Is this idea of "living the future" just a fantasy, or a hoax perpetrated by well-meaning, but naïve or desperate people? What are we to make of "evidence" in charismatic experience, especially the more subjective forms of prophecy or deliverance where scientific methods seem unable to grasp the depth of the experience?

How do we distinguish true and false experience of the Spirit? *Can we?* Are the skeptics right to question the authenticity of divine healing and other forms of charismatic experience? This chapter will set out to try and answer some of these questions. By looking at Vineyard charismatic experience, we will see that most Vineyard pastors and practitioners are well aware of the possibility of false miracles, deception, and even overstating the true outcomes of their experience. Even more than that, by examining this experience, we can begin to suggest some "ground rules" that, while not universal and certain, are nonetheless quite helpful in determining the truthfulness and source of modern-day miracles.

At first glance it is quite obvious that there are at least two distinct groups of charismatic phenomena in our study. The first group would be those in which "evidence" or evaluation is more easily found; that is, there is often a clear outcome of the experience. Either the proclaimed healing occurs or it doesn't, or the natural phenomena, as in Paul Cain's earthquake predictions, occur or not. The second group is more mysterious and subjective, as it refers to inner "spiritual" or "psychological" healings which are dependent on the report of the witness or individual to "authenticate" the validity of the experience. First, we will treat the more "objective" experiences, and then turn to the more private, mystical encounters.

In both Wimber's and Venter's healing models, there is an explicit "feedback loop" within the five-step prayer model that encourages the intercessor to solicit feedback from the individual in order to increase the effectiveness of the prayer. Further, Wimber actively encouraged participants to give reports as to the value of prayer that was received in conferences and other events.[1] Numerous reports from sources offer both negative and positive reinforcement of the process, as several Vineyard practitioners were not shy in offering accounts of "failed" healing prayers, as in the case of David Watson, Chris Wimber, and even John Wimber himself. In these cases, the "failure" was often attributed to the already– not yet nature of the kingdom, or there was a general appeal to the mysteries of God's sovereignty in these matters.

The more sensational, public nature of proclamations like those from Paul Cain made it quite simple for investigators like Ernie Gruen to determine their "accuracy". Even then, defenders of Cain, such as Wimber and Deere, often allowed that the experience itself was authentic, but suggested that sometimes Cain missed on the *timing* or *application* of the revelation.

Vineyard intercessors in our study also noted that through prior experience they have been able to track or evaluate the validity of charismatic events, even if they were of a more subjective nature. As

162

honest practitioners, we should be open to this kind of evidence, challenge, and even correction when needed. Some prophecies have powerful and immediate effect; at other times the effect is delayed.[2] The most significant form of evidence is the many instances when the prophetic words have startling accuracy or contain great detail that is meaningful to the individual. The intercessors related instances where the "knowledge" of the prophetic word contained such precise detail of events, places, names that there was no rational explanation for how the intercessor could possibly have gained this knowledge.

In the cases where there was no discernable immediate effect, several possible explanations were offered. Being fully aware of the subjective and imprecise nature of the process, the intercessors acknowledge the possibility of deception. Following the lead of Paul and John in the New Testament, who commanded believers to "test the spirits" or evaluate revelatory messages (1 Corinthians 14:32; 1 Thessalonians 5:18-22; I John 4:1). The process of sifting true from deceptive revelation involves testing the content of the prophecy to see if it is "sensible", and in accord with the teachings of scripture and the historic doctrines of the church.[3] Wimber was adamant that the "word" given should be evaluated by the person receiving prayer, and was wary of prophetic messages given in the form of: "Thus saith the Lord...".[4]

An intriguing broad theme within the concerns about evidence and deception is the relationship between the more dramatic occurrences in the "Toronto blessing", such as "resting in the spirit", extreme physical reactions (laughing, violent shaking, jumping etc.) and the effectiveness of the prayer or experience. Although Chevreau noted numerous instances where individuals obtained healing (physical, emotional, spiritual) while undergoing these intense manifestations, other Vineyard authors are more cautionary in attributing a *causal* relationship between the phenomena and healing. Venter believes that, even in these dramatic manifestations, *deception is a possibility* and therefore discernment is crucial; these experiences could be generated by the Spirit, by human persons, or even Satan.[5] He writes:

We must avoid two extremes with regard to manifestations: identifying spiritual phenomena too readily with God's Spirit or the demonic, without discerning the human element (that leads to a naive endorsement of what happens); dismissing the phenomena as "emotionalism" or "deception", not discerning the Spirit's work, resulting in critical indifference and rejection. The authenticity and effectiveness of the encounter should *never* be judged by the intensity of the human response, by the outward "shows of power" or lack thereof.[6]

However, Venter is equally opposed to merely dismissing manifestations out of hand owing to their strangeness, as this runs the equal risk of dismissing the possibility of the Spirit's work. While the scriptures do record many examples of physical responses to the presence of the Spirit,[7] it is not surprising that these instances are not exhaustive. Further, the ever-present element of the mystery of the kingdom entails that multiple forces could be at work.[8] Regardless of these possibilities, he holds that we may, with time and experience, perform this discerning task more effectively. By focusing not on the manifestations themselves, but on the *fruit* of the experience in lives of the requester and the intercessor, more certainty can be had.

Thus,

if the phenomena result in healing, cleansing, transformation, joy, peace, intimacy with Jesus, obedience to His Word, it is of God. If it leaves a person more depressed, fearful, selfish, disobedient, divisive, carnal, it is the fruit of fallen nature (Galatians 5:19-21) and the "wisdom of the devil" (James 3:14-16).[9]

Therefore, if the prophecy has an emotional, spiritual, or cognitive effect on a person, the intercessor can then be more confident that the message was true. However, Vineyard practitioners related occasions where a "word" to individuals had little effect at the time, even though the intercessors were quite convinced they had heard a clear message from the

Spirit, and so concluded that the individual was unable or unwilling to recognize the message. In other cases of healing, the healing itself was *progressive* or occurred at some point *after* the initial event.

In many cases, the intercessors related that after valid prophetic words were given, persons experienced a release from anxiety, fear, depression, anger or other negative emotional states, and an increase in positive emotional states such as love, peace, joy, calm, courage, and faith. However, Wimber was adamant that the occurrence of manifestations was not *certain* evidence of anything, as "these experiences do not ensure healing; healing is an internal work of the Holy Spirit".[10]

Here, it is important to recall that the uniqueness of prophecy lies in its characterization of three-way communication. Indeed, the individual mentally processes the prophecy spoken to them by the intercessor. Raising the very question: "Does this make any sense to you?" *presupposes* not only the possibility of error, but also that the individual can, and should, undergo the testing and verification process. In this "feedback loop" not only does the particular prophetic word *given at the moment* undergo testing, but the *prophetic process itself* becomes subject to verification and falsification. While one could certainly think of numerous cases where experiences like this have been an occasion for abuse, mind control, or punishment (the obvious cases of doomsday cults come to mind), closer examination would most likely reveal that, at some point, these words were not tested as scripture instructs.

TWELVE
Idolatry in Vineyard Experience

The word "idolatry" is certainly a loaded term. For some, this might bring up images of the ancient Hebrews worshipping the Canaanite god Baal. We might also think of Paul's churches struggled with worshipping in the temple of Artemis or other Hellenistic deities. In its simplest form, idolatry is the act of putting something, anything, in the place that only God can occupy. So for our purposes, we can think of idolatry as the act or thought of putting anything- our reputations, our desires, our ministries, even our desire to see the Holy Spirit act – in the place where only the sovereign Lord should occupy. With this definition in mind, how might we be tempted to act or think in idolatrous ways?

Certainly few, if any, Vineyard authors proposed that the charismatic experience would be an unending fullness of the total power of God; if anything, early "failures" in healing were clear testimony of the exact opposite.[1] As we have seen, Wimber placed a strong emphasis on God's sovereignty in the practice of the *charismata*, thus making room for the possibility of healing not occurring. Thus, not only was the already–not yet nature of the kingdom of God a factor in the effectiveness of healing, but the very "strength" or perceived depth of any particular experience could vary as well.[2] The issue of God's presence in the midst of suffering is important as well. This was certainly evident in the corporate mourning over the illnesses and deaths of David Watson, Chris Wimber, and John Wimber.[3] Thus, a lack of healing does not necessarily mean God is not present or concerned with human suffering, as even in the cases of praying for the terminally ill, God's presence might still be felt.[4]

The corporate experience of an absence or withdrawal of God's presence is noted by Vineyard authors. Wimber spoke of a "waxing and waning" of the presence of God. Speaking of the experience of the Anaheim Vineyard, he wrote: "There were times when we had a great sense of nearness and times in which there seemed to be a *withdrawal to some degree*". [5] While there was often little explanation of withdrawal beyond the appeal to sovereignty and mystery, the encouragement to prevail in the faith in the midst of absence and suffering is prevalent in the Vineyard literature.

Wimber frequently reacted against those who attempted to designate him as a *healer* or *prophet,* as in his mind this violated his understanding of the *charismata* as *gifts* of the sovereign Spirit. As we noted, his very early ministry success did cause him to swell with self-pride at one point, which had numerous negative consequences. Beyond personal grandiosity, how else might we see self-pride in the Vineyard?

It seems quite obvious that *idolatry* in the form of *self-pride* would be evidenced by the placing of *oneself in the place of the Holy Spirit,* as this would attack the sovereignty of the Spirit. This might show up in the Vineyard as a *profound rejection* of the mystery of the kingdom of God, possibly by collapsing the eschatological tension to the "already" side of the equation.

....

By rejecting the mystery of the kingdom of God, we collapse the eschatological tension of the already-not yet and risk placing ourselves in the place only God can occupy.

....

How might this be so? If it's true that fundamental to Vineyard practice is a commitment to live in the *tension* of the kingdom here and not yet, then an over-realized eschatology would entail placing more *responsibility* and *weight* for the success of healing on *either the intercessor or the person requesting prayer.* For example, like the disciples in John 9, someone may believe that an illness or misfortune is a direct result of sin; thus, only confession of sin would release healing and restore *shalom.* An unfortunate step beyond this would be to "blame the victim" if *the prayer for healing did not work* – a claim that John Wimber, Alexander Venter, Gary Best and others stridently argued against! Sadly, in some churches (especially those that see healing as guaranteed in the atonement), when healing prayer is not successful, people often look for a reason, and too often the "reason" is a lack of faith, or the presence of sin in the life of the sick person.

This type of victim-blaming adds theological insult to injury, and has no place in Vineyard healing practice. Many people have been hurt by these kinds of words when they have suffered or have had loved ones suffer. When I have witnessed or heard about these kinds of prayers, I often wonder if the people praying are more concerned about *their own faith being challenged* then they are about the well-being of the person they are praying for. What I mean is this: when we offer healing prayer for a sick person, if we believe that all healing comes from the sovereign Spirit, then whether or not the healing comes, it's not up to us. While we may grieve for those who don't receive healing, our personal faith, holiness, or relationship with God is not on trial. God heals, not us. Therefore, God is responsible. It goes off the tracks when we *demand or require God to move in order to bolster our own faith or reputation.* This attempt to put ourselves in the place that God alone can occupy, is a form of idolatry and a distortion of biblical healing. In other forms of charismatic experience (deliverance from spirits, prophecy, etc.), *a refusal to allow for mystery, for the reality of suffering, the limitations of human understanding, or possible absence of the Spirit's power, would also reject the tension of the kingdom dynamic and could also be considered idolatry.*

How else might idolatry materialize in Vineyard theology and practice? What about the move to the opposite pole of the kingdom scale, i.e. an adoption of a "consistent" or *completely future* eschatology, which would entail collapsing the pole to the "not yet" side? This would be characterized by an *acceptance* of disease, misfortune, and unhealthy psychological or spiritual behaviors. If this led to an abandonment of the practice, or even the possibility, of healing or restoration of peoples and communities, it would be, at the very least, a *rejection of the Vineyard birthright.* In effect this would be akin to abandoning the task of "the redemption of the world", and a refusal to obey the command of Jesus to "heal the sick" (Matthew 10:8).

Yet another possibility of idolatry is the claiming that any charismatic experience comes from the sovereign Spirit, but primarily to persons who are special or "unique". This idea makes the Spirit as being nearly incomprehensible to most humans, *with the exception of a specially gifted few*. In the Vineyard context, this would be a move beyond even cessationism, for it would necessitate the rejection of the Spirit given to *all who profess Christ*. Could we say, then, that this temptation of idolatry would be unthinkable in the Vineyard? What if an especially gifted person refused to acknowledge the present–future tension of the Spirit's work? John Wimber had to fight the idolatrous temptation to enhance his reputation as "a healer" or "a prophet" uniquely gifted by the Spirit. While this temptation is not unique to the Vineyard, this form of idolatry could very well arise among people who expect and move in the presence and gifts of the Spirit.

Conclusion: What do our Experiences Tell us? Eschatology in the Vineyard

It has become evident in this study that throughout Vineyard history, certain characteristics of the charismatic experience can be defined. The work of the Spirit within the presence of the already–not yet kingdom is the defining characteristic of living the future kingdom. The works of the Spirit require the foundation of inaugurated eschatology; the theology of the kingdom must be enacted by the works in order to maintain its own inherent logic. We have seen that collapsing to either pole of the dynamic tension, that is to say, adoption of a "triumphalist" pneumatological practice and a realized eschatology, is a move towards idolatry; so also a cessationist pneumatological practice or a completely futuristic eschatology would be disobedient to our call. The Vineyard practitioner must dwell in the difficult tension of the kingdom that is here but still coming. This is what makes ministry on this side of Jesus' final *parousia* so difficult. We strive to *expect* healing – to see the Holy Spirit change circumstances, to see people released from addictions or pain that hurt them and the people around them. Many times the healing does come. However, we need to accept the reality that we cannot guarantee any healing or move of the Spirit. Sometimes, perhaps too often, the hoped-for healing doesn't come.

....

When healing doesn't come, we neither "blame the victim" for not having enough faith, nor do we accuse them of holding secret sins in the lives.

....

Healings, like all works of God, are a mystery. The Holy Spirit is sovereign, and chooses to move as he wishes. When these difficult and painful situations arise, we have two choices. We can get discouraged and quit praying for the sick, or we can trust God, and obediently continue to pray for the sick, trusting the results to him. We must, at any cost, avoid the temptation to resolve the tension of the already–not yet by collapsing to either a triumphalist view of the "already", or give in to the defeatist view of the "not yet". The Vineyard minister is called to live between these two worlds.

Section V: Extending Vineyard Kingdom Theology

As it moves into its fourth decade, the Vineyard has reached a point where theological maturity is not only overdue, but necessary. A major goal of this work has been to provide one set of answers to questions such as: "What are the central theological distinctives of the Vineyard", and: "How are these different from other churches and theological perspectives?" The Vineyard, like many emerging movements, certainly struggled with theological self-definition. The diversity of traditions, approaches, and theological structures that make up the movement bring a broad range of theological views and perspectives into the movement. Thus the question becomes: "What exactly is the 'theological center' to which the Vineyard is moving?" Also, we now understand what John Wimber and other Vineyard leaders sought to accomplish when they formed this new church which became a movement. We understand the importance of culturally relevant mission and the tensions that Wimber and other faced when they attempted to create new practices and models out of their kingdom values. We've seen what Living the Future meant for these early Vineyard pioneers, but what does living the future look like in our day? How might the Vineyard begin to address the crucial theological and practices issues of our age?

THIRTEEN

Vital Elements of Vineyard Theology and Practice

An Inaugurated, Enacted Eschatological Vision of the Kingdom of God

....

The kingdom of God was inaugurated in the mission of Jesus, is fundamentally eschatological as it points towards God's ultimate triumph, and it is enacted through the Holy Spirit in the life of the church.

....

We have seen that the central distinctive of the Vineyard movement is the *inaugurated, enacted eschatological kingdom of God. This is living the future reality of the kingdom of God.* It is true that, with the orthodox Christian traditions, the Vineyard holds a high Christology and sees the birth, life, death and resurrection of Jesus Christ as the principal events in history; however, the story of Jesus also highlights the coming of the kingdom – the sign of a future event, when "all will be all in all". This kingdom metanarrative requires a solid theology of the Holy Spirit. The coming and work of the Spirit *is eschatological,* as the "first fruits" of a future comprehensive consummation. The coming of the kingdom of the triune God means that the power and presence of the future has forced its way into the present – hence, the "presence of the future". Rudolf Bultmann stated: "In every moment slumbers the possibility of being the eschatological moment."[1] The essential truth of his claim is evidenced in Vineyard practice – *every moment can be a moment when the powers of the eschatological kingdom of God may be enacted in the present.*

A Kingdom Breaking Through in the Present

In the case of the Vineyard, then, what does it mean to engage theology "from the ground up?"[2] What makes its theology "distinctively Vineyard",

175

as it were? Perhaps another way to diagnose this is to ask: "What does the kingdom do?" In our study of the parables of the kingdom, we saw essentially that the kingdom, *grows*, *builds*, and *forcibly advances*. It could also be said that the kingdom of God advances *violently* against the enemy. In examination of Vineyard practice, we have seen that living the future implies that there was an explicit connection between healing, restoration and wholeness, overcoming exclusion, division and sickness as signs of kingdom advancement.

With Pentecostals and Charismatics, the Vineyard shares a common belief that *God acts today in much the same way he has throughout history* – we know and experience the creating and sustaining Spirit of life intervening in God's world. John Wimber taught his parishioners "to do what the Father is doing". Explicit in this formulation is the claim that God is *always* at work, *always* pressing in on the present, *always* making the breakthrough of his kingdom a powerful reality. More than this, the *tension* of the kingdom's presence sets Vineyard practice apart from other continuationist groups. As we have seen, in praying for the sick, for example, the present–future tension of the Spirit enables *both* the possibility of healing and provides a theological explanation for when the healing *does not come*. This present–future tension of the Spirit is found throughout other forms of Vineyard practice and experience as well.

Any extension of Vineyard theology into other ideas must maintain this eschatological tension in order to remain authentically Vineyard. If this is so, then human experiences such as suffering, struggle, and the "withdrawal" of God's presence would be expected in light of the conflict or warfare between kingdoms that Wimber embraced from the work of Kallas. Whether we study anthropology, hermeneutics or justice, collapsing to either an entirely *realized* conception or an entirely *future* one, or *denying the reality of human suffering or conflict,* would cease to be a truly Vineyard approach. While the foundational kingdom theology and pneumatological practice of the Vineyard may be in place, there are many theological ideas that have yet to be explored from the kingdom perspective. Several contemporary scholars who immediately emerge as possible theological friends are N.T. Wright in kingdom studies, and

Graham Twelftree and Craig Keener in Pneumatology. I shall touch briefly on several areas where these scholars can extend and challenge Vineyard theology.

Contemporary Versions of the Kingdom Story

While there has been, as yet, little reason to abandon the consensus view exemplified by George Ladd, studies on the kingdom have continued to examine the teachings of Jesus on this and other topics. Perhaps the best examples are the continuing "Third Quest", the related "Jesus Seminar", and works written in response and reinforcement of the respective positions.[3] N.T. Wright has arguably become the most vocal opponent of the liberal-leaning "Jesus Seminar". The first three volumes of his magisterial multi-volume work, *Christian Origins and the Question of God*, dealt with the kingdom theme extensively.[4] It would be impossible to adequately address the major themes of this work in several pages; hence, I will restrict this reflection to some comments as to the potential for his work to extend Vineyard eschatology. Wright's work is well-known among Vineyard pastors and leaders, and has been a theological influence on the movement for many years.[5] It would be no understatement that, from the Vineyard perspective, Wright is a most compelling ally of kingdom theology and inaugurated eschatology.

Overall it is clear that Wright reinforces the inaugurated eschatology consensus view typified by Ladd. His work does not attempt to overturn or revise this consensus, but adds considerable understanding of late Second-Temple Judaism that sheds light on the Jewish expectation of the kingdom.[6] Wright helpfully dissects the contrary positions of Second-Temple Judaism regarding kingdom expectations, which naturally leads to the even-greater disparity with Jesus' conceptions of the kingdom.[7] Wright elaborates on the points made by Kallas about the essential nature of conflict between kingdoms being the horizon against which Jesus identifies the real enemy of God's people as *not* the present Roman occupiers, but the cosmic usurper, Satan.[8] Wright supports Wimber's contention that this fight is an essential sign of the kingdom's presence, as "a present reality, in which people can share, but which still awaits some sort of final validation".[9] These elements function more as reinforcement for the consensus view, so in some respects Wright's voluminous accounts reinforce and add depth to the conclusions of Ladd's proposals more so than advancing new theses. Where Wright does provide new territory for the Vineyard scholar to explore, is his expansion of the kingdom concept to cosmic realms; indeed, his retelling of the kingdom growth parables to include cosmic realms is a principal concern in his *Surprised by Hope: Rethinking Heaven, the Resurrection, and the Mission of the Church.*[10] This popular level work reforms and extends the conclusions of *The Resurrection of the Son of God*, and offers a vision of restoration and renewal of creation that could extend enacted eschatology in new ways. Wright's expansive vision of the kingdom encompasses an entirely renewed creation, for "space is to be redeemed, time is to be redeemed, and matter is to be redeemed".[11] Wright sees the renewal of matter, especially, being a foil for Platonic/Gnostic tendencies that still plague western thought by *denying the good of God's created world*. This renewal of creation is universal and all-encompassing, and includes the re-ordering of the material world into its eschatological purpose, or a "Cosmic Christology".[12] While there has been some reflection on a theology of creation and creation care within the Vineyard, formal theological reflection interacting with creation renewal has not yet been developed.[13] Wright would be a worthy conversation partner and resource for a project to develop such a theology of the renewal of creation.[14]

The possibility of modern miracles has taken on new life in the academy in recent years; this development may provide Vineyard apologists with much valuable material to extend our Pneumatology in new and fruitful directions. Craig Keener is a wonderful scholar and teacher who has emerged as a prolific writer focusing on Gospel and Pauline studies. Not only is his recent volume, *Miracles: The Credibility of the New Testament Accounts*, a solid theological defense of the biblical concept of miracles, but it also includes stunning accounts of modern-day miracles that reinforce his theological and exegetical case.[15] Keener advances a simple two-part thesis in this work: first, he argues that eyewitnesses throughout history and all over the world offer miracle claims, and secondly, supernatural explanations should not be excluded *a priori* as suitable explanations for these miracle claims.[16] He readily acknowledges that not *all* claims should be given equal weight, but that first-hand eyewitness testimony can be investigated, evaluated, and in many cases *the most reasonable conclusion is that a miracle did indeed occur*. Keener is not unaware of the historic skepticism towards his thesis; thus he takes considerable care in deconstructing the scholarly presupposition against the possibility of miracle and divine action. As one would expect, the claims of David Hume are brought to the fore; Keener relies on profuse critiques of Hume's work that have been amassed in recent decades. While Hume's arguments held wide sway during the Enlightenment, it is quite evident that his work is a product of the modern West, and lies outside the broad scope of both ancient and non-Western belief systems. Keener contends that "the particular arguments once used by Spinoza, Hume and others to form a modern consensus against miracles made sense only on the philosophical and scientific presuppositions of their era, not those of our own." Just as mechanistic scientific principles of the Newtonian age have been questioned in quantum mechanics, so also the modern bias against God acting in the world must be questioned in light of accounts within and without the enlightenment-influenced Western world.

The result of this reading of modernity brings Keener to a fascinating question. If the Humean Enlightenment claim against the possibility of miracles is indeed in question, what might we learn from the Majority Worldview regarding the possibility of God acting in the world? This question is answered by offering a stunning quantity of accounts of modern-day miracles. In nearly 900 pages of scholarly text, Keener recounts innumerable first-hand accounts of miracles from both the Majority World and the West, including the United States. He personally investigated many of these stories, interviewing the participants, and in some cases, even observed the miraculous event himself.[17] He amassed not only a considerable list of possible miracle accounts, but a reasoned evaluation of the reliability of the eyewitnesses as well. While some case studies offer "confirmed" medical reports of healing, (that is to say, the condition or disease is medically documented as being present, then absent after healing prayer), many accounts are in poor, remote, or inaccessible Majority World circumstances that challenge Western worldview predisposition to "scientific" verification. Keener's model of strict investigation and evaluation of miracle claims is a humble and honest example that Vineyard practitioners should follow. We need not be afraid or hostile towards those who might question or be skeptical towards our claims of miracles; for the reputation of God and his work is partially dependent on our faithful reporting of his work amongst us. If we exaggerate or manipulate our stories of God's work, not only will our credibility eventually be damaged as the truth is revealed, but the reputation of the Holy Spirit's work could be damaged as well.

The sheer number and reliability of the witnesses beg the question of what we are to make of these ancient, modern, and contemporary claims of healing. The countless reports of healing in contemporary Pentecostal, Charismatic, and Third-Wave churches share much in similarity with the stories in the gospels and Acts. Is this mere coincidence or psychological suggestion? Keener contends that emotional manipulation is highly unlikely, owing to the sheer number of witnesses, the unsophisticated nature of many of the cases, and the underlying supernatural worldview of the participants. If indeed, we take the supernatural worldview of the Majority World seriously, then the best explanation for many of these accounts is that a miracle occurred, for the supernatural explanation is much less "novel" in the Majority World than it is to Western sensibilities.[18] Even Western-trained anthropologists have documented numerous claims of the "miraculous" challenging their supposedly "neutral" scientific presuppositions. Keener is well aware of the limitations of his approach in that he has taken eyewitness accounts often at face value. However this is not problematic as in many of the cases there is little to be gained by lying; thus, he is largely creating an "inference to the best explanation" account. The sheer mass of accounts is staggering – Keener offhandedly notes "millions of claims!"[19] This fact alone demands that the nature of these accounts be taken seriously, as they cover an impressive swath of experience. For a Vineyard scholar or practitioner,

Keener's compelling book provides a very different kind of material than our previous study.

Graham Twelftree was a Vineyard pastor in Australia, and has held academic positions in America at Regent University, and the United Kingdom. He is currently the academic dean at the London School of Theology. Dr Twelftree has emerged as a specialist not only in Jesus studies, but also in the study of the miraculous. His interest in the miraculous is shown in his first published academic work, *Jesus the Miracle Worker: A Historical and Theological Study.*[20] Twelftree examines the gospel accounts of the miracles of Jesus, and the historical study of these miracles in contemporary scholarship. As Keener would do later, Twelftree engages modern and contemporary skeptics of miracles, and notes that in much of the recent "quests" the subject of the miracles had almost entirely been ignored. He also builds an impressive argument for the idea that in many cases, it was the *miracles* that best explain the popularity of Jesus and the crowds that followed him, rather than the quality or force of his *teaching* which has often been the focus of historical Jesus research. At this point in time, Twelftree's book was probably the most helpful one available to interested Vineyard scholars. In his most recent book, Dr Twelftree turns his attention to the apostle Paul in *Paul and the Miraculous: A Historical Reconstruction.* Once again, Twelftree discovers that much of Pauline research has ignored both miraculous events in Paul's life and Paul's theological understanding of miracles. Whereas historically, scholars have tended to see Paul primarily as an academic (one of *them*!), a true picture of Paul demands that we take seriously his view and experience of the miraculous. Once again, Dr Twelftree has provided new material that has been too-often overlooked in academic research.

It is clear that through the works of Wright, Keener, and Twelftree, the Vineyard's theology of the kingdom and Pneumatology can be enriched and extended. Strengthening its theological self-identification will certainly assist the movement as it continues in ecumenical conversations; but at this point in its history, the Vineyard lacks a fully developed ecclesiology that will firm up its self-understanding. I will offer a potential way forward for this development of an ecclesiology based on inaugurated, enacted eschatology. Following this, the bulk of the chapter will contend that the Vineyard is uniquely equipped to engage with some of the crucial issues of our day (the so-called "post-modern" world) from a fresh perspective, as a commitment to the mystery and tension of the kingdom has a great deal to add to topics like hermeneutics, Christian anthropology, and justice.

Towards a Vineyard Ecclesiology

In recent years, an interesting conversation has developed within the Vineyard movement: Should the Vineyard be content to adopt free-church ecclesiology uncritically, or can the relationship between the kingdom and the church be reconsidered "from the ground up?" The Vineyard does have a clear distinction between the kingdom and the church. As the kingdom is the dynamic reign of God, the kingdom is cosmic, universal, and over all creation. The church is comprised of the people of the kingdom at a particular time and place, ordered in structured social relationships.[21] The church, then, "demonstrates the presence of the kingdom"[22] and is in itself a *prolepsis* (first fruit) of the future community of God, a foretaste of perfect communal relationships as they will exist in the fully realized kingdom of God. Thus, the church and the kingdom are not the same; the expanse of the kingdom reign is far greater than the church.

A potential weakness in the Vineyard movement's ecclesiology is its vague organization which has resulted in uncertain conceptions of offices, denominational structures, leadership, and authority. Much of this is also related to the Vineyard identifying itself as an *association* instead of a formal *denomination,* but it may be time to revisit these concepts. More explanation is in order. Perhaps a good question that could be asked is: "What traits, tendencies, or hidden assumptions are in the Vineyard that may inhibit its ability to move forward theologically and organizationally?"

I would suggest that the Vineyard has a sort of anti-institutionalism that needs to be examined as we move forward into the next decades. That is to say, within our heritage lies a subtle distrust, fear, or loathing of

182

structure. A principal fear of the movement is the "routinization of charisma" made famous by sociologist Max Weber. This fear is not irrational. One of the many lessons that John Wimber picked up during his time at the Fuller Institute of Church Growth is that the pattern of denominational growth often culminates in the establishment of an institution that loses the vitality of its charismatic founders. Weber wrote that religious movements inevitably lost the charismatic vitality of their youth, eventually becoming institutions rather than enduring movements. When "prophetic movements" developed a level of structure that ensured their economic, social, or political survival, this structure in turn inhibited their dynamic will to innovate, to evolve, and to move into new areas of thinking or ministry. Weber put it this way:

> Primarily, however, a religious community arises as a result of routinization of a prophetic movement, namely as a result of the process whereby either the prophet himself or his disciples secure the permanence of its preaching and the dispensation of grace. Hence they insure also the economic existence of the enterprise and its staff, and thereby monopolize its privilege of grace and charge for its preservation.[23]

As a church planting movement, the Vineyard has proved countless times that successful church planters and pastors do indeed need a set of skills, knowledge and abilities; even if they are not professionally trained (i.e. in a seminary). However, many of these skills are best learned or developed "on the job", as it were, in situations where the aspiring pastor can test their abilities, and learn through their successes and their failures. It is possible that the success of non-formally trained pastors, combined with this fear of the "routinization of charisma" – expressed in a form of anti-institutionalism – has devalued scholarship and academic excellence in the past. However, this fear of routinization, combined with the loose organizational structure, has led to a fuzzy ecclesiology that leaves much to be desired. A question immediately arises, however, when one begins down this path:

"Can the Vineyard develop and maintain a more robust ecclesiology and yet remain an association and still hold at bay the routinization of charisma?"

That is, is Weber's "routinization of charisma" claim truly an "inevitable" process? The growth of vitality and continued charismatic development in the Vineyard movement after John Wimber's passing surely challenges Weber's thesis. Rather than *weaken* the movement, a stronger ecclesiology will empower the movement and provide further resources to *resist routinization* and maintain the distinctive identity of the Vineyard.

A mature Vineyard ecclesiology would have the following characteristics. The mission of the church should be evident from a now-familiar refrain in this study, which is, "doing the works and preaching the words of Jesus".[24] This missional self-understanding needs little addition as it is firmly entrenched in Vineyard DNA and evident in recent practitioners such as Robby Dawkins and Alexander Venter. This conception of the Vineyard *ekklesia* has been a strength since Wimber's early years of leadership, as Wimber first suggested a centered-set form of association rather than a formal denominational structure for the Vineyard movement.

It is an open question whether or not this relational, centered-set ecclesiology (i.e. with minimal formal structures of identification, adherence, membership, etc.), is still relevant and sustainable in the global, diverse body of the Vineyard. Maintaining relational affiliation and common purpose and values in a hundred churches located in the Western United States focused on middle class, white, baby-boomer demographics was relatively simple compared to maintaining unity of purpose and identity within the present spread and diversity of churches in the global Vineyard.

All this is not to imply there is *no structure* or hierarchical authority in the current organization. The Statement of Faith is fundamentally Nicene, with little mention of *how* a church should structure itself according to government, the sacraments, etc.[25] As expected, this implies a wide variety of practice in Vineyard churches regarding formal membership in a local congregation, how the offices and leadership of the church are structured, how ordinances like baptism and the Eucharist are practiced, and how ordination is granted to pastors. It is expected that common values and kingdom theology will be maintained, whereas particular practices may differ across cultures, societal groups, or countries.[26] Some issues appear to be settled: the role of women being equal to men as far as roles in ministry are concerned, for example. A church that proclaimed otherwise would be out of step with the proclaimed values of the movement.[27]

A comprehensive Vineyard ecclesiology would thus have to build on the foundational values and theology already established (everybody gets to play, the ministry of the Spirit, inaugurated eschatology, culturally relevant mission, etc.), be aware of the strengths and weaknesses of the centered-set model, and yet be elastic enough to incorporate global expressions of "what it means to be a Vineyard" in *cultures dramatically different from middle-class suburban America*.[28] Hopefully, this book has been a step forward in identifying important aspects of Vineyard theology and practice; however it is clear that much work is yet to be done in this area.

Towards a Vineyard Theology of Justice

Theological ethics constructed from the kingdom background may help our post-Christian culture plot a course through the difficult issues in racial, economic, and social justice. A robust inaugurated eschatology should provide resources to the pressing and exceedingly difficult questions related to justice and privilege. The Vineyard has always had a focus on *serving* the poor and marginalized, but what more can be done to *empower* marginalized or traditionally under-represented populations or victims of systemic oppression? [29] While there have been several justice-oriented conferences and initiatives in the movement, a comprehensive theology of justice has not yet been developed.[30]

185

> We must continue to ask: "What might it mean to enact the justice of the kingdom?"

A Vineyard theology of justice would need to contain the following elements that would empower it to speak to a number of current, pressing issues in the church and society.[31]

First, a Vineyard theology of justice would find its *foundation* in the Old Testament conception of the kingdom of the "Lord that loves justice" (Isa. 61:8), which looks forward to the final triumph of righteousness. The Vineyard retelling of the Exodus story is that it is the first major revelation of the kingdom of God;[32] thus it is clear that the working of justice and release from oppression lie deep within the story of the Hebrew people. The demands of justice within Hebrew society and most specifically, on its kings, religious rulers, and persons of wealth are brought to the front in the major and minor Hebrew prophets; but these protests are grounded in a picture of the eschatological kingdom of justice that acted as a *standard to which the current rulers could be held.*

The demands of the Mosaic Law to administer justice[33] can be traced back to the call of Abraham and the very founding of the Hebrew identity itself.[34] The call to enact justice is therefore an act of obedience, much like the act of obedience in praying for the sick. The rule of justice is idealized in Solomon's dream when he asked for "understanding to discern justice" instead of riches or revenge.[35] Sadly, the ideal did not last, for we see in the prophetic rebuke of Isaiah 1:17 that the call to "seek justice, rebuke the oppressor" had been lost by Judah's rulers. The call of the prophets demanded that Judah and Israel's rulers enact justice and return to the LORD; indeed the final judgment against both kingdoms was partially owing to their failure to obey the demands of *righteousness and justice.* Throughout these prophetic protests, the charge of guilt was accompanied by the proclamation of a future hope, when the Servant of the Lord will "bring forth justice".[36] The expectation of the kingdom of God thus included the enacting of justice as a central feature of the Messiah's reign.[37] Thus, the yearning for justice is essential to the already–not yet

186

eschatological paradigm, as it is rooted in the story of God's people.

Secondly, an inaugurated eschatological conception of justice for the Vineyard must have a firm understanding of *who and what* it struggles against; for the battle for justice is primarily undertaken against "principalities and powers" that war against God's good creation. While unjust rulers and systems enslave and harm people, a Vineyard theology would see the essential force behind these rulers in much the same way Jesus did – as the demonic enemy whose desire is to steal, kill and destroy God's creation.[38] Wimber understood this dynamic through his study of Ladd and Kallas, and it is reinforced through popular Vineyard literature.[39]John Wimber commonly expressed this idea as, "a person is never your real enemy....even when he acts like one". Thus, a Vineyard theology of justice would see human perpetrators as victims of a sort, even though they are co-regents of evil held accountable for their acts of injustice.[40] Thus, other persons must be understood as agents and victims deserving grace and forgiveness, and much reflection must be done on the ethical requirements of Jesus to love our enemies and pray for the persecutors.

Living the future kingdom of justice now needs to be both *realistic* and *transformative, truthful* and yet *compassionate, conscious* of suffering, yet always *pointing* towards the *future hope* of the fullness of the kingdom. The suffering of those under the realm of injustice must not be underappreciated or blandly accepted, but understood, entered into, and mutually endured. Yet even in the sympathizing with the victims of oppression, the call to kingdom transformation is equally important. Thus, it would not be acceptable either to accept or glamorize suffering; instead, a Vineyard enacting of justice would recognize the reality of suffering even in the call to transformation as it looks forward to the time when God will be "all in all". The refusal of the haughty and arrogant to acknowledge *injustice* (Isaiah 3) is certainly unacceptable, but so would be the omission of the call to transformation for *both* the oppressor and the victim of oppression, as *both* are called to be transformed into the image of Jesus. John Wimber understood that imitating the compassion of Jesus was necessary for his healing ministry; the same would be true of working for justice. Those moments, when justice is achieved, would be seen as signs of the Holy Spirit, who is always working to make all things new. This future kingdom of justice provides a source of hope and strength for both the victim of injustice and those practitioners working *for* justice.

Finally, an inaugurated eschatological theology of justice would be *comprehensive*. While institutional oppression, racism, and hatred of peoples immediately come to mind when considering the realm of justice, a Vineyard theology of justice would go both deeper and wider. Modern-day slave trafficking, the rights of women worldwide, and economic issues related to globalization would all be in view. Principal questions relating to the meaning of kingdom identity over and above national, political, or social identity, would have to be considered. Jesus' critiques of empire, nationalism, and political identity would have to be brought thoughtfully into this discussion. For example, it is quite clear that dispensational eschatology has influenced how American Christians approach foreign policy, especially the modern nation of Israel. A theology of justice based on inaugurated eschatology would most likely challenge this, and suggest that human rights for Palestinians might challenge unqualified support for the nation of Israel.[41]

The effect of globalization on emerging nations has been well-documented. A theology of justice would need to engage these issues of economic justice, fair versus so-called "free" trade, and the exploitation of the natural and economic resources of poorer nations to support modern Western economies. The call to clothe and care for the widow and the orphan entails that we critically examine how consumerism, consumption and free-market forces work against the poor, marginalized and vulnerable of the world. Justice practitioners would most likely find themselves at odds with an American consumerist culture that blindly accepts corporate goals of achieving ever-lower costs of production in order to maximize investor returns and price-to-earnings ratios. A theology of justice may not only consume less, but would consume *differently,* with attention to the hidden costs of production and distribution that often harm the world's poor.

Connected to the issue of economic justice are the issues of modern-day slavery, human trafficking, and sexual oppression. Vast economic inequalities among developing nations create desperate conditions for the poor, often creating the conditions for exploitation and injustice. It has been said that there are more humans enslaved today (as many as 21 million), than in the time of Wilberforce and Newton.[42] The modern abolition movement has gained considerable momentum in recent decades; the Vineyard movement is not unaware of this issue – slavery and human trafficking is one of the issues of concern for the Vineyard Justice Network. Connected also to this issue is that of immigration, as desperate people attempt to gain entry and citizenship in Western democracies. As some Vineyard churches have begun to engage with this issue on a high level, a robust theology of justice will support and define these efforts.[43] A particularly unsettling facet of this issue is the plight of impoverished women in the developing world, as they are more likely to be victimized and oppressed than men.[44]

While the Vineyard in the United States has made considerable efforts to become more racially diverse, the fact remains that the movement is still predominately a Caucasian movement.[45] Issues of racial injustice and prejudice have again taken center stage in recent years, with many wondering how much progress has been made since the civil rights movement of the 1960s. Dr Christena Cleveland is a social psychologist and popular author and teacher. Her recent work, *Disunity in Christ: Uncovering the Hidden Forces that Keep Us Apart*, is focused on issues of privilege, difference, and reconciliation in the American church.[46] While written on a popular level, her work is heavily supported by social science research on the perspectives of various ethnic and population groups in the United States. People in all ethnic groups have group identity markers from early childhood; hence undoing these prejudices is no easy task. Her research does reveal a challenge for the Vineyard, which is primarily headed by white males. She found that it was particularly difficult for the privileged to recognize *their own* privileged status; this made conversation on inequality particularly difficult. Dr Cleveland writes:

This is a tall order that requires a real and fierce conversation on the elephant in the church: privilege and power differentials. For some reasons, high status people (in my experience, particularly white men) have a hard time seeing and admitting that they are in fact high-status people. Even more troubling, I've found that many white male pastors and seminary students have an even harder time admitting that these privilege and power issues exist in the church and are even perpetuated by the church.[47]

A Vineyard theology of justice would be woefully inadequate if voices like Dr Cleveland's, which open up conversations about privilege, power and reconciliation, were not included in the dialogue. The growing multi-ethnic and Latino Vineyard churches are certainly needed in this conversation as well. Despite the occasional, overwhelmingly-discouraging notes in her research, she still holds out hope that through mutual interaction, recognition of privilege, and effort, racial unity and understanding in the church can be achieved.

Finally, a Vineyard theology of justice would be *comprehensive* in that it would include concern for God's good creation, as environmental issues are often linked to human well-being. In many cases, the poor and marginalized peoples of the world suffer most from environmental upheaval and change. Rather than seeing God's creation as merely a "bag of resources" to be exploited for immediate gain, a theology of environmental justice would maintain that care for the earth and care for the inhabitants of the earth are inextricably linked.[48] Unfortunately, evangelical theology that believes in the destruction of planet earth, ("It's all going to burn!"), has often contributed to the exploitation, rather than the preservation, of the environment.[49] Seeing the negative consequences of environmental destruction on the world's poor, and on all persons, is most important, considering the interwoven issues of environmental change on food production, trade, and economic livelihood.

This brief proposal for constructing a theology of justice that is authentically Vineyard may offer a way forward, but a number of objections could be raised. A critic might say that the ideas I have presented are absurdly brief and simplistic. It is true that as one engages the issue of the ethics of the kingdom of God, a whole host of difficult issues arise that resist a simple treatment. Many of these objections that surface are not only related to the issue of justice, but also, they depend on basic ideas of human rights, and more importantly, human identity.

....

The issues of justice and human rights are inevitably caught up in the idea of what is means to be a human person.

....

Therefore, the construction of kingdom ethics quickly becomes the question of ethics defined *by whom* and *for whom*, and it is exactly at this point that conversations about justice often go off the tracks.

It is essential then, for the Vineyard to develop a robust *theological anthropology* to answer basic questions of human nature and human dignity.

Towards a Vineyard Theological Anthropology

Just a century ago, Western culture was in pretty solid agreement that a person was made in the image of God, and thus had an inherent dignity and worth. Much has changed in the last century. Late modern Western culture has no clear consensus on what it means to be a person.[50] The disintegration of the idea of *imago dei* has led to a diversity of concepts of personhood. Therefore, there has never been a greater need for the church to offer a viable theological anthropology. While traditionally Christian theological anthropology has grounded itself firmly in a doctrine of creation, might we also utilize resources from incarnational Christology *and* eschatology to develop a fuller picture of being human? The question of the day could be phrased: "Can the Vineyard offer a picture of humanity that is biblically-grounded, theologically true, and relevant to the late modern Western culture in which we find ourselves?"

To begin, a Vineyard theological anthropology would forward the idea of an already–not yet person, because we are *eschatological people in the process of realization.*[51] This assumes a starting point, which in orthodox

Christian theology has been the *imago dei* – humanity created in the image of God with Godlikeness. From this intrinsic dignity of persons as image-bearers of God comes a particular ideal of human flourishing. Broader than the exercise of freedom or personal volition, Christianity believes that the highest goal of humanity is to be transformed into the image of the Son, as the Son is the archetype of the human in perfect relationship with God.[52]

Thus, Christology, anthropology and eschatology come together. However, it is obvious that the reality of human existence falls far short of this ideal; even the best person experiences life that falls far short of this ideal. This picture of humanity is therefore a *transition* between states. If this is so, which qualities *in this transformation* change, and which are preserved? Further, is this idea of the human adequate *only* for those who share eternity with God? In other words, if becoming more like Jesus is the highest goal of humanity, and it is only fully realized in kingdom of God, what can we say about the final state of the unredeemed?[53]

Can we develop a logically-coherent Christian anthropology based on the concept of an eschatological person in the process of realization? What does a person who is *living the future within their very person* look like? A Vineyard approach must bring together the previous thoughts by offering a relational, embodied, *and* eschatological theological anthropology. Human persons belong to all that is created by God, and thus share in the essential dependent nature of all of creation; implied in this dependency is *relationality*. Job 34:13-15 states: "If it were his intention and he withdrew his spirit and breath, all humanity would perish together and mankind would return to the dust". Humans are dependent creatures: we exist because of the will and sustaining life of God.

While social anthropologies are not new, they could reinforce Vineyard commitment to rationality, communal practice, and the "everyone gets to play" idea. A number of evangelical theologians like Anthony Thiselton, Stanley Grentz, and Amos Yong have all explored the possibilities of relational anthropologies.[54] Yong demonstrates that even profoundly cognitively-disabled persons have relational capacity, manifested in "relationships of interdependence with others", frequently with the caregiver(s) of the disabled person.[55] We have seen that Vineyard practice is heavily communal, intersubjective, and focused on the presence of the relational Spirit of God in the community of believers. Therefore a Vineyard theological anthropology would be greatly enhanced by these recent studies in relational anthropology.

Much of this book has considered the Vineyard practice of divine healing. The very nature of praying for healing of the body implies that there is something *intrinsically good* about physical creation, while impaired health and disease are at odds with the realized eschatological nature of human persons. Further, much of human involvement via relationality entails the body, as we move, touch, dance, embrace, lay hands on, or otherwise physically express our participation in the kingdom of God. The intrinsic good of materiality also enables Vineyard concern for feeding the poor, improving the living conditions of the impoverished, and even care for God's creation.

Wimber infused into the Vineyard psyche the awareness of James' injunction that true worship was expressed in caring for the material needs of the poor and destitute (James 2:15-17). The holistic paradigm of "healing the whole person" and the interconnectedness of spiritual, emotional, and physical issues in divine healing, imply that persons cannot be reduced to material properties *or* relations only. Healing often comes within the community, and the healing of broken relationships (i.e. forgiveness, mercy, compassion, etc.), frequently accompanies physical healing. Even in this, waiting for the final consummation of the kingdom allows for treating the suffering and the disabled with humility and compassion. With Yong, a Vineyard theologian could strenuously contend that all human persons reflect the *imago dei* regardless of their physical, relational or cognitive capacities, both now and in the eschaton.[56]

Finally, a Vineyard anthropology would have to be eschatological. The trajectory of eschatological consummation of creation primarily includes the *subjects* (persons) of the kingdom. If the reigning Christ is the archetypical realization of true humanity, the nature of that eschatological human identity must be given careful thought. It is true that scripture is limited as to what exactly this identity will look like; thus, there will always be an element of mystery. Certainly this existence will be one of relational wholeness just as the Trinitarian relations are whole. In addition, we know that our spiritual bodies will still be physical in some way, as this is the very hope of the resurrection (1 Corinthians 15:44, 46). Eschatological reality will no doubt be different in essence and ability, but to go further is to speculate on deep mystery. There is much about the nature of God's fully actualized kingdom or reign that is beyond human understanding.

Such a relational, embodied anthropology would need yet another element to be authentically Vineyard: it would need to be conversant and intelligible to the spirit of the age, and empower Vineyard thinkers to speak into late modern culture which is desperately in need of Christian witness. Information saturation has yielded a world more aware than ever of the plight of modern slaves, the worldwide oppression of women, and the impact of globalization, urbanization, and modern enterprise on the world's most vulnerable peoples.

Terms like universal human rights, fair trade, honor killings, and child marriage have entered our vocabularies and everyday conversations. This growing awareness and activism is good and we are right to applaud it. In a world in desperate need of an enacted
theology of justice, the need for a concept of the person to ground theological ethics has never been greater.

What is Worship?

A great deal of further study needs to be done on the Vineyard worship experience. By worship, I do not mean the term in general terms, as in the duty of the individual Christian to give honor to God, or the life of sacrifice and service given to God. I mean specifically the *experience* of the presence of the divine through the performance of music, dance, etc. Put more precisely, in the Vineyard context, "worship" means intentional, participatory, personal or corporate involvement in singing, listening, and prayer, characterized by an intimate, relational style that is said to "invite" the presence of God into the experience of the individual or community. Next to his legacy of praying for the sick, perhaps John Wimber's greatest contribution outside of the Vineyard is his influence on the worship and music practices of the global church. Vineyard worship style and content has influenced much of the recent changes in Evangelical worship styles, replacing traditional piano or organ-based hymns, performed by choirs, with modern, rock-influenced, guitar and drum-based songs. Wimber's background as a professional jazz musician led him to re-evaluate existing music forms and develop a new approach that he felt was more relevant to the post-hippie culture of Southern California in the 1970s. While several attempts have been made to develop a theology of Vineyard worship, to my knowledge a theological study of Vineyard worship has not been published.[57]

A study of worship in the Vineyard would have much in common with the study of charismatic experience, as the two are often experientially intertwined in Vineyard practice. Wimber created a form where, usually at the conclusion of a church service or meeting, he would have the worship ministry team play intimate songs at a softer volume while the prayer ministry team would engage with those coming forward for prayer. Wimber believed that the charismatic experience of prayer ministry could be encouraged or enhanced by the music which played in the background during the ministry time. Even in his "kinship" groups, or smaller, home based meetings, Wimber encouraged this connection between worship and charismatic ministry.

As mentioned previously, Vineyard anthropology posits a thoroughly embodied human experience, evidenced by the valuing of physical healing and the interconnectivity between physical, emotional, and spiritual states. Vineyard worship also is often embodied, including dance and physical movements like participants raising hands, swaying rhythmically, clapping, bowing or kneeling, or even lying prostrate or resting quietly. The effect of the music and the physical response can be quite formative, as certain styles of songs may elicit particular physical responses. Such physical responses are common in the scriptures: the exhortations of the Psalmist: "Oh, clap your hands, all you peoples! Shout to God with the voice of triumph!" (47:1) and, "Oh come, let us worship and bow down; Let us kneel before the Lord our Maker" (95:6) encourage such physical responses in worship; in fact, both refrains have been included in Vineyard worship songs. The performance of the musicians is embodied as well, as the various instruments used (guitars, drums, piano, etc.) all require and stimulate physical response.

John Wimber professed that the goal of worship was to increase or make room for intimacy with the Spirit; thus, *the music* performed or sung was designed to be *participatory*. For Wimber, this meant a contemporary, soft-rock style, with simple lyrics, in an easy-to-sing key and register, which did not require the audience to have the musical proficiency of a trained choir. While his background as a professional musician encouraged the worship leaders to be highly skilled, he encouraged Vineyard songwriters to achieve "intimacy with simplicity". He avoided musical performers who put the focus on themselves or their musical gifts. A Vineyard musician's task was "to lead the people to the throne and then get out of the way".

To enable this, Wimber encouraged his musicians to move through a progression from louder, dramatic, anthems or "call to worship" songs, finishing with slower, quieter, contemplative songs that "encouraged" intimacy. More would need to be said on what Vineyard worshipers mean by *participatory*. John Wimber was emphatic that his worship leaders did not place the focus on themselves or their musical performance, because he saw this as an *impediment to the participation of the audience.*

....

The key element in Vineyard worship is participation by everyone: Everybody gets to Play.

....

He abhorred "concert" type formats, with a high number of "observers" watching a "band" "perform" music; to Wimber this was unacceptable. The stated goal of intimacy and "making room" for the presence of the Spirit *for everyone* ("everybody gets to play") trumped the demonstration of any particular expression of skill or ability on the part of the worship leaders. The key element here is *trumped*. In other words, as a musician himself, Wimber certainly understood the connection with the Holy Spirit

196

that a musician feels when they are expressing their creative gifts in worship. So quite likely this *could include* particular "demonstrative" elements like a guitar or drum solo, a beautifully sung phrase, or other things. Where Wimber would draw the line (admittedly a quite subjective one) is when that guitarist or vocalist's expression would *inhibit or restrict* the participation of the audience. At this point, the music would cross the line into pure performance, and this was the danger Wimber was concerned about.

So we see, that all the accompanying elements: the lyrics, the musicians playing drums, guitars, piano, the congregants singing, the worship leaders singing, etc., should all focused on "welcoming" and experiencing a heightened presence of the Spirit. As the Vineyard has gradually become more diverse ethnically; worship forms reflective of these communities have become more common in multicultural Vineyards. Hence, influences from gospel, hip-hop, and Latino music are often incorporated into the familiar and traditional rock-guitar Vineyard genre. These various forms may all contribute nuances or practical emphases that are not included in the soft-rock style of worship. We have much to learn from styles of music and cultural approaches *to worship* that can expand the Vineyard's traditional approach.

A full study of Vineyard worship would also need to include a study of the relationship between the lyrics of the songs and kingdom theology, as the words and phrases should reflect the theology of the movement. Exactly how the lyrics contribute or influence the experience and proclaimed goals of the Vineyard would contribute to the depth of understanding and open new connections between values and experience.

We saw that, in many cases, evidence in other practices took fairly objective and observable forms (either a person was healed, or not, and either the prophecy came true, or not); "evidence" of the Spirit's working in worship may be harder to determine. Thus, questions would emerge such as: "If the stated goal is "intimacy" or encouraging the presence of the Spirit, how do we know when worship is 'effective'?" and, "How is the *presence of the Spirit* enabled or reinforced by worship?" In the same way that Wimber recognized the sovereignty of God in the practice of healing, he acknowledged that different worship experiences had varied degrees of intensity or perceived "power" or presence of the Spirit.[58] Thus, the issues of absence and withdrawal could be just as real in worship as they are in the charismatic experience.

A kingdom "theology of worship" would therefore cross stylistic and musical differences, and assist pastors and worships leaders so that they might better understand worship from theological and practical perspectives. Focusing on the theological aspects of worship would not be enough, for some measure of *effectiveness* would have to been considered as well. Considering the growth of Vineyard music beyond its soft-rock roots, these measures would have to apply to other forms of music as well. So we could ask, "What does *effective* Vineyard hip-hop music look like?" Or, "What does 'authentically Vineyard' *gospel* music look like?" "How might drum-based musical forms enable *intimacy with the Spirit*, even if this intimacy looks different from what we are used to in our guitar-based songs?" These are all questions that need to be asked as Vineyard worship continues to move in diverse paths and follow the lead of the Spirit dwelling within all human cultures.

FOURTEEN
Living the Future

This book has been a modest attempt to provide an introduction to the theology of the Vineyard movement, which we have characterized as a church *living the future reality of the kingdom in the present day even in the midst of suffering, evil, and disappointments.* In pursuing the thesis that the inaugurated, enacted, eschatological kingdom of God is the central theological distinctive of the Vineyard movement, a number of discoveries have come to light. It was first established that in order to understand the Vineyard movement, and hence its theology; it was necessary to understand the history and thought of its founder, John Wimber. Wimber's personal theology was a mixture of many influences, including his secular family history, his coming to faith in the Evangelical Quaker movement, his discovery of the teachings of George Eldon Ladd, and the charismatic empowerment of the Holy Spirit. Obviously, Wimber's influence on Vineyard theology cannot be underestimated.

In order to understand the influence of Ladd, it was necessary to recover the story of how Ladd's views of the already–not yet kingdom of God became the consensus perspective in Evangelical theology. The study of eschatology in the twentieth century served not only to describe this consensus, but also revealed competing perspectives on the kingdom that were adopted or inherited by other faith traditions that are theological cousins of the Vineyard, specifically classical Pentecostalism and American Evangelicalism.

We discovered that, while both of these traditions clearly were aware of inaugurated eschatology, other convictions in these movements made the full adoption of the conclusions of inaugurated eschatology quite difficult. For Pentecostalism, early flirtations with dispensationalist theology made inclusion of Ladd's work a nearly schizophrenic process;

and limited the full implications of what inaugurated eschatology offered. On the Evangelical side, the adoption of dispensationalism brought with it a predilection towards cessationism as well.

Coming into the process as late as he did, Wimber was not as burdened with these constricting perspectives, and was thus able to fully adopt Ladd's theology with less theological stress. Even after his death, other Vineyard pastors and academics continued to teach, revise, and develop the kingdom theme in the Vineyard, as we saw most notably in the work of Derek Morphew. Thus, theological reflection did not cease with John Wimber's passing.

As some called Wimber the founder of the "Signs and Wonders" movement, it was essential to investigate his Pneumatology, and his subsequent influence on the theology regarding the work of the Spirit in the Vineyard. While convictions regarding the *person* of the Spirit fell within the orthodox, Trinitarian tradition, significant differences were revealed between the Vineyard's conception of the baptism of the Holy Spirit with both Pentecostalism and Evangelicalism.

The twentieth century "return to the Spirit" in theology provided a fertile source of investigation to determine which options were available to Wimber as he began to shed his cessationism, and which paths were chosen by Pentecostalism and Evangelicalism. It was shown that Wimber, once again, critically fused elements from both traditions into this theology of the baptism of the Spirit, for he understood the need to fully integrate this theology with his eschatology.

As noted, many observers wondered if, after Wimber's untimely death, the Vineyard movement as a whole would retain the identity or DNA imprinted in it by Wimber. The most robust way of determining this was to investigate the practice and experience of the Vineyard from the time of Wimber's entry into power ministry up to the present day. We discovered that there was much coherence between the early Vineyard practices of Wimber with many Vineyard practitioners and influencers today. This section of our study also revealed essential characteristics of Vineyard identity that could only be discovered by a careful study of experience.

Lastly, with the essential qualities of Vineyard eschatology,

Pneumatology, and practice in place, I offered several suggestions as to where future theological projects should be directed. As the first generation of Vineyard leaders, most familiar with Wimber, are passing on leadership of the movement to younger leaders who probably have never met him, it is crucial for the movement to hold on to the DNA of its beginning, even as it enters into the theological disputes of the present day. Hence, issues of ecclesiology, justice, and anthropology *can* and *must* be engaged from the foundation of inaugurated eschatology. Whatever theology emerges in the future must be founded on essential Vineyard distinctives. The overarching aim of this study was to provide such a foundation.

It has often been said that the Vineyard leadership has had the unique ability to "exegete culture"; that is, to understand the fears and ideals that lay behind cultural trends and shifts. I have argued that eschatology is the *central theological locus* of the Vineyard. The inbreaking of the kingdom and the *enacted* reality of the kingdom, cannot be divorced from Vineyard theology and practice. All the fears and dystopian worries of late modernity call not only for a theology of hope, but also for a hope that is enacted and evidenced in the lives of suffering humanity.

As Vineyard pastors and scholars, we can begin to engage these troubled grounds of ecclesiology, justice, anthropology, and the environment, amongst many others, as we have much to offer to a world deeply in need of hope. We can avoid theological "routinization of charisma" by maintaining a firm grip on the foundations of the inaugurated, enacted eschatological kingdom *and* the vitalizing presence of the Holy Spirit. Living the future means boldly entering into these challenging conversations in late modernity and contributing our unique voice and perspective into the questions of our age.

Amen Lord! Bring your kingdom!

Chart of Kingdom Perspectives

Kingdom Perspectives					
ALREADY ←			**TENSION →**		**NOT-YET**
School	*Existential*	*Lives of Jesus*	*Realized*	*Synthesis*	*Consistent*
Scholars	Bultmann	Reimarus, Straus, Wrede	Dodd	Kummel, Jeremias, Cullmann, Ladd	Weiss, Schweitzer
Who Brings it?	Man	Man	God – Man's help	God & Church	Entirely God
When?	Now, but individually	Now in History	Ministry of Jesus – Now	Fulfillment without Consummation	End of Time – Future
What does it look like?	Persons living in dependence on God	Father-hood of God & Brother-hood of Man	Spread of the Gospel = Evangelism	Process of Realization (Messy!)	Cataclysmic! – Apocalyptic End
Churches	?	Social Gospel	Classical Pentecostals	Vineyard Third Wave New Wine	Dispensation ~ Evangelicals
Gift of Holy Spirit	?	?	Latter Rain Restorationist	Given by Spirit to fulfill Mission	Cessationism or "Soft" Cessationism
Healing	Not Physical	Society	In Atonement	Available, but not *Guaranteed*	In Future

BIBLIOGRAPHY

Abbot, W.M. Ed. "The Dogmatic Constitution on the Church: *Lumen Gentium.*" ". Ch. VII, §48. *The Documents of Vatican II.* New York: Herder and Herder, 1966.

Althouse, Peter. *Spirit of the Last Days: Pentecostal Eschatology in Conversation with Jürgen Moltmann.* London: T & T Clark, 2003.

Anderson, Allan. *An Introduction to Pentecostalism: Global Charismatic Christianity.* Cambridge: Cambridge University Press, 2004.

_____. "Pentecostal Approaches to Faith and Healing" *International Review of Mission* Vol.   XCI No. 363: 523-534.

Anderson, Robert Mapes. *Vision of the Disinherited: The Making of American Pentecostalism.* New York, NY: Oxford University Press, 1979.

Arnott, John. *The Father's Blessing.* Orlando, FL: Creation House, 1994.

Badcock, Gary D. *Light of Truth and Fire of Love: A Theology of the Holy Spirit.* Grand Rapids, MI: Eerdmans, 1997.

Baer, Jonathan R. "Redeemed Bodies: The Functions of Divine Healing in Incipient Pentecostalism" *Church History* 70:4 (Dec 2001).

Barbour, Robin. *The Kingdom of God and Human Society.* Edinburgh: T&T Clark, 1993.

Barth, Karl. *Church Dogmatics.* Vols. 1-14. Edited by Geoffrey Bromiley and Thomas F. Torrance. Edinburgh: T. & T. Clark, 1936-1977.

Bass, Clarence B. *Backgrounds to Dispensationalism: Its Historical Genesis and Historical Implications.* Grand Rapids, MI: Eerdmans, 1960, repr. Grand Rapids, MI: Baker Book   House, 1977.

Bateman, Herbert W. IV. *Three Central Issues in Contemporary Dispensationalism.* Kregel Publications, 1999.

Bauckham, Richard and Trevor A. Hart. *Hope against Hope: Christian Eschatology at the Turn of the Millennium.* Grand Rapids, MI: W.B. Eerdmans, 1999.

Baxter J. Sidlow. *Divine Healing of the Body.* Grand Rapids, MI: Zondervan, 1979.

Beasley-Murray, George Raymond. *Jesus and the Kingdom of God.* Grand Rapids, MI; Exeter, Devon: W.B. Eerdmans, Paternoster Press, 1986.

_____. "Demythologized Eschatology" *Theology Today.* 14 (1957): 61-79.

Bebbington, David. *The Dominance of Evangelicalism: The Age of Spurgeon and Moody.* Downers Grove, IL: Intervarsity, 2005.

Bennett, Dennis and Rita. *How to Pray for Inner Healing for Yourself and Others.* Old Tappen, NJ: Revell Books, 1984.

_____. Bennett, Dennis. *The Holy Spirit and You.* Plainfield, NJ: Logos, 1971.

_____. *Nine O'Clock in the Morning.* Plainfield, NJ: Logos International, 1970.

_____. "The Gifts of the Holy Spirit" in *The Charismatic Movement* Ed. Michael P. Hamilton. Grand Rapids, MI: Eerdmans Publishing Company, 1975.

Berkley, Robert F. "ΕΓΓΙΖΕΙΝ, ΦΘΑΝΕΙΝ, and Realized Eschatology". *Journal of Biblical Literature.* LXXII, (June, 1963): 177-87.

Bertone, Larry. "Seven Dispensations or Two-Age View of History: A Pauline Perspective" in *Perspectives in Pentecostal Eschatologies: World Without End.* Peter Althouse and Robby Waddell, eds. Eugene, OR: Pickwick Publishers, 2010.

Best, Gary. *Naturally Supernatural: Joining God in His Work.* Kenilworth, South Africa: Vineyard International Publishing, 2007.

Bibliography

Beverley, James A. *Holy Laughter and the Toronto Blessing: An Investigate Report.* Grand Rapids, MI: Zondervan, 1995.

_____. *Revival Wars: A Critique of Counterfeit Revival.* Toronto, Canada: Evangelical Research Ministries, 1997.

Bialecki, Jon. "The Kingdom and its Subjects: Charisms, Language, Economy, and the Birth of a Progressive Politics in the Vineyard". PhD Diss., Anthropology, University of California: San Diego, 2009.

Bickle, Mike. *Growing in the Prophetic: A Practical, Biblical Guide to Dreams, Visions, and Spiritual Gifts.* Lake Mary, FL: Charisma House, 1996.

Blaising, Craig and Darrel Bock. *Progressive Dispensationalism: an up-to-date Handbook of Contemporary Dispensational Thought.* Victor Books: Wheaton, IL, 1993.

Blumhofer, Edith. *Aimee Semple McPherson: Everybody's Sister.* Grand Rapids, Eerdmans, 1993.

Bornkamm, Gunther. *Jesus of Nazareth.* Irene and Fraser McLusky trans. New York: Harper & Row, 1960.

Braithwaite, Joseph Bevan. *Memoirs of Joseph John Gurney; With Selections from His Journal and Correspondence.* 2 vols., Philadelphia: Lippincott and Grambo, 1855.

Bright, John. *The Kingdom of God, the Biblical Concept and its Meaning for the Church.* Nashville: Abingdon-Cokesbury Press, 1953.

Bruce F.F. *1 & 2 Thessalonians*, Word Bible Commentary. Dallas, TX: Word Books, 1982.

_____. *Paul: Apostle of the Heart Set Free.* Grand Rapids, MI: Eerdmans, 1977.

Bruner, Frederick Dale. *A Theology of the Holy Spirit: The Pentecostal Experience and the New Testament Witness.* Grand Rapids, MI: Eerdmans, 1970.

Buchanan, George Wesley. *Jesus, the King and his Kingdom.* Macon, GA: Mercer, 1984.

Bultmann, Rudolf. *Jesus and the Word.* Eng. Trans. Louise Smith. New York: Scribners, 1934.

_____. *Theology of the New Testament.* Eng. Trans. Kendrick Grobel. New York: Scribners, 1951-55. 2 vols.

207

_____. *Jesus Christ and Mythology*. New York Scribner's, 1958.

_____. "History and Eschatology in the New Testament," *New Testament Studies*, I (September, 1954): 9-16.

_____. "New Testament and Mythology" in *Kerygma and Myth: A Theological Debate*. London, S.C.K., 1953.

Burgess, Stanley M. ed. *The New Dictionary of Pentecostal and Charismatic Movements*. Grand Rapids, MI: Zondervan, 2003.

Cantalamessa, Raniero S.J. *Sober Intoxication of the Spirit*. Cincinnati, OH: Servant Publications, 2005.

Cargill, Timothy B. "Beyond the Fundamentalist-Modernist Controversy: Pentecostals and Hermeneutics in a Postmodern Age". *PNEUMA: The Journal of the Society for Pentecostal Studies*. 15:2 (Fall 1993): 163-187.

Cartledge, Mark. "The Symbolism of Charismatic Glossolalia", *Journal of Empirical Theology* 12:1 (1991).

_____. *Speaking in Tongues: Multi-Disciplinary Perspectives*. London: Paternoster Press, 2006.

Chafer, Lewis Sperry. *Systematic Theology*. Dallas: Dallas Theological Seminary, 1944.

Chan, Simon. "Evidential Glossolalia and the Doctrine of Subsequence", *Asian Journal of Pentecostal Studies* 2:2 (1999): 195-211.

Chappell, Paul G. "Tongues as the Initial Evidence of Baptism in the Holy Spirit: A Pentecostal Perspective", *Criswell Theological Review* 4:1, (Fall 2006): 41-54.

_____. "Healing Movements" in *Dictionary of Pentecostal and Charismatic Movements*. Stanley Burgess, Gary McGee, Patrick Alexander, eds. Grand Rapids, MI: Zondervan, 1988.

Chevreau, Guy. *Catch the Fire*. Toronto, Canada: HarperCollins, 1994.

_____. *Share the Fire: The Toronto Blessing and Grace-Based Evangelism*.Shippensburg, PA: Revival Press, 1997.

Chilton, Bruce. *Pure Kingdom: Jesus' Vision of God*. Grand Rapids, MI: Eerdmans; Society for Promoting Christian Knowledge, 1996.

_____. *The Kingdom of God in the Teaching of Jesus*. Issues in religion and theology; 5. Philadelphia; London: Fortress Press; SPCK, 1984.

Bibliography

_____. *God in Strength: Jesus' Announcement of the Kingdom*. Studien zum neuen testament und seiner umwelt : Serie B ; bd. 1. Freistadt: F.Plochl, 1979.

Cho, Youngmo. *Spirit and Kingdom in the Writings of Luke and Paul*. London, UK: Paternoster, 2005.

Christenson, Larry. *Welcome, Holy Spirit: A Study of Charismatic Renewal in the Church*. Minneapolis; MN: Augsburg Pub. House, 1987.

_____. *The Charismatic Renewal among Lutherans: A Pastoral and Theological Perspective*. Minneapolis: Lutheran Charismatic Renewal Services: distributed by Bethany Fellowship, 1976.

_____. *Speaking in Tongues and its Significance for the Church*. Minneapolis: Bethany Fellowship, 1968.

Cleveland, Christena. *Disunity in Christ: Uncovering the Hidden Forces that Keep Us Apart*. Downers Grove, IL: Intervarsity, 2013.

Crutchfield, Larry V. *The Origins of Dispensationalism: The Darby Factor*. Lanham MD: University Press of America, 1992.

Coffey, David Michael. *"Did You Receive the Holy Spirit When You Believed?" Some Basic Questions for Pneumatology*. Milwaukee, WI: Marquette University Press, 2005.

Congar, Yves. *I Believe in the Holy Spirit*. 3 Vols. New York, NY: Seabury Press, 1983.

Conzelmann, Hans. *An Outline of the Theology of the New Testament*. New York: Harper and Row, 1969.

Coulter, Dale M. "Pentecostal Visions of the End: Eschatology, Ecclesiology, and the Fascination of the Left Behind Series", *Journal of Pentecostal Theology,* 14.1 (2005) 81-98.

Cox, Harvey. *Fire From Heaven: The Rise of Pentecostal Spirituality and the Reshaping of Religion in the Twenty-First Century*. Reading, MA: Addison-Wesley Pub., 1995.

Cullmann, Oscar. *Christ and Time*. Philadelphia: Westminster, 1950.

_____. *The Christology of the New Testament*. London: SCM, 1971.

Dabney, D. Lyle. "Naming the Spirit: Towards a Pneumatology of the Cross." *Starting with the Spirit*. Gordon Preece and Stephen Pickard, eds. Hindmarsh, S. Aust.: Australian Theological Forum, 2001, 28-58.

_____. "Starting with the Spirit: Why the Last Should Now be First". *Starting with the Spirit*. Gordon Preece and Stephen Pickard, eds. Hindmarsh, S. Aust.: Australian Theological Forum, 2001, 3-27.

_____. "Why Should the Last be First? The Priority of Pneumatology in Recent Theological Discussion". *Advents of the Spirit: An Introduction to the Current Study of Pneumatology*. Bradford E. Hinze and D. Lyle Dabney eds. Milwaukee, WI: Marquette University Press, 2001: 240-261.

Darby, John Nelson. *Collected Writings. Vol. 2*. Sunbury, PA: Believers Bookshelf, 1971.

Davids, Peter H. "God, Satan and the Bible." *Equipping the Saints*. Vol. 7 No. 1 (1993).

_____. "Have You Completed Basic Training?" *Equipping the Saints*. Vol.1 No. 4 (1987).

_____. "Suffering, Endurance and Relief". *Equipping the Saints*. Vol. 3, No. 4, (July-August 1986).

_____. "What is Biblical Revival?" *Equipping the Saints*. Third Quarter, (1994).

Dawkins, Robby. *Do What Jesus Did: A Real-life Field Guide to Healing the Sick, Routing Demons and Changing Lives Forever*. Minneapolis, MN: Chosen Books, 2013.

Dayton, Donald W. *Discovering an Evangelical Heritage*. New York: Harper and Row, 1976.

_____. *Theological Roots of Pentecostalism*. Metuchen, NJ: Scarecrow Press, 1987.

Deere, Jack. *Surprised by the Power of the Spirit: A former Dallas Seminary Professor Discovers that God Speaks and Heals Today*. Grand Rapids, MI: Zondervan, 1993.

_____. *Surprised by the Voice of God*. Grand Rapids, MI: Zondervan, 1996.

_____. *The Vineyard's Response to the Briefing*. Vineyard Position Paper 2. 1992.

Del Colle, Ralph. *Christ and the Spirit: Spirit-Christology in Trinitarian Perspective*. Oxford: Oxford University Press, 1994.

_____. "Pentecostal/Catholic Dialogue: Theological suggestions for Consideration". *PNEUMA: The Journal of the Society for Pentecostal Studies*. 25:1 (2003) 93-96.

_____. "Postmodernism and the Pentecostal-Charismatic Experience." *Journal of Pentecostal Theology*. 8:17 (2000) 97-116.

_____. "The Holy Spirit: Presence, Power, Person." *Theological Studies* 62 (2001) 322-340.

_____. "The Outpouring of the Holy Spirit: Implications for the Church and Ecumenism." In *The Holy Spirit, the Church, and Christian Unity: Proceedings of the Consultation Held at the Monastery of Bose, Italy, 14-20 October, 2002*. Leuven: Leuven University Press, 2005, 247-66.

_____. "Wither Pentecostal Theology? Why a Catholic is Interested". *PNEUMA: The Journal of the Society for Pentecostal Studies*. 31:1 (2009): 35-46.

D'Elia, John A. *A Place at the Table: George Eldon Ladd and the Rehabilitation of Evangelical Scholarship in America*. Oxford; New York: Oxford University Press, 2008.

DeWitt, Calvin. *Earth-Wise: A Biblical Response to Environmental Issues*. 2nd Edition. Grand Rapids, MI: Faith Alive Publishers, 1994, 2007.

Dodd, C. H. *History and the Gospel*. London: Nisbet, 1952.

_____. *The Parables of the Kingdom*. 3rd ed., rev. ed. London: Nisbet, 1936.

_____. *The Apostolic Preaching and its Development*. London: Hodder and Stoughton, 1936, 1967.

_____. *The Coming of Christ*. Cambridge, 1951.

Dunn, James D. G. *Baptism in the Holy Spirit: A Re-examination of the New Testament Teaching on the Gift of the Spirit in Relation to Pentecostalism Today*. Naperville, IL: A. R. Allenson, 1970.

_____. *Christology in the Making: A New Testament Inquiry into the Origins of the Doctrine of the Incarnation*. Philadelphia, PA: Westminster Press, 1980.

_____. *Jesus and the Spirit: A Study of the Religious and Charismatic Experience of Jesus and the First Christians as Reflected in the New Testament.* London: S.C.M. Press, 1975.

_____. *Jesus Remembered: Christianity in the Making Volume I.* Grand Rapids, MI: Eerdmans, 1993.

_____. *New Testament Theology: An Introduction.* The library of biblical theology. Nashville, TN: Abingdon Press, 2009.

_____. "Review of Frederick D. Bruner, A Theology of the Holy Spirit". *The Expository Times* 83:4 (January, 1972).

_____. *The Christ and the Spirit: Collected Essays of James D.G. Dunn.* 2 Vols. Grand   Rapids, MI: Eerdmans, 1998.

_____. *The Christ and the Spirit: Volume. 2 Pneumatology.* Grand Rapids, MI: Eerdmans,   1998.

Dunn, James D. G., Graham Stanton, Bruce W. Longenecker, and Stephen C. Barton. *The Holy Spirit and Christian Origins: Essays in honor of James D.G. Dunn.* Grand Rapids, MI.: William B. Eerdmans Pub. Co., 2004.

Du Plessis, David *The Spirit Bade Me Go.* Plainfield, NJ: Logos, 1970.

_____. "Final Report of the International Roman Catholic/Pentecostal Dialogue (1977-1982)". *PNEUMA: The Journal of the Society for Pentecostal Studies.*12 (Fall 1990) 97-115.

Ervin, Howard M. *Conversion-Initiation and the Baptism of the Holy Spirit.* Peabody, MA: Hendrickson Publishers, 1984.

Epp, Eldon Jay. "Mediating Approaches to the Kingdom: Werner George Kummel and George Eldon Ladd." *The Kingdom of God in 20th Century Interpretation.* Wendell Willis, ed. Peabody,   MA: Hendrickson, 1987.

Faupel, David W. *The American Pentecostal Movement.* Wilmore, KY: B.L. Fisher, 1972.

_____. *The Everlasting Gospel: The Significance of Eschatology in the Development of Pentecostal Thought.* Sheffield: Sheffield Academic Press, 1996.

_____. "The Function of Models in the Interpretation of Pentecostal Thought. *PNEUMA: The Journal of the Society for Pentecostal Studies.* 2:1 (Spring, 1980) 51-71.

Fee, Gordon D. *God's Empowering Presence: The Holy Spirit in the Letters of Paul.* Peabody, MA: Hendrickson Publishers, 1994.

_____. *The First and Second Letters to the Thessalonians* [NICNT] Grand Rapids, MI: Eerdmans Publishing Co., 2009.

Finney, Charles Grandison. *Memoirs of Reverend Charles G. Finney Written By Himself.* New York: A.S. Barnes, 1876.

Foster, Richard. "The Lamb's War", *Equipping the Saints.* Vol. 3 No.2 (Spring, 1989).

Fox, George. *The Works of George Fox.* 8 vols., Philadelphia: Marcus T. C. Gould, 1831.

Gaffin, Richard B. *Perspectives on Pentecost: Studies in New Testament Teaching on the Gifts of the Holy Spirit.* Phillipsburg, NJ: Presbyterian and Reformed Publishing Company88, 1979.

Gaffin, Richard B. and Wayne A. Grudem. *Are Miraculous Gifts for Today? Four views.* Counterpoints. Grand Rapids, MI.: Zondervan Pub., 1996.

Gathercole, SJ. 'The Critical and Dogmatic Agenda of Albert Schweitzer's 'The Quest for the Historical Jesus'. *Tyndale Bulletin* 51.2 (2000) 261-283.

Gaustad, Edwin S. *The Great Awakening in New England.* New York: Harper and Brothers, 1957.

Gee, Donald. *Concerning Spiritual Gifts.* Springfield, MO: Gospel Press, 1972.

Gentry, Kenneth L. and Wayne A. Grudem. *The Charismatic Gift of Prophecy: A Reformed Response to Wayne Grudem.* 2nd ed. Memphis, Tenn.: Footstool Pub., 1989.

Goff, James Jr. "Initial Evidence in the Theology of Charles Fox Parham". *Initial Evidence: Historical and Biblical Perspectives on the Pentecostal Doctrine of Spirit Baptism* Gary McGee, Ed. Peabody, MA: Hendrickson, 1991.

Graham, Billy. "The Holy Spirit". *The Collected Works of Billy Graham.* New York: Inspirational Press, 1993.

Gray, John. *The Biblical Doctrine of the Reign of God.* Edinburgh: T. & T. Clark, 1979.

Green, Michael. *I Believe in the Holy Spirit.* Grand Rapids, MI: Eerdmans, 1975.

Grentz, Stanley J. *Theology for the Community of God.* Grand Rapids, Eerdmans, 1994.

_____. *The Social God and the Relational Self: A Trinitarian Theology of the Imago Dei.* Louisville, KT: Westminster John Knox, 2001.

Grudem, Wayne. *The Gift of Prophecy in the New Testament and Today.* Rev ed. Wheaton, Ill.: Crossway Books, 2000.

_____. *The Gift of Prophecy in 1 Corinthians.* Washington, D.C.: University Press of America, 1982.

_____. *The Vineyard's Response to The Standard.* Position Paper 3. (1992).

Gurney, Joseph John. *Observations on the distinguishing views and practices of the Society of Friends.* 7th   Loon ed. New York: William Wood, 1869,1986.

_____. *A Peculiar People* [Observations on the religious peculiarities of the Society of Friends]. Richmond, Ind.: Friends United Press, 1979; 1824.

Hamm, Thomas. *Quaker Writings: An Anthology 1650-1920.* London: Penguin Book, 2010.

_____. *The Transformation of American Quakerism: Orthodox friends, 1800-1907.*   Bloomington, IN: Indiana University Press, 1988.

Hiebert, Paul. *Anthropological Insights for Missionaries.* Grand Rapids, MI: Baker, 1985.

Hocken, Peter D. "A Charismatic View of the Distinctiveness of Pentecostalism." In *Pentecostalism in Context: Essays in Honor of William W. Menzies.* Edited Wonsuk Ma and Robert P. Menzies. Sheffield: Sheffield Academic Press, 1997, 96-106.

Hollenweger, W.J. *Pentecostalism: Origins and Developments Worldwide.* Peabody, MA: Hendrickson, 1997.

_____. *The Pentecostals: The Charismatic Movement in the Churches.* Minneapolis, MN: Augsburg, 1972.

Howitt, Quinton. *Christianity and the Poor.* CreateSpace Independent Publishing Platform 2011.

Hunter, Harold. *Spirit-Baptism: A Pentecostal Alternative.* New York: University Press of America, 1983.

Bibliography

Jackson, Bill. *The Quest for the Radical Middle*. Kenilworth, South Africa: Vineyard International Publishing, 1999.

Jackson, John Paul. "Prophetic Reformation", *Equipping the Saints*. Vol. 7 No. 4 (Fall 1993).

Jacobsen, Douglas G. *Thinking in the Spirit: Theologies of the Early Pentecostal Movement*. Bloomington, IN: Indiana University Press, 2003.

Jeremias, Joachim. *Jesus' Promise to the Nations*. Franz Delitzsch lectures ; 1953. 1st English ed. Naperville, Ill: A. R. Allenson, 1958.

_____. *New Testament Theology. [translated from the German by John Bowden]*. The new testament library. [Neutestamentliche Theologie. English.]. London: S.C.M. Press. 1971.

_____. *The Parables of Jesus*. New York: Charles Scribner's Sons, 1963.

_____. *The Prayers of Jesus*. Studies in biblical theology, 2d ser. 6. [Abba. English. Selections.]. Naperville, Ill: A. R. Allenson, 1967.

Jeremias, Joachim and K. C. Hanson. *Jesus and the Message of the New Testament*. Fortress classics in biblical studies. Minneapolis: Fortress Press, 2002.

Jones, Rufus Matthew. *Rethinking Quaker Principles*. Pendle Hill pamphlet. Vol. 8. Wallingford, Pa.: Pendle Hill, 1940.

_____. *The Later Periods of Quakerism*. London: Macmillan and Co., Limited, 1925.

_____. *The Life and Message of George Fox, 1624-1924 ; a Tercentenary address*. New York: Macmillan Co., 1924.

Johns, Cheryl Bridges. *Pentecostal Formation: A Pedagogy Among the Oppressed*. Sheffield: Sheffield Academic Press, 1993.

Johnson, Allan G. *Privilege, Power and Difference*. Boston, Mass.: McGraw-Hill, 2006.

Lloyd-Jones, Martyn. *The Baptism and Gifts of the Spirit*. ed. Christopher Catherwood. Grand Rapids, MI: Baker Books, 1996.

Joy, John. "The Outpouring of the Holy Spirit in the Catholic Charismatic Renewal: Theological Interpretation of the Experience." *Antiphon* 9.2 (2005) 141-65.

Kallas, James. *The Significance of the Synoptic Miracles*. Greenwich, CT: The Seabury Press, 1961.

_____. *Jesus and the Power of Satan*. Philadelphia, PA: Westminster, 1968.

_____. *The Satanward View: A Study in Pauline Theology*. Philadelphia, PA: Westminster Press,   1966.

_____. *The Real Satan*. Minneapolis, MN: Augsburg, 1975.

Kärkkäinen, Veli-Matti. "Evangelization, Proselytism, and Common Witness: Roman Catholic-Pentecostal Dialogue on Mission, 1990-1997" *International Bulletin of Missionary Research*. January, 2001.

_____. *Pneumatology: The Holy Spirit in Ecumenical, International, and Contextual Perspective*. Grand Rapids, MI: Baker Academic, 2002.

Keener, Craig. *Miracles: The Credibility of the New Testament Accounts*. 2 vols. Grand Rapids, MI: Baker Academic, 2011.

Kelsey, David. *Eccentric Existence: A Theological Anthropology – 2 Volumes*. Louisville, KT: Westminster John Knox Press, 2009.

_____. "The Human Creature". *The Oxford Handbook of Systematic Theology*. John Webster, Kathryn Tanner, Iain Torrance, eds.. Oxford: Oxford University Press, 2007.

Kraft, Charles. *Christianity and Culture: A Study in Dynamic Biblical Theologizing in Cross-Cultural Perspective*. Maryknoll, NY: Orbis Books, 1979.

_____. *Christianity with Power*. Ann Arbor, MI: Vine Books, 1989.

_____."Communicating and Ministering the Power of the Gospel Cross-Culturally: The Power of God for Christians who Ride Two Horses." *The Kingdom and the Power*. ed. Gary S. Grieg and Kevin Springer. Ventura, CA; Regal Books, 1993.

_____. "Shifting Worldviews, Shifting Attitudes." *Equipping the Saints* Vol. 1 No. 5 (1987).

_____. "Why the Vineyard Should move into Cross-Cultural Ministry." *First Fruits* Nov/Dev 1985.

Kraus, C. Norman. *Dispensationalism in America: Its Rise and Development*. Richmond, VA: John Knox Press, 1958.

Kummel, Werner George. *Promise and Fulfillment: The Eschatological Message of Jesus*. London: SCM Press, 1957.

_____. *The New Testament: The History of the Investigation of its Problems.* London: SCM Press, 1973.

_____. *The Theology of the New Testament According to its Major Witnesses.* New York: Abingdon, 1969.

Ladd, George Eldon. *A Commentary on the Revelation of John.* Grand Rapids: Eerdmans, 1972.

_____. "Historic Premillennialism" in *The Meaning of the Millennium* ed. Robert G. Clouse Downers Grove, IL: Intervarsity Press, 1977.

_____. *The Blessed Hope: A Biblical Study of the Second Advent and the Rapture.* Grand Rapids, MI: Eerdmans, 1959.

_____. *The Pattern of New Testament Truth.* Grand Rapids, MI: Eerdmans, 1968.

_____. *The Presence of the Future; the Eschatology of Biblical Realism.* Grand Rapids, MI: Eerdmans, 1974.

Ladd, George Eldon and Donald Alfred Hagner. *A Theology of the New Testament.* Rev. ed. Grand Rapids, MI: Eerdmans, 1993.

Land, Steven J. "A Pentecostal Perspective." In *Pentecostal Movements as an Ecumenical Challenge.* London: SCM Press, 1996, 85-93.

_____. *Pentecostal Spirituality: A Passion for the Kingdom.* Sheffield: Sheffield Academic Press, 1993.

Lederle, H.I. *Treasures Old and New: Interpretations of "Spirit-Baptism" in the Charismatic Renewal Movement.* Peabody, MA: Hendrickson Publishers, 1988.

Le Shana, David C. *Quakers in California; the effects of 19th century revivalism on Western Quakerism.* Newberg, OR: Barclay Press, 1969.

Lewis, David. *Healing: Fiction, Fantasy or Fact?* London: Hodder and Stoughton, 1989.

Lindsey, Hal. *The Late Great Planet Earth.* Grand Rapids, MI: Zondervan, 1970.

_____. *There's a New World Coming.* Eugene, OR: Harvest House, 1973, 1984.

Lloyd-Jones, David Martyn. *God the Holy Spirit.* Great doctrines of the bible. Vol. 2. Wheaton, Ill.: Crossways Books, 1997.

_____. *Healing and Medicine*. Eastbourne, U.K.: Kingsway Pub., 1988; 1987.

_____. *Revival*. Basingstoke: Marshall Pickering, 1986.

_____. *The Kingdom of God*. Wheaton, Il: Crossway Books, 1992.

Lundström, Gösta. *The Kingdom of God in the Teaching of Jesus; a History of Interpretation from the Last Decades of the Nineteenth Century to the Present Day*. English ed. ed. Edinburgh: Oliver and Boyd, 1963.

Lunn, Pam. "Do we Still Quake? An Ethnographic and Historical Inquiry" *Quaker Studies* 12:2 (March 2008) 216-229.

MacArthur, John F. *Charismatic Chaos*. Grand Rapids, MI: Zondervan, 1992.

Macchia, Frank D. *Baptized in the Spirit: A Global Pentecostal Theology*. Grand Rapids, MI: Zondervan, 2006.

_____. "Astonished by Faithfulness to God: A Reflection on Karl Barth's Understanding of Spirit Baptism." In *The Spirit and Spirituality: Essays in Honour of Russell P. Spittler*. Edited Wonsuk Ma and Robert P. Menzies. London: T & T Clark International, 2004.

_____. "The Time is Near! Or, Is It? Dare We Abandon Our Eschatological Expectation?" *PNEUMA: The Journal of the Society for Pentecostal Studies* 25:2 (2003): 161-63.

_____. "Salvation and Spirit Baptism: Another Look at James Dunn's Classic." *PNEUMA: The Journal of the Society for Pentecostal Studies* 24:1 (2002): 1-6.

_____. "The 'Toronto Blessing': No Laughing Matter." *Journal of Pentecostal Theology* 8 (1996): 3-6.

_____. "A Pentecostal Perspective." In *Pentecostal Movements as an Ecumenical Challenge*. London: SCM, 1996, 63-69.

_____. "God Present in a Confused Situation: The Mixed Influence of the Charismatic Movement on Classical Pentecostalism in the United States." *PNEUMA: The Journal of the Society for Pentecostal Studies* 18:1 (1996): 33-54.

_____. "The Spirit and Life: A Further Response to Jürgen Moltmann." *Journal of Pentecostal Theology* 5 (1994): 121-27.

_____. "The Spirit and the Kingdom: Implications in the Message of the Blumhardts for a Pentecostal Social Spirituality." *Transformation* 11 (1994): 1-5, 32.

_____. "The Question of Tongues as Initial Evidence: A Review of *Initial Evidence*, Edited Gary B. McGee." *Journal of Pentecostal Theology* 2 (1993): 117-27.

MacNutt, Francis. *Healing.* Notre Dame, IN: Ave Maria, 1974.

_____. *The Power to Heal.* Notre Dame, IN: Ave Maria, 1977.

Mansfield, Patti Gallagher. *As By A New Pentecost - The Dramatic Beginnings of The Catholic Charismatic Renewal.* Steubenville, Ohio: Franciscan University Press, 1992.

Manson, Thomas Walter. *The Sayings of Jesus: As Recorded in the Gospels According to St. Matthew and St. Luke.* London: SCM Press, 1949.

_____. *The Servant-Messiah: A Study of the Public Ministry of Jesus.* Cambridge Eng.: University Press, 1953.

_____. *The Teaching of Jesus: Studies of its Form and Content.* 2 reprint ed. Cambridge: University Press, 1951; 1935.

Marcus, Joel. *The Mystery of the Kingdom of God.* Dissertation series society of biblical literature. Atlanta, GA: Scholars Press, 1986.

Marsden, George M. *Reforming Fundamentalism: Fuller Seminary and the New Evangelicalism.* Grand Rapids, MI: Eerdmans, 1987.

_____. *Understanding Evangelicalism and Fundamentalism.* Grand Rapids, Eerdmans, 1991.

Martin, David. *Pentecostalism: The World Their Parish.* Oxford: Blackwell Publishers, 2002.

_____. *Tongues of Fire: The Explosion of Protestantism in Latin America.* Oxford: Blackwell, 1990.

McDonnell, Kilian. *Charismatic Renewal and Ecumenism.* New York, NY: Paulist Press, 1978.

_____. *Presence, Power, Praise: Documents on the Charismatic Renewal.* Collegeville, MN: Liturgical Press, 1980.

_____. *The Other Hand of God: The Holy Spirit as the Universal Touch and Goal.* Collegeville, MN: Liturgical Press, 2003.

McDonnell, Kilian and George T. Montague. *Christian Initiation and Baptism in the Holy Spirit: Evidence From the First Eight Centuries.* Collegeville, MN: Liturgical Press, 1991.

McGee, Gary B. "'New World of Realities in Which We Live': How Speaking in Tongues Empowered Early Pentecostals." *PNEUMA: The Journal of the Society for Pentecostal Studies* 30:1 (2008): 108-35.

McLaughlin, William G. Jr. *Modern Revivalism: Charles Grandison Finney to Billy Graham.* New York: The Ronald Press Co., 1959.

McQueen, Larry. "Early Pentecostal Eschatology in the Light of *The Apostolic Faith*, 1906-1908". *Perspectives in Pentecostal Eschatologies: World Without End.* Peter Althouse and Robby Waddell, eds. Eugene, OR: Pickwick Publishers, 2010.

Menzies, Robert P. *Empowered for Witness: The Spirit in Luke-Acts.* Sheffield: Sheffield Academic Press, 1994.

Mittelstadt, Martin William. *The Spirit and Suffering in Luke-Acts: Implications for a Pentecostal Pneumatology.* London: T & T Clark International, 2004.

Moltmann, Jürgen. *The Coming of God: Christian Eschatology.* London: SCM Press, 1996.

_____. *The Spirit of Life: A Universal Affirmation.* London: SCM Press, 1992.

_____. *The Trinity and the Kingdom.* New York: Harper and Row, 1981.

_____. "The Trinitarian Personhood of the Holy Spirit", *Advents of the Spirit: An Introduction to the Current Study of Pneumatology.* ed. Bradford Hinze & D. Lyle Dabney. Milwaukee, WI: Marquette University Press, 2001.

Morphew, Derek. *Breakthrough: Discovering the Kingdom.* Cape Town: Struik Christian Books, 1991.

_____. *Different but Equal? Going Beyond the Complementarian/Egalitarian Debate.* Cape Town: South Africa, Vineyard International Publishing, 2009.

_____. *South Africa and the Powers Behind.* available as an E-book from Vineyard Institute.

_____. *The Mission of the Kingdom: The Theology of Luke-Acts.* . Cape Town: South Africa, Vineyard International Publishing, 2011.

_____. *Kingdom Theology and Human Rights*. CreateSpace Independent Publishing Platform, 2015.

Morris, Leon. *The First and Second Epistles to the Thessalonians*. [NICNT] Grand Rapids, MI: Eerdmans, 1991.

Mumford, John. "Vineyard Movement Founder". *John Wimber: His Influence and Legacy*. ed. David Pytches. London: Cox and Wyman, 1998.

Nathan, Rich. *Who is My Enemy? Welcoming People the Church Rejects*. Grand Rapids, MI: Zondervan, 2002.

Noll, Mark. *American Evangelical Christianity: An Introduction*. London: Blackwell, 2001.

_____. *A History of Christianity in the United States and Canada*. Grand Rapids, MI: Eerdmans, 1992.

Pannenberg, Wolfhart. *Theology and the Kingdom of God*. Philadelphia: Westminster Press, 1969.

_____. *Systematische Theologie*. 3 Vols. Göttingen: Vandenhoeck & Ruprecht, 1988-93.

Parham, Charles. *A Voice Crying in the Wilderness*. Baxter Springs, KS: Robert L. Parham, 1944.

Park, Andy. *To Know You More: Cultivating the Heart of the Worship Leader*. Downers Grove, IL: Intervarsity Press, 2002.

Percy, Martyn. "Adventure and Atrophy in a Charismatic Movement: Returning to the 'Toronto Blessing'". *Journal of Contemporary Religion*. 20:1 (2005): 71-90.

Perrin, Norman. *Jesus and the Language of the Kingdom: Symbol and Metaphor in New Testament Interpretation*. Philadelphia: Fortress Press, 1976.

_____. *The Kingdom of God in the Teaching of Jesus*. The New Testament library. Philadelphia: Westminster Press, 1963.

Pinnock, Clark H. *Flame of Love: A Theology of the Holy Spirit*. Downers Grove, IL: InterVarsity Press, 1996.

Poloma, Margaret M. "Inspecting the Fruit of the 'Toronto Blessing': A Sociological Perspective". *PNEUMA: The Journal of the Society for Pentecostal Studies*. 20:1 (Spring, 1998): 43-70.

_____. *Main Street Mystics: The Toronto Blessing and Reviving Pentecostalism.* Walnut Creek, CA: AltaMira Press, 2003.

Pytches, David. *John Wimber: His Influence and Legacy.* London: Cox and Wyman, 1998.

_____. *Some Say it Thundered: A Personal Encounter with the Kansas City Prophets.* Nashville, TN: Thomas Nelson, 1991.

Ranaghan, Kevin & Dorothy. *Catholic Pentecostals.* Paramus, N.J.: Paulist Press, 1969.

Reimarus, Fragments Charles H. Talbert ed. London: SCM Press, 1971.

Ridderbos, Herman N. *The Coming of the Kingdom.* Philadelphia: Presbyterian and Reformed Pub. Co., 1962.

Ritschl, Albrecht. *The Christian Doctrine of Justification and Reconciliation.* 3rd ed. Edinburgh: T & T Clark, 1900.

Robeck, Cecil M. Jr. "William J. Seymour and 'The Bible Evidence'" *Initial Evidence: Historical and Biblical Perspectives on the Pentecostal Doctrine of Spirit Baptism.* Gary McGee, ed. Peabody, MA: Hendrickson, 1991.

Robinson, Tri. *Saving God's Green Earth: Rediscovering the Church's Responsibility to Environmental Stewardship.* Norcross, GA: Ampelon, 2006.

Ruthven, Jon Mark. *On the Cessation of the Charismata: The Protestant Polemic on Postbiblical Miracles.* Sheffield: Sheffield Academic Press, 1993.

Ryrie, Charles C. *Dispensationalism, Revised and Expanded.* Chicago, IL: Moody Publishers, 2007.

_____. *Dispensationalism Today.* Chicago: Moody Press, 1965.

Saucy, Mark. *The Kingdom of God in the Teaching of Jesus in 20th Century Theology.* Dallas: Word Publishing, 1997.

Schlosser, Jacques. *Le règne de Dieu dans les dits de Jésus.* Etudes bibliques. Paris: J. Gabalda, 1980.

Schleiermacher, Friedrich. *The Christian Faith.* ed. H.R. Manckintosh and J. Stewart Edinburgh: T & T Clark, 1928.

Schnackenburg, Rudolf. *God's Rule and Kingdom* [Gottes Herrschaft und Reich. English.]. New York: Herder & Herder, 1963.

Schweitzer, Albert and Ulrich Neuenschwander. *The Kingdom of God and Primitive Christianity* [Reich Gottes und Christentum. English.]. New York: Seabury Press, 1968.

_____. *The Quest for the Historical Jesus.* New York: MacMillan, 1910, 1968.

Sheppard, Gerald T. "Pentecostals and the Hermeneutics of Dispensationalism: The Anatomy of an Uneasy Relationship" *PNEUMA: The Journal of the Society for Pentecostal Studies.* 6:1 (Fall 1984): 5-33.

Smalley, Stephen. "The Delay of the Parousia". *Journal of Biblical Literature* 83.1 (March 1964): 41-54.

Smith, Chuck. *The History of Calvary Chapel.* Costa Mesa, CA: The Word for Today Press,   1990.

_____. *Charisma vs. Charismania.* Costa Mesa, CA: The Word for Today Press, 1992.

Stott, John R.W. *Baptism and Fullness: The Work of the Holy Spirit Today.* Downers Grove, IL: Intervarsity Press, 1964, 1978.

Strong, Augustus. *Systematic Theology.* Old Tappan, NJ: Revell, 1960, 21st printing.

Stronstad, Roger. *The Charismatic Theology of St. Luke.* Peabody, Mass.: Hendrickson Publishers, 1984.

_____. *The Prophethood of All Believers: A Study in Luke's Charismatic Theology.* Sheffield: Sheffield Academic Press, 1999.

Suenens, Léon Joseph. *Ecumenism and Charismatic Renewal: Theological And Pastoral Orientations.* South Bend, IN: Servant Books, 1978.

_____. *Charismatic Renewal and Social Action.* London: The Anchor Press, 1979.

Swindoll, Chuck. *Flying Closer to the Flame: A Passion for the Holy Spirit.* Dallas, TX: Word   Books, 1993.

Synan, Vinson. "A Healer in the House? A Historical Perspective on Healing in the Pentecostal/Charismatic Tradition", *Asian Journal of Pentecostal Studies* 3/2, (2000):189-201.

_____. *In the Latter Days: The Outpouring of the Holy Spirit in the Twentieth Century.* Ann Arbor, MI: Servant Books, 1984.

_____. *The Holiness-Pentecostal Movement in the United States.* Grand Rapids, MI: Eerdmans, 1971.

Thiselton, Anthony. *Interpreting God and the Postmodern Self.* Edinburgh: T&T Clark, 1995.

_____. *The Hermeneutics of Doctrine.* Grand Rapids, MI: Eerdmans, 2007.

Thomas, John Christopher. "Pentecostal Theology in the Twenty-First Century." *PNEUMA: The Journal of the Society for Pentecostal Studies* 20:1 (1998): 3-19.

_____. "The Charismatic Structure of Acts." *Journal of Pentecostal Theology* 13:1 (2004): 19-30.

Thompson, Matthew K. *Kingdom Come: Revisioning Pentecostal Eschatology* [Journal of Pentecostal Theology Supplemental Series No. 37]. Dorset, UK: Deo Publishing, 2010.

Torrey, R.A. *Divine Healing.* Grand Rapids, MI: Baker Book House, 1974.

Trueblood, Elton. *The People Called Quakers: The Enduring Influence of a Way of Life and Thought.* New York: Harper & Row, 1966.

_____. *The Essence of Spiritual Religion.* New York: Harper and brothers, 1936.

Turner, Max. "Interpreting the Samaritans of Acts 8: The Waterloo of Pentecostal Soteriology and Pneumatology?" *PNEUMA: The Journal of the Society for Pentecostal Studies* 23: 2 (2001): 265-86.

_____. *Power from on High: The Spirit in Israel's Restoration and Witness in Luke-Acts.* Sheffield: Sheffield Academic Press, 1996.

Twelftree, Graham. *A Historical and Theological Study: Jesus the Miracle Worker,* Illinois: InterVarsity Press, 1999.

_____. *In the Name of Jesus: Exorcism among Early Christians.* Grand Rapids, MI: Baker, 2007.

_____. *Jesus the Exorcist: A Contribution to the Study of the Historical Jesus.* Tübingen: Mohr and Peabody: Hendrickson, 1993.

_____. *People of the Spirit: Exploring Luke's View of the Church.* Baker Academic, 2009.

_____. *The Cambridge Companion to Miracles.* Cambridge University Press, 2011.

_____. *Paul and the Miraculous*. Grand Rapids, MI: Baker Academic, 2013.

Venter, Alexander. *Doing Church: Building from the Bottom Up*. Cape Town, South Africa: Vineyard International Publishing, 2000.

_____. *Doing Healing: How to Minister God's Kingdom in the Power of the Spirit*. Cape Town, South Africa: Vineyard International Publishing, 1998.

_____. *Doing Reconciliation: Racism, Reconciliation, and Transformation in Church and World*. Cape Town, South Africa: Vineyard International Publishing, 2004.

Wacker, Grant. *Heaven Below: Early Pentecostals and American Culture*. Cambridge, MA: Harvard University Press, 2001.

Wagner, C. Peter. *Churchquake! : How the New Apostolic Reformation is Shaking up the Church as we Know it*. Ventura, Calif.: Regal, 1999.

_____. *How to Have a Healing Ministry without Making Your Church Sick*. Ventura, CA: Regal Books, 1998.

_____. *Look out! The Pentecostals are Coming*. 1st ed. Carol Stream, Ill.: Creation House, 1973.

_____. *Signs & Wonders Today*. Altamonte Springs, FL: Creation House, 1987.

_____. *Spiritual Gifts & Church Growth*. 2nd ed. Pasadena, Calif.: Charles E. Fuller Institute of Evangelism & Church Growth, 1982.

_____. *The Third Wave of the Holy Spirit*. Ann Arbor, MI: Vine Books, 1988.

Wallace, Dan. "The Uneasy Conscience of a Non-Charismatic Evangelical". *Who's Afraid of the Holy Spirit: An Investigation into the Ministry and Spirit of God Today* ed. Daniel B. Wallace and M. James Sawyer. Dallas, TX: Biblical Studies Press, 2005.

Walvoord, John F. "Realized Eschatology". *Bibleotheca Sacra* (October, 1970): 313-23.

_____. *The Rapture Question*. Grand Rapids, MI: Dunham Publishing Co., 1957.

Warfield, B.B. *Counterfeit Miracles*. New York: Charles Scribner and Sons, 1918, 1972.

_____. "Miracle" in *Dictionary of the Bible.* ed. J.D. Davis. Old Tappan, NJ: Revell, 1955, 1972.

Warren, M.C. "Eschatology and History". *International Review of Missions.* 41:3 (July 1952): 337-50.

Weber, Max. *The Sociology of Religion.* Boston, MA: Beacon Press, 1993.

Weiss, Johannes. *The Preaching of Jesus on the Kingdom of God.* Translated Richard H. Hiers & D. Larrimore Holland Philadelphia: Fortress Press, 1971.

Welker, Michael. *The Work of the Spirit : Pneumatology and Pentecostalism.* Grand Rapids, MI: William B. Eerdmans Pub. Co., 2006.

White, John. "Characteristics of Revival." *Equipping the Saints.* Vol. 5 No. 1 (1991).

_____."Flee from the Wrath to Come." *Equipping the Saints.* (First Quarter, 1995).

_____. "MC 510: A Look Inside, Part I" in *First Fruits* (July, 1985).

_____. "MC 510: A Look Inside, Part II" in *First Fruits* (September, 1985).

_____."Relinquishment of Adult Children." *Equipping the Saints.* Vol. 5 No. 2 (1991).

_____. "Renewal and Revival." *Equipping the Saints.* (Third Quarter, 1994)

_____. "The Critical Spirit.", *Equipping the Saints.* (Fourth Quarter, 1994)

_____. *When The Spirit Comes With Power; Signs and Wonders Among God's People.* London: Hodder & Stoughton, 1988.

Williams, Don. *Bob Dylan: The Man, the music, the Message.* Old Tappen, NJ: Revell, 1985.

_____. "Friend and Encourager". *John Wimber: His Influence and Legacy.* ed. David Pytches. London: Cox and Wyman, 1998.

_____. *Signs, Wonders, and the Kingdom of God.* Ann Arbor, MI: Servant Books, 1989.

_____. *Start Here: Kingdom Essentials for Christians.* Ventura, CA: Regal Books, 2006.

_____. *Twelve Steps with Jesus.* Venture, CA: Regal Books, 1994.

Bibliography

Williams, J. Rodman. *Renewal Theology: Systematic Theology From a Charismatic Perspective.* 3 Vols. Grand Rapids, MI: Zondervan, 1996.

Wills, Wendell. The Kingdom of God in 20th Century Interpretation. Boston, MA: Hendrickson Press, 1987.

Wilson, Ken, and Rich Nathan. *Empowered Evangelicals.* Norcross, Georgia: Ampelon Publishing 2009.

Wimber, Carol. *John Wimber: the Way it Was.* London: Hodder & Stoughton, 1999.

Wimber, John. *Baptism in the Holy Spirit* (1991), Audio Resource available from Wimber.org

_____. *Everyone Gets to Play.* ed. Christy Wimber. Norcross, Georgia: Ampelon Publishing 2009.

_____. "Facing the '90's" *Equipping the Saints.* Vol.3 no3. (Summer 1990).

_____. "Healing". Audio Resource available from Wimber.org

_____. *I'm a fool for Christ- Whose Fool are You?* Vineyard Resources.

_____. "Introducing Prophetic Ministry", *Equipping the Saints.* Vol. 3, No.4 (Fall,1989).

_____. *Kingdom Evangelism: Proclaiming the Gospel in Power.* Ann Arbor, MI.: Vine Books, 1989.

_____. *Kingdom Fellowship: Living Together as the Body of Christ.* Ann Arbor, MI.: Vine Books, 1989.

_____. *Kingdom Suffering: Why do People Suffer.* Ann Arbor, MI.: Vine Books, 1990.

_____."Learning from our Elders." *Vineyard Reflections.* 1(Winter 1994).

_____. *Power Healing.* San Francisco: Harper & Row, 1987.

_____. *Power Evangelism.* San Francisco: Harper & Row, 1986.

_____. *Power Points.* New York: HarperCollins, 1991.

_____. "Releasing Lay People". *Equipping the Saints.* Vol. 3 No. 4, July-August 1986.

_____. "Season of New Beginnings", *Equipping the Saints.* (Fall, 1994).

_____. "Second Coming I". Sermon at Anaheim Vineyard. Audio Resource 1982).

227

_____. "Second Coming II". Sermon at Anaheim Vineyard, Audio Resource. (1982)

_____. "Sent into the Harvest Field", *Equipping the Saints*, Vol. 1, No. 5 (October 1987).

_____. "Staying Focused: The Vineyard as a Centered Set" *Vineyard Reflections,* 1995-1996.

_____. "The Church Jesus Builds" *Voice of the Vineyard.* (Spring, 1997).

_____."The Five-Fold Ministry." *Vineyard Reflections.* August 1997.

_____. "The Kingdom of God: Establishing Christ's Rule." *First Fruits.* January/February 1986.

_____. "The Kingdom of God and Social Justice." *Equipping the Saints* (1995).

_____. *The Holy Spirit and the Church* (1977), Audio Resource available from Vineyard Resources.

_____. *The Holy Spirit's Work in Believer's* (1986), Audio Resource available from Wimber.org

_____. *The Way In is the Way On.* ed. Christy Wimber. Norcross, Georgia: Ampelon Publishing 2006.

_____. "Warfare in Kingdoms", Audio Resource available from Wimber.org

_____. "Why Christians Suffer". *Equipping the Saints.* Vol. 2 No. 1, (Winter 1988).

Wimber, John, and Kevin Springer. *Study Guide to Power Healing.* San Francisco: Harper & Row, 1987.

Wimber, John and Dr. C. Peter Wagner, Course Syllabus, *MC 510/610,* Fuller Theological Seminary, Winter 1985.

Wink, Walter. *Naming the Powers: The Language of Power in the New Testament.* The Powers vol. 1. Philadelphia, PA: Fortress Press, 1984.

_____. *Unmasking the Powers: The Invisible Forces that Determine Human Existence.* The Powers vol. 2. Philadelphia, PA: Fortress Press, 1986.

_____. *Engaging the Powers: Discernment and Resistance in a World of Domination.* The Powers vol. 3. Philadelphia, PA: Fortress Press, 1992.

Witherington, Ben III. *The Problem with Evangelical Theology: Testing the Exegetical Foundations of Calvinism, Dispensationalism, and Wesleyanism.* Waco TX: Baylor University Press, 2005.

Witt, Stephan. "Where the Spirit of the Lord is, There is Freedom". *Equipping the Saints.* (Fall,   1994): 13.

Wright, N.T. *The New Testament and the People of God.* Minneapolis: Fortress Press, 1992.

_____. *Jesus and the Victory of God.* Minneapolis: Fortress Press, 1996.

_____. *Paul and the Faithfulness of God.* London/Minneapolis: Fortress, 2013.

_____. *Surprised by Hope: Rethinking Heaven, the Resurrection, and the Mission of the   Church.* London: HarperOne, 2008.

Yong, Amos. *The Spirit Poured Out on All Flesh: Pentecostalism and the Possibility of Global Theology.* Grand Rapids, MI: Baker Academic, 2005.

_____. "Rapture." In *The Encyclopedia of Protestantism*, vol. 3. Edited Hans J. Hillerbrand. New York, NY: Routledge, 2004, 1590-91.

_____. "The Marks of the Church: A Pentecostal Re-Reading." *Evangelical Review of Theology* 26:1 (2002): 45-67.

_____. *Spirit-Word-Community: Theological Hermeneutics in Trinitarian Perspective.* Burlington, VT: Ashgate, 2002.

_____. "Tongues of Fire in the Pentecostal Imagination: The Truth of Glossolalia in Light of R. C. Neville's Theory of Religious Symbolism." *Journal of Pentecostal Theology* 12 (April 1998): 39-65.

_____. Theology and Down Syndrome: Reimaging Disability in Late Modernity. Waco, TX: Baylor University Press, 2007.

Yong, Amos, Dale T. Irvin, Frank D. Macchia, and Ralph Del Colle. "Christ and Spirit: Dogma, discernment, and dialogical theology in a religiously plural world" *Journal of Pentecostal Theology* no. 1 (2003).

"Word and Spirit, Church and World: The Final Report of the International Dialogue Between Representatives of the World Alliance of Reformed Churches and Some Classical Pentecostal Churches and Leaders 1996-2000." *PNEUMA: The Journal of the Society for Pentecostal Studies* 23:1 (2001): 9-43.

"*Final Report* of the International Roman Catholic/Pentecostal Dialogue (1972-1976)." *PNEUMA: The Journal of the Society for Pentecostal Studies* 12:2 (1990): 85-95.

"*Perspectives on Koinonia*: Final Report of the International Roman Catholic/Pentecostal Dialogue (1985-1989)." *PNEUMA: The Journal of the Society for Pentecostal Studies* 12: 2 (1990): 117-142.

"Evangelism, Proselytism and Common Witness: The Report from the Fourth Phase of the International Dialogue (1990-1997) between the Roman Catholic Church and Some Classical Pentecostal Churches and Leaders." *PNEUMA: The Journal of the Society for Pentecostal Studies* 21:1 (1999): 11-51.

NOTES

<u>Chapter 1:</u>

[1] Wimber's impact undoubtedly spread beyond the Vineyard to the broader "third wave" movement, which will be described below, and the Anglican renewal widely known as the "New Wine" movement.

[2] For biographical information on John Wimber see the book *John Wimber: The Way it Was,* by Carol Wimber, John's wife. (London: Hodder & Stoughton, 1999) hereafter *TWIW.*

[3] Carol Wimber, *TWIW,* 31. A fine resource from a first-hand source who did extensive research on the Vineyard is Bill Jackson's *The Quest for the Radical Middle: A History of the Vineyard* (Cape Town, South Africa: 1999), hereafter, *Quest* 44.

[4] John Wimber, *Power Points,* (New York: HarperCollins, 1991), 17. Hereafter *PP.*

[5] Carol Wimber, *TWIW,* 59ff.

[6] Wimber, *PP* 22-23.

[7] In his book *Power Evangelism* (San Francisco: Harper & Row, 1986), Wimber states his conversion occurred in 1962, xv. Hereafter, *PE.* However, Carol Wimber states that they were converted in 1963, *TWIW,* 64-65.

[8] John Wimber, *Power Healing* (San Francisco: Harper & Row, 1987), 23. Hereafter, *PH.*

[9] Cessationism is the theological belief that miracles and signs and wonders like healing, speaking in tongues, prophecy and other "gifts" ceased, or ended after the age of the apostles. More will be said about this in a following chapter.

[10] It was in this time at Yorba Linda Friends Church, as Wimber began to study the scriptures for himself, that he had a conversation with one of the elders of the Friends church, in which Wimber inquired, "when do we get to do the stuff?", referring to the signs and wonders that marked the ministry of Jesus and the early church. At the time, he was disappointed by, but accepted nonetheless, the answer from the cessationist elder "We don't do that anymore". This concept of "doing the stuff" later became a foundational myth of Vineyard identity. Sermons and video teachings of Wimber retelling this story are copious on the internet.

[11] Jackson, *Quest,* 51.

[12] It is interesting to note there is some discrepancy in the dating of this event. In *Power Evangelism,* John Wimber states this occurred in 1974, but Dr. Wagner states this occurred in 1975 in his book *How to Have a Healing Ministry Without Making Your*

Church Sick, (Ventura, CA: Regal Books, 1998). Carol Wimber believes that Dr. Wagner is right, see *TWIW*, 98. Bill Jackson concurs based on his research and a personal conversation with Dr. Wagner, *Quest*, 53.

[13] Carol Wimber, *TWIW*, 98; Wimber, *PH, 28-29*; Wagner, *Healing Ministry*, 47.

[14] Cited in Jackson, *Quest*, 53; Wimber, *PH* 29-30.

[15] Wimber, *PP* 59.

[16] *Charismata* is the Greek word in the New Testament that can be translated "gifts of the Spirit" or "spiritual gifts".

[17] Wimber, *PH* 43.

[18] Carol Wimber, *The Way it Was*, 120; Jackson, *Quest*, 63.

[19] Jackson, *Quest*, 84ff.

[20] Carol Wimber notes there is some confusion as to the exact date of this separation, as in *Power Evangelism* John Wimber relates this happened in 1974, whereas Peter Wagner recalls it happening in 1975. Carol suggests that Wagner's timetable may be the more reliable. Jackson, *Quest*, 63; Wimber, *PE* 45; TWIW, 98.

[21] For more information on Dr. Chuck Smith and Calvary Chapels see Chuck Smith, *The History of Calvary Chapel* (Costa Mesa, CA: The word for Today Press, 1990); idem, *Charisma vs. Charismania* (Costa Mesa, CA: The word for Today Press, 1992).

[22] Wimber writes in *Power Healing* that by 1977, he had become convinced that divine healing was operative for the contemporary church. *PH*, 44. In Bill Jackson's view, Wimber had begun to promote "in the front room what Calvary was doing only in the back room". *Quest*, 85.

[23] See chapter 2 on the process of Wimber's rejection of dispensationalism, and his differences with Calvary Chapel's and Chuck Smith's eschatology. Also consult Jackson, *Quest*, 88.

[24] Jackson, *Quest*, 85-6.

[25] Carol Wimber's account of this separation notes that this experience was painful for John, as he did not think what he was doing at YLCC was much different than the other Calvary Chapels. *TWIW*, 157-8.

[26] Jackson, *Quest*, 81-88.

[27] Dr. Wagner speaks of this experience in his book *The Third Wave of the Holy Spirit* (Ann Arbor, MI: Vine Books, 1988), 25-30. The material for this course was eventually formed into Wimber and Springer's book *Power Evangelism*. See Carol Wimber's recounting of MC 510 in *TWIW* 166-68.

[28] Wimber recounts this time in numerous writings, sermons, and teachings. In this course syllabus, the introduction to the class states; "This course will focus on developing a better understanding of the purpose of the wide range of signs and wonders that have existed throughout the history of the Church…this course is designed primarily for individuals interested in more than new information. *It is aimed especially at those who desire to understand, develop and allow for a miraculous ministry as God directs and empowers them*". (Italics mine) John Wimber and Dr. C. Peter Wagner, Course Syllabus, MC 510/610, Fuller Theological Seminary, Winter 1985, introduction. In other words, the course as developed by Wimber and Wagner was not merely academic, but practical, in that, after Wagner taught on the subject in a traditional didactic fashion, he would turn the class over to Wimber for "clinic time" at which point Wimber would demonstrate prayer ministry by praying for students in the classroom, and teaching and coaching them as they prayed for other students.

[29] This incident is recounted by John Wimber in *PH*, 3-4, and Carol Wimber in *TWTW* 75-76.

[30] Wimber, *PH*, 44-55. Wimber recounts this in his introductory talk at the 1985 'Signs and Wonders" Conference in Anaheim, California. This video and audio are available from Vineyard resources as "I'm a fool for Christ- Whose Fool are You?'

[31] This first healing incident was followed by Wimber's "Honeycomb" vision, which has become a defining myth of the Vineyard identity. Wimber recounts it in his book *Power Healing*: As Wimber drove from the woman's house, he saw a vision in the sky: "Then I was jolted out of my jubilant mood by an incredible vision. Suddenly in my mind's eye there appeared to be a cloud bank superimposed across the sky. But I had never seen a cloud bank like this one, so I pulled my car over to the side of the road to take a closer look. Then I realized it was not a cloud bank, it was a honeycomb with honey dripping out on to people below. The people were in a variety of postures. Some were reverent; they were weeping and holding their hands out to catch the honey and taste it, even inviting others to take some of their honey. Others acted irritated, wiping the honey off themselves, complaining about the mess. I was awestruck. Not knowing what to think, I prayed, "Lord, what is it?" He said, "It's my mercy, John. For some people it's a blessing, but for others it's a hindrance. There's plenty for everyone. Don't ever beg me for healing again. The problem isn't on my end, John. It's down there". 52.

[32] The concept is rooted in mathematical set theory, but Hiebert saw its application to anthropology. Hiebert discusses the concept in his book *Anthropological Insights for Missionaries* (Grand Rapids, MI: Baker, 1985).

[33] Wimber introduced this concept to Vineyard pastors in a training seminar he called "Building the Church from the Group Up". The material for the seminar was eventually formalized in Alexander Venter, *Doing Church: Building from the Bottom Up* (Cape Town, South Africa: Vineyard International Publishing, 2000) hereafter, *DC*. Venter has an extended discussion of set theory in his section "Three Sociological Models of Community" 50-61. Wimber reinforced this in a series of articles titled "Staying Focused: The Vineyard as a Centered Set" from 1995-1996 in *Vineyard Reflections*. Jackson states that Wimber publicly taught this concept to the movement leaders in 1989, see *Quest* 244-45.

[34] Ibid., 53. The centered set model is foundational to understanding Vineyard ecclesiology, organizational structure, and developing theology, and thus will be referenced throughout this project.

[35] Jackson, *Quest*, 101. Jackson's list includes the following items: worship, Scripture, fellowship, ministry, caring for the poor, training, a non-religious style, church renewal, church planting, and spiritual gifts.

[36] Ibid., 236-37. Alexander Venter states he first heard the code formalized in 1991. Venter further argues that Wimber intended to put the code into 10 unique items that pastors and churches could easily understand and replicate. I will return to the genetic code and its impact on Vineyard practice in a later chapter.

[37] The so-called "Kansas City Prophets" era of the Vineyard movement is well chronicled in Bill Jackson's *Quest for the Radical Middle*, chapters 10-13. In this period of time, John Wimber received several significant prophecies that encouraged him to "stir up" the gift of prophecy in the Vineyard. Men like Bob Jones, Paul Cain, and Jon Paul Jackson were involved with Mike Bickle's Kansas City Vineyard, and took center stage in the movement's conferences and publications for a time. As several personal moral failures occurred, and numerous well publicized prophecies failed, Wimber became gradually disenchanted with the "Prophets" and began to restrict their activity.

[38] Venter, *DC*, 236.

[39] While most Vineyard churches practice believers baptism, Wimber was happy to accommodate child baptism in England.

Chapter 2

[1] As the Society of Friends has a rich, diverse, and global expression that has developed over nearly 500 years, this section will focus primarily on the beliefs and practices of Yorba Linda Friends Church, as Wimber's exposure to the Society of Friends was primarily through the lens of YLFC.

[2] The term "Quaker" was originally a derogatory term placed on the followers of George Fox by critics. The Society of Friends is the preferred name of the adherents.

[3] According to Quaker Information Center of the Earlham School of Religion. Information retrieved from the Center's website on 6/2010 at http://www.quakerinfo.org/quakerism/branchestoday.html.

[4] For information on the history and religious development of the Society of Friends, consult: Margaret Hope. Bacon, *The Quiet Rebels : The story of the Quakers in America*. (Philadelphia, PA: New Society Publishers, 1985); Hugh Barbour and J. William Frost. *The Quakers*, Denominations in America Vol. 3. (New York: Greenwood Press, 1988); *The Journal of George Fox*. (Cambridge: The University press, 1911); Thomas D. Hamm, *The Quakers in America*. Columbia contemporary American religion series. (New York: Columbia University Press, 2003); Elton Trueblood, *Robert Barclay*. 1st ed. (New York: Harper & Row, 1967; 1968); Trueblood, *The People Called Quakers*. 1st ed. (New York: Harper & Row, 1966).

[5] This conflict and change within the Society of Friends is brilliantly traced by David C. Le Shana, *Quakers in California; the effects of 19th century revivalism on Western Quakerism*. (Newberg, Or.: Barclay Press, 1969) and Thomas D. Hamm, *The Transformation of American Quakerism: Orthodox friends, 1800-1907*. (Bloomington: Indiana University Press, 1988).

[6] For more on the impact of the Second Great Awakening and revivalism in America, consult Edwin S. Gaustad, *The Great Awakening in New England* (New York: Harper and brothers, 1957); William G. McLaughlin, Jr., *Modern Revivalism: Charles Grandison Finney to Billy Graham* (New York: The Ronald Press Co., 1959).

[7] While the division began in 1827, the conflict came to a head at the famed Yearly meeting in Newport, Rhode Island in 1845. Quakerism became divided between the "Gurneyites", or followers of the Englishman Joseph Gurney, who had been heavily influenced by American Revivalism, and the followers of John Wilbur, or "Wilburites". The Gurneyites strain would eventually constitute the Evangelical Friends of the Twentieth century. See the discussion on Gurney below.

[8] Ibid., 137-38; Rufus Jones, *Quakerism vol II*, 930-33. The text of the Richmond declaration can be found online at http://www.quakerinfo.com.

⁹ Arthur O Roberts, *The Association of Evangelical Friends; A Story of Quaker Renewal in the Twentieth Century* (Newberg, OR: Barclay Press, 1975).

¹⁰ For example, on the issue of eschatology, it is obvious that what Wimber learned from YLFC was the dominant Protestant Dispensationalist/Cessationist "rapture theology," which is quite different from traditional Quaker views of the kingdom of God, which tended towards a realized eschatology and emphasized the ethical demands of the kingdom- worked out in Quaker history as opposition to slavery, caring for prisoners, pacifism, and working towards a more just society. In Quaker parlance, this became known as "The Lamb's War". An admirable exposition of early Quaker millenarianism, realized eschatology, and the concept of The Lamb's War is T.L. Underwood's essay "Early Quaker Eschatology" in *Puritans, The Millennium, and the Future of Israel: Puritan Eschatology 1600 to 1660* Ed. Peter Toon (London: James Clark & Co. 1970).

¹¹ A long accusation against the Society of Friends was that they had no professional "ministers" or pastors. William Barkley in his *Apology* stated, "That which we oppose, is the distinction of clergy and laity, which in the Scripture is not to be found", Proposition 10. Elton Trueblood is credited by some as coining the phrase "Quakers didn't abolish the priesthood...they abolished the laity" in defense of this Quaker belief. Trueblood was the Quaker author that Wimber quoted most often. He also favored the devotional writings of Hannah Whithall Smith, especially her *The Christian's Secret of a Happy Life,* which he quotes several times in *TWIWO*, 38, 42. Smith was greatly influenced by revivalist Quakerism.

¹² This phrase nearly reproduces a statement of Trueblood's; "A minister was simply one who ministers," *People,* 110.

¹³ In a personal conversation with Dr. Richard Foster, he recalled that in these meetings, Wimber "would wait, and wait, and wait some more" for the Spirit to move, and give charismatic guidance.

¹⁴ *TWIW,* 95. Dr. C. Peter Wagner was also a Quaker at this time, and was at many of these meetings, according to Carol Wimber *TWIW,* 110.

¹⁵ Dr. Richard Foster has personally related a story about an occasion when Wimber visited the house of David Watson, the Anglican vicar of St. Michael-le-Belfry in York in 1984 or 1985. According to Foster, a Quaker woman had visited one of Wimber's meetings at Watson's church and invited Wimber to her Quaker service. When Wimber visited this church he was given a prophetic "word" that stated "you will receive the Quaker blessing". Wimber understood this as a bestowing

of the power of Holy Spirit that accompanied the early Quaker meetings that was experiencing as physical manifestations of trembling or shaking under the power of the Spirit. Foster, Richard, phone interview with author, May 2012.

[16] This eventually of course led to a separation between Wimber's group and the church, which was painful for both sides. See Carol Wimber's account in *TWIW*, p115ff. In her recollection, there were about 60 individuals that left Yorba Linda Friends Church and joined the Wimbers in their new group.

[17] The influential Quaker author, Richard Foster, who was a close friend of John Wimber, wrote an article titled "The Lamb's War" in an *ETS* issue dedicated to social justice, serving the poor, and alleviating poverty. Vol. 3 No.2 (Spring, 1989). The South African Vineyard Pastor Alexander Venter, who himself worked as a white South African against apartheid, was John Wimber's research assistant in the 1980s in Anaheim. Out of his work with Wimber, Venter coalesced Wimber's writing on church planting into a monograph called *Doing Church* that has been used by countless Vineyard pastors worldwide. Venter reproduces an early document of Wimber's "The Church that I would join" (1982) which includes a section on "a ministering to the poor church" (230) in which Wimber (via Venter) states, ""it becomes of major importance that we reach out to the oppressed poor. It is our commission to minister to them, as an expression of our health and what God has done for us...". Wimber uses the phrase "The Lamb's War" as a *leitmotif* in his 1995 *Equipping the Saints* article "The Kingdom of God and Social Justice" in an issue dedicated to social justice and caring for the poor.

[18] Carol Wimber, *TWIW 104-05.*

[19] George Fox wrote of this commitment in 1661, "He that hath commanded us...that we shall not kill, so that we can neither kill men, nor swear for or against them". Reprinted in Hamm, *Quaker Writings,* 324. In *A Procession of Friends* (Garden City, New York: Doubleday, 1972).

[20] Vol. 2 No 3, (Summer 1988).

[21] *TWIW*, 112ff. Jackson suggests that Wimber's Quaker background was influential in this decision as well, see *Quest,* 153ff.

[22] See Vineyard pastor Rich Nathan's book, *Who is my Enemy: Welcoming People the Church rejects* (Grand Rapids, MI: Zondervan, 2011) for a contemporary treatment of this perspective.

Chapter 3

[1] Carol Wimber cites John's original skepticism, and then unending questioning of Gunnar Payne throughout the *TWIW*.

[2] Of course, the precise meaning of what an "evangelical" is has come into significant dissension within the movement itself over the last decades. For the purposes of this paper, the definition provided by David Bebbington is useful, though perhaps not all-encompassing. He cites the following elements as normative: conversionism, biblicism, activism, and crucicentrism, *Evangelicalism in Britain: a History from 1730s to the 1980s* (London: Unwin Hyman, 1989).

[3] Wimber, Carol *TWIW*, 60.

[4] Wimber wrote, "In the first year of my Christian life, I followed Gunnar around, learning to do everything he did" *PE*, 82. Wimber later wrote "Through example and teaching, Gunnar spliced the value of evangelism into my spiritual 'Genetic Code'". *PP*, 163-64

[5] Numerous citations reference Wimber leading "many hundreds" of people to Christ during his time at Yorba Linda Friends Church. *PH*, 23; *PP*, 163.

[6] Wimber, Carol, *TWIW*, 90.

[7] Once again, Wimber's emphasis on "everybody gets to play" and the democratization of ministry spoken of earlier meant that in his view, evangelism and witness were not only the domain of a select "gifted" few; rather, all Christians are called and gifted to be witnesses for Christ. For example in his article "Sent into the Harvest Field", *ETS*, Vol. 1, No. 5 (October 1987) Wimber wrote "All Christians are called as workers into the ripe harvest fields... All are called into evangelism, no matter where we live and work". In one of his final public addresses to the Vineyard just before his death, Wimber spoke of the central important of evangelism, church planting, and missions. This address can be found in *VOV* (Spring, 1997) "The Church Jesus Builds".

[8] Wimber strongly emphasizes the influence of Gunnar Payne numerous times. See *PE*, 82; section A above.

[9] Jackson, *Quest*, 63. See the extended discussion in section A above.

[10] For years afterword John Wimber and other Vineyard leaders were known for wearing their Hawaiian shirts in public speaking events. John Mumford, now the leader of the Vineyard Churches in the United Kingdom, speaks of the effect of Wimber's beach attire - "a rather awful Hawaiian shirt" on his staid British audiences in "Vineyard Movement Founder", *John Wimber: His Influence and Legacy*. ed. David Pytches, (London: Cox and Wyman, 1998) 198.

[11] Wimber's experience in the Institute of Church Growth gave him exposure to thousands of Churches in North America and beyond. He would become convinced that one of the elements of successful, growing congregations was their willingness to be open to and engage culture, rather than shield themselves off from potentially negative influences of the surrounding secular culture.

[12] For more on the cultural and theological milieu embroiling Fuller Seminary in the years during Wimber's work at the Institute of Church Growth, see George M. Marsden, *Reforming Fundamentalism: Fuller Seminary and the New Evangelicalism* (Grand Rapids, MI: Eerdmans, 1987), idem, *Understanding Evangelicalism and Fundamentalism* (Grand Rapids, Eerdmans, 1991).

[13] See Venter, *Doing Church,* 233; Jackson, *Quest,* 107; Wimber, "Facing the '90's" *ETS* Vol.3 no3. (Summer 1990). In the chapters on eschatology and Pneumatology, significant time will be spent elaborating the many ways that Wimber diverged from the current options in Evangelical theology and practice, however, there is little doubt that he saw the Vineyard as a broadly "Evangelical" movement, and part of the wider Evangelical Protestant church. See Rich Nathan and Ken Wilson, *Empowered Evangelicals,* (Norcross, Georgia: Ampelon Publishing 2009) for their helpful discussion of the features of Evangelicalism that Wimber attempted to instill into the Vineyard.

[14] Wimber, "I had always avoided Pentecostal and Charismatic Christians, in part because it seemed that controversy and division often surrounded their ministries. Also, as a dispensationalist, I believed that the charismatic gifts had ceased at the end of the first century", *PE,* 17-18.

[15] Wimber, *PH,* 21, "most of the contemporary healers appeared foolish, weird, or bizarre".

[16] Jackson, *Quest,* 70; Wimber, *PH,* 3-4.

[17] Wimber, *PH* 30. Carol Wimber speaks of these reputable men as being crucial to the "breakdown of our prejudices towards Pentecostals and Charismatics", *TWIW,* 109ff.

[18] The Catholic Charismatic movement was influenced by, and in turn greatly influenced, the events of Vatican II, which has been rightly called one of the more significant events in Catholic Pneumatology in the last century. Helpful works include Fr. Donald Gelpi, S.J., *Pentecostalism: A Theological Viewpoint* (Costa Mesa, CA: Paulist Press, 1971); Fr. Raniero Cantalamessa, *Sober Intoxication of the Spirit* (Cincinnati, OH: Servant Publications, 2005).

[19] For more on the complicated relationships between Pentecostalism, Fundamentalism, Evangelicalism, and the Charismatic movement, helpful sources include: Stanley M. Burgess, Ed. *The New Dictionary of Pentecostal and Charismatic Movements* (Grand Rapids, MI: Zondervan, 2003); W.J. Hollenweger, *The Pentecostals: The Charismatic Movement in the Churches* (Minneapolis, MN: Augsburg, 1972); idem, *Pentecostalism: Origins and Developments Worldwide* (Peabody, MA: Hendrickson, 1997); Harvey Cox, *Fire from Heaven: The Rise of Pentecostal Spirituality and the Reshaping of Religion in the Twenty-first Century* (Reading, MA: Addison-Wesley 1995).

[20] Particularly influential for Wimber were McNutt's works, *Healing* (Notre Dame, IN: Ave Maria, 1974), and *The Power to Heal* (Notre Dame, IN: Ave Maria, 1977).

[21] Dennis Bennett was the priest of St. Mark's Episcopal Church in Van Nuys, California when in 1960, he announced to his congregation that he had experienced the baptism of the Holy Spirit. He is widely credited for being one of the early figures in the Charismatic movement. Dennis and Rita Bennett, *How to Pray for Inner Healing for Yourself and Others* (Old Tappen, NJ: Revell Books, 1984).

[22] Donald Gee, *Concerning Spiritual Gifts* (Springfield, MO: Gospel Press, 1972).

[23] Recalling that the Charismatics were primarily believers within established theological traditions and churches that had experienced a form of spiritual renewal, there were many more academically trained, reputable, "sophisticated" if you will, Charismatics at the time than traditional Pentecostals. Hence Wimber developed deep, respectful friendships with leaders of the Charismatic movement, even as the movement itself was waning from its heyday in the 1960s and 1970s.

[24] These were both denominational publications of the Vineyard movement.

[25] Carol Wimber tells of a fascinating occurrence when John, Peter Wagner, and Eddie Gibbs visited a Pentecostal faith-healing church in Appalachia that practiced handling dangerous vipers and consuming poison as evidence of "faith", *TWIW*, 102ff.

[26] Wimber, *PH*, 20-21.

[27] More complete discussions of the relationship between Pentecostal eschatology and Pentecostal Pneumatology will be undertaken in following chapters.

[28] In the course readings of MC 510, Wimber included a section from J. Sidlow Baxter's work *Divine Healing of the Body* (Grand Rapids, MI: Zondervan, 1979) that detailed the course of divine healing through church history. Wimber modifies Baxter's conclusions, and disagrees with him on some points. For example, Wimber was concerned that Baxter overlooked the Gospels in his survey of New Testament healing models. *PH*, 280.

[29] A major inspiration for this insight was Father Francis McNutt's book *Healing*, in which McNutt makes a case for healing being normative practice in the Church body, sometimes led, but not necessarily only performed by, priests. Wimber credits McNutt and Dennis Bennett for helping him to see the healing gift as not restricted to the domain of an especially gifted few. *PH*, 50.

[30] Wimber, *PH, 50.*

[31] For example, I understand that if I was *learning and developing this gift,* then mistakes or failure were *part of the process of learning* just as one makes mistakes learning a new skill or technique in sports or a musical instrument. Further, this must mean that *God is ok with my mistakes and my learning,* which fits in perfectly with the already-not yet view of the kingdom of God.

[32] Among other issues, Wimber would part with the Pentecostals over the so-called "second blessing" doctrine; Wimber held that "conversion and Holy Spirit baptism are simultaneous experiences," *PP*, 136. Wimber's views evolved over time however, and were quite nuanced.

[33] Wimber died in 1997 after a two year battle with cancer at the age of 59. In the last years of his life he struggled with numerous health issues that limited his travel and ministry.

[34] Christianity Today, 1997 .

[35] During Wimber's time, the national board of the Vineyard U.S. began "releasing" AVC's (Association of Vineyard Churches) in countries worldwide, as part of the "International Vineyard Consortium. See Jackson, *Quest,* 340ff for an explanation of this process. At the time of this writing, Vineyard International consists of 10 independent AVC's; U.S.A., Canada, United Kingdom/Ireland, Germany/Austria/Switzerland, South Africa, Costa Rica, Australia, New Zealand, Benelux, and Norden (Scandinavia) . These AVC's take responsibility for ecclesial governance and church planting in their respective geographical regions. See www.vineyard.org.

[36] Pytches, *JW,* 32-33.

[37] Examples of influential churches are quite abundant, including Dr. Joel Hunter's Northland Church in Orlando, Florida, with over 20,000 members; New Life Church in Colorado; Willow Creek Evangelical Association in the Chicago, Illinois area; and Bill Johnson's Bethel churches based in Redding, California. Churches that are formally affiliated with the Vineyard, such as Mike Bickle's Kansas City Fellowship, and the Toronto Airport Network would likely be understood as Third Wave as well.

---

38 http://christianchurchestogether.org

39 The so-called "Toronto Blessing" began in winter of 1994 with a visitation of the Spirit at the Toronto Airport Vineyard led by Pastor John Arnott. As the renewal spread throughout Vineyard churches worldwide, there were numerous conflicts and criticisms that arose. Eventually Wimber and the Vineyard National Board withdrew their official endorsement from the Toronto Vineyard. See Jackson's balanced discussion in *Quest*. Helpful sources from an insider on the blessing include Guy Chevreau, *Catch the Fire: The Toronto Blessing-An Experience of Renewal and Revival* (Toronto: HarperCollins Canada, 1994), and idem, *Share the Fire: The Toronto Blessing and Grace-Based Evangelism* (Shippensburg, PA: Revival Press, 2007).

40 Jackson deconstructs this well in *Quest*. While Wimber's voice was the only one heard in the earlier controversies, as the National Board had invested significant time in dealing with Mike Bickle and the Kansas City prophets, and even more so with John Arnott and the Toronto Airport Vineyard, his perspective and persona was certainly dominant . See Jackson, *Quest, 326ff.* Todd Hunter, who was Wimber's assistant at the time, wrote the document "Withdrawal of endorsement of the Toronto Airport Vineyard" in 1995.

41 As there was no longer one dominant voice that could control the decision making process, the decisions for the movement became more corporate and discussion oriented. This involved a corporate public comment period (open to scholars, pastors, and laypersons) where opinion papers were solicited, published publicly, and discussed at many levels of the organization. The national board made the final decision at the termination of this process. Influential position papers were submitted by historic leaders like Rich Nathan, Dr. Don Williams, and Dr. Peter Davids, but numerous papers from pastors were considered as well.

42 The end result of this process in 2005 was a statement on women in ministry that essentially granted every possible role to women, including that of National Director of Vineyard U.S. It is also notable that previously dominant perspectives like that of Dr. Wayne Grudem (who strongly opposed the move to allow women to serve at any level) were considered as viable options among many.

43 As early as 1995 the Vineyard held an international conference focused on justice in Winnipeg, Canada. The issue of justice and caring for the poor has been addressed in frequent articles in Vineyard publications.

44 This initiative was first developed as the Vineyard Anti-Slavery Task force (VAST), and in 2013 was re-launched as the Vineyard Justice Network (VJN).

---

[45] Tri Robinson, *Saving God's Green Earth: Rediscovering the Church's Responsibility to Environmental Stewardship* (Norcross, GA: Ampelon, 2006).

[46] Dr. DeWitt is a past executive Director of the Ausable Institute in Mancelona, Michigan which is a non-profit Christian organization dedicated to environmental stewardship and protection. See www.ausable.org.

Chapter 4

[1] Among the more recent kingdom of God studies in the last decades consult: Mark Saucy, *The Kingdom of God in the Teaching of Jesus* (Dallas: Word Publishing, 1997) ; Bruce Chilton, *Pure Kingdom: Jesus' Vision of the Kingdom of God* (Grand Rapids, Eerdmans, 1996); George Beasley-Murray, *Jesus and the Kingdom of God* (Grand Rapids, Eerdmans, 1986). The year 1963 was an especially fruitful one in Kingdom of God studies, with 3 major works published in English: Norman Perrin, *The Kingdom of God in the Teaching of Jesus* (London: SCM Press, 1963); Gösta Lundström, *The Kingdom of God in the Teaching of Jesus: A History of Interpretation from the Last Decades of the Nineteenth Century to the Present Day* (London, Oliver and Boyd, 1963); and George Eldon Ladd, *Jesus and the Kingdom: The Eschatology of Biblical Realism* (New York: Harper and Row, 1963)(Revised and reprinted as *The Presence of the Future* (Grand Rapids, MI: Eerdmans, 1974), hereafter *TPOF*. For the purposes of this study, the 1974 (revised) version will be utilized.

[2] Albrecht Ritschl, *The Christian Doctrine of Justification and Reconciliation* 3rd Ed. (Edinburgh :T & T Clark, 1900) 8.

[3] Translated by Richard H. Hiers & D. Larrimore Holland (Philadelphia: Fortress Press, 1971) page number references belong to this version. At a mere 67 pages, *Preaching of Jesus* is tantalizingly short, and straightforwardly written, which perhaps explains its lukewarm reception by the German academy. Regardless, Schweitzer argues that it is one of the most important books written in German theology. See Albert Schweitzer, *The Quest for the Historical Jesus* (New York: MacMillan, 1910, 1968) 328-39.

[4] Weiss, *Preaching of Jesus*, 73.

[5] Ibid., 105.

[6] One of Weiss' stated goals was to return the concept of Jesus' "overwhelming heroic greatness" to Jesus studies, which he believed had been cast aside in the "lives of Jesus "project.

[7] Ibid., 131.

[8] Hence Schweitzer's construction of "thoroughgoing" or "consistent" eschatology. This intuition sees its full development in Schweitzer's later *The kingdom of God and Primitive Christianity* (New York: Seabury Press, 1968) where he traces the kingdom of God in the old Testament prophets, extra-Biblical eschatology, late Judaism, Jesus, and Paul. This manuscript was finalized by Schweitzer in 1950-51, but only discovered after his death.

[9] Schweitzer contends that much of previous quest had ignored this critical evidence, such as the influence of Jewish apocalyptic literature from Daniel onward. He states, "what else, indeed, are the Synoptic Gospels, the Pauline Letters, the Christian apocalypses than products of Jewish apocalyptic?" *Quest*, 367.

[10] Ironically Schweitzer seems to, in the final analysis, include Weiss in the cast of characters that have misconstrued the quest. He mentions Weiss in several brief references in *Quest*, but rarely in his decisive conclusion. Gathercole writes of Schweitzer "On the other hand, having praised Weiss, Schweitzer comes to bury him". S.J. Gathercole, 'The Critical and Dogmatic Agenda of Albert Schweitzer's 'The Quest for the Historical Jesus' *Tyndale Bulletin* 51.2 (2000) 277.

[11] Quest, 23.

[12] Schweitzer, *Quest*, 330ff.

[13] It is well recognized that Schweitzer's *Quest* put the definite end on the "lives of Jesus" project, as he relentlessly argues that the various Since the Gospels relate that immediate expectancy of the Kingdom, which obviously did not come, Schweitzer thought that the Gospel accounts had been edited to de-emphasize the immediate sayings, and to explain the historical problem of the "non-occurrence of the *Parousia*". *Quest*, 360. Therefore, what was important was not the "historical Jesus", but the "spiritual Jesus" who lived on in the hearts of men, because "the abiding and eternal in Jesus is absolutely independent of historical knowledge and can only be understood in contact with His Spirit". He further adds "Jesus as a concrete historical personality remains a stranger to our time", 401.

[14] Ibid., 370-371.

[15] *Ibid.*, 398. The matter of what Schweitzer's own view of the Kingdom is has been hotly debated. While he ardently expounds the *konsequente Eschatologie* view in *Quest*, his later work *The Mystery of the Kingdom of God* is more nuanced. Here, Schweitzer seems to allow for a transformed existence on earth that is the kingdom of God. N.T. Wright is extremely critical of Schweitzer's understanding of Jewish

apocalyptic. Wright argues that Schweitzer understands apocalyptic as "the climax of Israel's history, involving the end of the space time universe," whereas recent studies in Jewish Apocalyptic have revealed the idea of a transformation and re-creation of the current cosmos. See Wright, *Jesus and the Victory of God* (Minneapolis: Fortress Press, 1996) 207ff. For a response to Wright's view, see Gathercole, "Critical and Dogmatic Agenda" who argues that Wright does not adequately represent Schweitzer's position.

[16] C.H. Dodd, *The Parables of the Kingdom* (London: Nisbet, 1935, 1961). Dodd returns to the issue of eschatology in his *The Apostolic Preaching and its Development* (London: Hodder and Stoughton, 1936, 1967); *History and the Gospel* (London: Nisbet, 1952); *The Coming of Christ* (Cambridge: Cambridge University Press, 1951).

[17] Dodd's work brought to light the connection between the parables and the kingdom of God that had not previously been expressed. Norman Perrin notes that "after Dodd any interpreter of the parables had to become self-conscious about his understanding of Jesus' use of the kingdom of God". See *Jesus and the Language of the Kingdom* 97-98.

[18] Dodd, *The Parables of the Kingdom*, 32-33. In comparing the various Gospel sources Dodd claims that the "earliest traditions" are "explicit and univocal" in support of the realized view. By examining the Q material, Dodd believes, one will find that the realized view dominates overwhelmingly. Robert F Berkley has considerable doubts about Dodd's attempt to carry his argument on his interpretation of the Greek verb ἤγγικεν "to draw near". Berkley painstakingly catalogs the considerable ambiguity of ἤγγικεν in both New Testament and Qumran documents, and finds that Dodd's claim that "to draw near" supports his realized eschatology is not as strong a case as he would wish. See his "ΕΓΓΙΖΕΙΝ, ΦΘΑΝΕΙΝ, and Realized Eschatology " *Journal of Biblical Literature* LXXII, (June, 1963) 177-87. For a dispensationalist appraisal of these claims by Dodd, consult John F. Walvoord, "Realized Eschatology" *Bibleotheca Sacra* (October, 1970) 313-23, who challenges Dodd on many points, summarizing with an expected dismissal of Dodd's program: "It may be concluded that in the concept of the person and work of Christ, Dodd is seriously divergent from traditional orthodoxy," and later refers to Dodd's eschatology as "bankrupt". 322-23.Both Kenneth Clark 'Realized Eschatology" *Journal of Biblical Literature* 56 (March 1957) 367-83 and Clarence Craig "Realized Eschatology" *Journal of Biblical Literature* (September 1940) 17-26 are

heavily critical of Dodd's forced exegesis as well. Clark argues that Dodd's insistence that "has come" is the best understanding of *ephthasen* is faulty, contending that the comparable literature suggests "drawn near" is a better understanding. This discussion will be resumed in the discussion below in the Vineyard's understanding of the four kingdom tenses, as discussed by Derek Morphew.

[19] Matthew 12:28 and Luke 11:20. Dodd also argues strongly that the use of *ennigken*, "at hand" used in Mark 1:15 is another example of the earliest and most reliable textual tradition, which is contested. Dodd is adamant that *ennigken* must be understood as "arrival," rather than merely "near". See also George Beasley-Murray, *Jesus and the Kingdom of God*, (Grand Rapids, MI: Eerdmans, 1986), 70-74.

[20] Dodd, *The Parables of the Kingdom*, 30.

[21] Dodd completely refutes the "social" program of the Kingdom as modeled by Kant and Ritschl. He argues that the "Growth Parables" such as the Sower, the Tares, the Leaven, the Secret Seed and the Mustard Seed are a "commentary on the actual situation in the ministry of Jesus" and not to be interpreted "as implying a long process of development introduced by the ministry of Jesus and to be consummated by His second advent". The Kingdom of God has come by "no human effort, but by an act of God". However, Dodd curiously adds that since the Kingdom has now come, there is a need for human effort, as "the harvest waits for the reapers". Ibid., 155.

[22] Ibid., 80. Early in his writing, Dodd also suggests that the apocalyptic sayings were probably generated by the early church as a way to explain the failure of the mission of Jesus. It was the fundamental misunderstandings of the disciples about the mission that forced them to interpret literally what was meant figuratively, See Dodd, *The Apostolic Preaching*, 55. George Ladd notes that in his later writings, Dodd seems less adamant about his purely realized eschatology, as he seems to make room for the eschatological Kingdom consummated at the end of history. See Ladd, *The Presence of the Future*, 20.

[23] Dodd states "it is at least open to the reader to take the traditional apocalyptic imagery as a series of symbols standing for realities which the human mind cannot directly apprehend". Dodd, *The Parables of the Kingdom* 81.

[24] Ibid., 82-83.

[25] Ibid., 155-59.

[26] Rudolf Bultmann, *Jesus and the Word*, trans. L. Smith and Erminie Huntress (New York: Scribner's, 1934); *Theology of the New Testament*, trans. Kendrick Grobel

(New York: Scribner's, 1951); *The Presence of Eternity* (New York: Harpers, 1957); *Jesus Christ and Mythology* (New York Scribner's, 1958). For secondary literature on Bultmann's view of the Kingdom, the surveys by Norman Perrin, Gösta Lundström, and Mark Saucy are helpful. Bultmann's essay in *Kerygma and Myth* (London, S.C.K., 1953) also details his program of demythologizing the teaching of the Kingdom. For a response, see G.R. Beasley-Murray "Demythologized Eschatology" *Theology Today* 14 (1957) 61-79. Ladd engages Bultmann's eschatology on a number of points as well in *The Presence of the Future.*

[27] Bultmann succinctly rejects Dodd's realized eschatology by calling it "escape-reasoning" that "cannot be substantiated by a single saying of Jesus", *A Theology of the New Testament* I §3.

[28] For a full discussion of the problem of the delay of the *Parousia* by Bultmann, see his "History and Eschatology in the New Testament," *New Testament Studies*, I (September, 1954), 9-16.

[29] Bultmann, *Kerygma and Myth,* 3. The concept of Bultmann's "demythologizing" has been the subject of countless primary and secondary works. Critics such as George Beasley-Murray objected that in this attempt, Bultmann strikes at the very heart of the Gospel, and thus, ceases to be relevant to orthodox theology. G.E. Ladd was more sympathetic to Bultmann's pastoral motivation, and yet largely disagreed with the conclusions derived at via his de-mythologizing methodology. Bultmann defines his process of demythologizing in numerous works, including *Jesus and the Word, Jesus Christ and Mythology,* and his *Theology of the New Testament.* Critical approaches are Ladd's *The Presence of the Future,* Herman Ridderbos', *The Coming of the Kingdom,* and Beasley-Murray's "Demythologized Eschatology".

[30] Bultmann, *The Presence of Eternity,* 154.

[31] Bultmann, *Jesus and the Word.,* 41.

[32] Bultmann, *Jesus and the Word,* 51.

[33] Oscar Cullman, *Christ and Time,* (Philadelphia: Westminster Press, 1945), 30-31. Cullman states that Bultmann's *a priori* assumptions are colored not by historical study, but by the philosophy of Martin Heidegger. See also Stephen Smalley, "The Delay of the Parousia", *Journal of Biblical Literature* 83.1 (March 1964) 41-54; M.C. Warren, "Eschatology and History", *International Review of Missions* Vol. 41, Issue 3, (July 1952) 337-50.

[34] Cullman, *Christ and Time,* 84. As this book was written during WWII, no doubt

Cullman had the war in Europe in mind. Numerous authors have made the analogical connection to the relationship between the success of the Allied invasion of Normandy and the final end of the Third Reich eleven months later.

[35] See the chart offered by Cullmann to explain his view on 83 of *Christ and Time*, in which he contrasts the Jewish two-stage view of history with the three-stage view of Primitive Christianity.

[36] Cullmann says of this "such a distinction...finds no real support in the New Testament texts". Ibid., 148.

[37] Ibid., 152. Cullman states that this present-future tension is the essence of the cry of the Early Church *"Maranatha",* (Our Lord, Come) which is in the imperative mood. His primary influence in further Kingdom studies was his contribution to the understanding of time and the ages in the New Testament, and his attempt to mediate a position between the consistent and the realized school. Ladd applauds Cullman's insistence on the "three stage" view of time in Primitive Christianity, yet is critical of Cullman's conception as to what constitutes the kingdom of God.

[38] Kümmel, *Promise and Fulfillment: The Eschatological Message of Jesus,*(London: SCM Press, 1957), 16. Kümmel also discusses Jesus' teaching on the Kingdom in his *The Theology of the New Testament According to its Major Witnesses* (New York: Abingdon, 1969).

[39] Kümmel writes, "For this would result in a complete disintegration of Jesus' message that man through Jesus' appearance in the present is placed in a definite situation in the history of salvation advancing towards the end, and the figure and activity of Jesus would lose their fundamental character as the historical activity of the God who wishes to lead his kingdom upwards". Ibid., 148.

[40] Ibid., 114.

[41] Ibid., 155. It is interesting to note that for Kümmel, there was no sense that the disciples or the church should "carry on" the ministry of the work of the Kingdom, as the Kingdom was present only in the person of Jesus. See Ibid., 139-40.   Furthermore, Kümmel argued against an understanding of the "growth parables" that would suggest that the Kingdom itself would grow, increase, etc. Rather than growth, per se, these parables were meant to show the inevitable finality of the eschatological consummation of the Kingdom. For example, in speaking of the parable of the leaven in Matthew 13:33 (Luke 13:20) Kümmel writes that "in no case can the parable be used to justify the assumption that Jesus announced a gradual penetration of the world by the forces of the kingdom of God".

⁴² While Kümmel's influence has been noted in the study, this is not to imply that there weren't other figures who also contributed to a mediating position between Schweitzer, Dodd, and Bultmann.

⁴³ Jeremias, *The Parables of Jesus* (New York: Charles Scribner's Sons, 1963). Ladd and Ridderbos both acknowledged the obvious impact of Jeremias on their own work, although each also were careful to note that their work went beyond Jeremias' in the attempt to forge a true consensus between the consistent and the realized school. Ladd notes that Jeremias did not follow through on some of his insights and thereby did not fully engage the implications of the "already" side of the equation. See *TPOF*, XXX. Ridderbos acknowledges his debt to Jeremias as well, but makes more use of Kümmel's work.

⁴⁴ That is to say, in his examination of the teaching on the Kingdom in the parables, Jeremias did not push the eschatological themes off as later reconstructions by the church, as Dodd had done.

⁴⁵ Jeremias, *Parables*, 230. Jeremias notes that the phrase was not conceived by him, but by Ernst Haenchen, see the 230 note 3.

⁴⁶ Jeremias, *A Theology of the New Testament* (New York: Charles Scribner's Sons, 1971) 99-100.

⁴⁷ Ibid., 105. According to Jeremias, Jesus' gloss on the passages from Isaiah mean that he is expanding the concept of the Kingdom beyond the expectations even of the prophet- the Lepers as healed, and in Rabbinic terms, the lepers, the lame, and the blind were considered as "dead men".

⁴⁸ Ibid., 102. It is interesting to note that Jeremias does seem to overreach on the realized side of the quotient, as Ladd and others have noted. See Ladd, *TPOF*, 27-28. In his conclusion, Jeremias writes of the post-Easter events, that in seeing Jesus, the disciples *"experienced the parousia"*, 310. Apparently, Jeremias intends that in his glorification, the disciples believed that the fullness of the Kingdom had arrived. Ladd challenged Jeremias at this point, asking exactly how the "process" can be substantiated if the fullness had already obtained. Ladd wonders how there is *either* realistic *or* futuristic eschatology in this sense.

⁴⁹ Along with the D'Elia's biography of Ladd, also helpful is George Marsden's excellent study on Fuller Evangelical Seminary at this time, *Reforming Evangelicalism: Fuller Seminary and the New Evangelicalism* (Grand Rapids, MI: Eerdmans, 1995).

⁵⁰ In a letter to Otto Piper of Princeton Theological Seminary, Ladd wrote; "In spite of all that has been written on the subject, I have the conviction that there

remains something to be said. I am convinced that the world of scholarship has not yet found a sound position between the extremes of the apocalyptic and neo-prophetic schools, and I am convinced that the biblical position lies in this area.... I am trying to assimilate into my thinking all of the important literature in English, German, and French. The book will, of course, be written from a thoroughly conservative point of view, and for this reason I do not know how it will be received; for the modern world of scholarship is not usually generous to any volume which sustains a real effort to obtain a measure of objectivity". Quoted in D'Elia, *Ladd*, 122.

[51] This volume has been republished as *The Presence of the Future: The Eschatology of Biblical Realism*.

[52] Ladd states that while is it clear that the records we possess of the life of Jesus are products of the believing community, this fact does not necessarily lead to the conclusion that the "Jesus of History" has been completely lost in the "Christ of Faith". See *POTF*, xii; Ladd, *The New Testament and Criticism* (Grand Rapids, MI: Eerdmans, 1967).

[53] "The Gospels are both reports of what Jesus said and did, and interpretations of the meaning of his acts and words. The author (Ladd) is convinced that this interpretation corresponds to the events which occurred in history, and that the interpretation goes back to Jesus himself". *POTF*, xiii.

[54] For example, Ladd is careful to credit Bultmann's pastoral inclinations, but complains that in the end, his program of demythologizing presents an "unbiblical" picture of God and Christ. Similarly, Ladd applauds Schweitzer's correction of the "lives of Jesus" studies, but considers Schweitzer's conclusions to be modified by later interpreters to include more of the historical "presence" of the Kingdom. Ladd agrees with much of Dodd's correction to the consistent school, and yet notes that Dodd himself has accepted Jeremias' contention that his early work was too one-sided in favor of realized eschatology. *TPOF*, Ch. 1.

[55] His *Crucial Questions* of 1952 formed the basis of his life's work. Here, Ladd interacts with several conservative options of his day, including his first academic jousts with dispensationalism. A major theme of this work is the idea that the teachings of Jesus on the Kingdom as "both a present and a future reality," 66. See D'Elia, *Table*, for more on Ladd's view of this project and how it led to his *Jesus and the Future*.

[56] George Eldon Ladd and Donald Alfred Hagner, *A Theology of the New Testament*. Rev. ed. (Grand Rapids, MI: Eerdmans, 1993), 61. Hereafter, *ATNT*.

⁵⁷ Ladd cites the Minor Prophets as examples, as they often speak of "The Day of the Lord" as the eschatological future that none could miss, and yet, consistently speak of Yahweh as acting in the present day to build His kingdom and or restrain the forces of evil. While the Israelites often had a historical, this-worldly conception of God's acting solely in focus, the prophets contradicted this view by pointing beyond the circumstances of the present to the eschatological future. *TPOF,* 52-59.

⁵⁸ Ibid., 59.

⁵⁹ Ladd understands the message of Amos to illustrate this point succinctly, for even though he used poetic language that could be understood metaphorically, Amos speaks of the "day of the Lord" as being a dramatic, sensational, cataclysmic intervention of God on a cosmic scale that is impossible to miss. *TPOF,* 57.

⁶⁰ N.T. Wright describes the Rabbinic messianic expectation to be centered around the restoration of the elements of Torah, Temple, Jewish Identity, and Land. Wright, *The New Testament and the People of God,* (Minneapolis: Fortress Press, 1992) 224-32, hereafter *NTPG; Jesus and the Victory of God,* (Minneapolis: Fortress Press, 1996), 202-09 hereafter *JVG.*

⁶¹ This is evidenced by the incredulous rabbis that challenged Jesus proclamation and deeds; the conception of the Kingdom that they taught (and had been passed on to them by their teacher's) was vastly different from the preaching and acts of Jesus. Ladd cites the Rabbi's demand that Jesus explain himself in Luke 17. See Ladd, *TPOF,* 228 n. 25.

⁶² Ibid., 218.

⁶³ Ibid., 125.

⁶⁴ Ibid., 126-27.

⁶⁵ Ibid., 136-37.

⁶⁶ This saying was a popular idiomatic expression of Wimber's.

Chapter 5:

¹ For the purposes of this discussion, I shall use the term "classic dispensationalism" to refer to that school of thought that grew out of the teachings of John Nelson Darby, and popularized by C.I. Scofield in his popular Scofield Reference Bible. This view and its variants were dominant theological models in the 1960s-1980s in Protestant America, although dispensationalism's influence has waned considerably. The literature on dispensationalism is ubiquitous; helpful

introductions can be found in Craig Blaising and Darrell Bock, *Progressive Dispensationalism: an up-to-date Handbook of Contemporary Dispensational Thought* (Victor Books: Wheaton, IL, 1993); Other sources include: Clarence B. Bass, *Backgrounds to Dispensationalism: Its Historical Genesis and Historical Implications,* (Grand Rapids, MI: Eerdmans, 1960, repr. Grand Rapids, MI: Baker Book House, 1977); Larry V. Crutchfield, *The Origins of Dispensationalism: The Darby Factor* (Lanham MD: University Press of America, 1992); C. Norman Kraus, *Dispensationalism in America: Its Rise and Development* (Richmond, VA: John Knox Press, 1958);*Three Central Issues in Contemporary Dispensationalism* Edited By: Herbert W. Bateman IV (Kregel Publications , 1999); Charles C. Ryrie, *Dispensationalism, Revised and Expanded* (Chicago, IL: Moody Publishers , 2007); Idem, *Dispensationalism Today* (Chicago: Moody Press, 1965); J.N. Darby, *Collected Writings Vol. ,* William Kelly, ed. (Believer's Bookshelf, 1971); L.S. Chafer, *Systematic Theology* (Dallas: Dallas Theological Seminary, 1944) John F. Walvoord, *The Rapture Question* (Grand Rapids, MI: Dunham Publishing Co., 1957).

2 In recent decades, so-called "Progressive Dispensationalism" has emerged out of classical dispensationalism, but this form did not exist in 1982, when Wimber began to think theologically about the Vineyard identity.

3 Quite a number of Bible Colleges and Seminaries were decidedly dispensationalist in the mid-twentieth century. See Blaising and Block, *Progressive Dispensationalism,* 11-13.

4 Blaising and Bock, *Progressive Dispensationalism,* 119.

5 Ibid., 11.

6 For a refutation of Cessationism from a Pentecostal perspective, consult Jon Ruthevan, *On the Cessation of the Charismata: The Protestant Polemic on Post-Biblical Miracles* (Tulsa, OK; Word and Spirit Press, 2003, 2011.

7 B.B. Warfield, *Counterfeit Miracles.* It could be argued that classical or progressive dispensationalism systems do not necessarily entail cessationism; that is, cessationism is not a necessary element of the system. However, when John Wimber was constructing his theology this option did not exist. In a footnote in *Power Healing,* Wimber cites the Scofield Reference Bible (C.I. Scofield's notes on Acts 2), and other Dispensationalist works that taught cessationism, so he obviously was well acquainted with the theology and popular teachings. Wimber, *Power Healing,* 271-72.

8 Wimber Sermon, "Second Coming I" , 1982, retrieved from www.yorbalindavineyard.com. Carol Wimber notes the shift in her husband's

theology away from dispensationalism in her book *John Wimber: The Way it Was*. Wimber makes a brief note about dispensationalism and cessationism in *Power Healing*, 10. In *Power Evangelism* he acknowledges that his difficulty in accepting the miraculous gifts of the Spirit were partially because of his dispensationalism. Wimber, *Power Evangelism* 18.

[9] Hal Lindsey, *The Late Great Planet Earth* (Grand Rapids, MI: Zondervan, 1970). Lindsey's tremendously popular book combined dispensationalist views on the rapture, the tribulation, and the second coming of Jesus with current geo-political events and stories from popular news sources to show that the rapture was imminent.

[10] Wimber Sermon, "Second Coming I" , Anaheim Vineyard 1982, retrieved from www.yorbalindavineyard.com. For a discussion in Ladd as to the nature of Israel, the Church, and the Kingdom see G.E. Ladd, *The Gospel of the Kingdom*, 107-122. Pentecostal theologian.

[11] G.E. Ladd, *The Gospel of the Kingdom*, 118. In another book, Ladd states that he is not considered a dispensationalist because "I do not keep Israel and the Church distinct throughout God's program". Ladd, "Historic Premillennialism" in *The Meaning of the Millennium* Ed. By Robert G. Clouse (Downers Grove, IL: Intervarsity Press, 1977) 20.

[12] Ladd, *Gospel*, 120. A more detailed examination of Wimber's adaptation of Ladd's system will be done in the final section of this chapter.

[13] This paradox weighed on Ladd heavily, as he struggled to reconcile his growing understanding of the Kingdom with his fundamentalist-dispensationalist roots.

[14] He states that he at one time had over 200 books on the subject, and in his estimation the significant number of books on the subject of the End Times, the Rapture, etc. revealed the level of fascination in popular Christian culture. Wimber, "Second Coming II" Sermon at Anaheim Vineyard, 1982, retrieved from www.yorbalindavineyard.com. Carol Wimber notes that the issue of the rapture was a significant area of tension between the Wimbers and the Calvary Chapels, who held a very strong view of the pre-tribulation rapture of the church. Carol Wimber, *TWIW*, 156. Calvary Chapels still hold strongly to this view, as evidenced by their statement of faith published at www.calvarychapel.com/about.

[15] Wimber, "Second Coming II".

[16] It is important to note that as G.E. Ladd held to what he called "historic premillennialism," in which Christ returns to earth after the tribulation. He had little trouble merging his kingdom theology with premillennialism;, it was other aspects of

dispensationalism that Ladd struggled with. The issues in conflict for Wimber therefore, were not around typical areas of contention such as the timing of the millennium, or the tribulation, but on more primary issues noted above. Wimber understood the various conflicts and inconsistencies in Ladd's approach. See Ladd, *A Commentary on the Revelation of John* (Grand Rapids, MI: Eerdmans, 1972; Idem, "Historic Premillennialism" in *The meaning of the Millennium; idem, The Blessed Hope: A Biblical Study of the Second Advent and the Rapture* (Grand Rapids, MI: Eerdmans, 1959).

[17] Numerous commentators have questioned whether "rapture theology" can be sustained from the text. Also, in recent study, the dispensationalist translation of I Thess. 4 has been widely challenged, with many commentators point out that the context of Paul's use of σὺν αὐτοῖς ἁρπαγησόμεθα may likely not best be translated as "caught up" (NASB, NIV, RSV) or "catching away". See Ladd's discussion of this in *The Blessed Hope* 78. Also helpful is Ben Witherington III, who argues that *apantesis* does not have the connotation of "catching up" at all, but rather refers to Hellenistic custom of a greeting committee which meets a visiting dignitary outside of the city, and then escorts him into the city. See *The Problem with Evangelical Theology: Testing the Exegetical Foundations of Calvinism, Dispensationalism, and Wesleyanism* (Waco TX: Baylor University Press, 2005) 113-120. So also F.F. Bruce sees *apantesis* as the process of escorting a dignitary on an official visit (*parousia*) on the last state of his journey. See F.F. Bruce, *1 & 2 Thessalonians*, Word Bible Commentary, (Dallas, TX: Word Books, 1982) 102. Following Moffatt, Morris concedes the cultural and historical use of *apantesis*, but is cautious about applying the concept to saints escorting Christ to earth. Leon Morris, *The First and Second Epistles to the Thessalonians* [NICNT] (Grand Rapids, MI: Eerdmans, 1991) 145; J. Moffatt, *The First and Second Epistles to the Thessalonians* [The Expositor's Greek Testament] (Grand Rapids, MI: reprint 1979); E. Peterson, *apantesis TDNT* 1:380-81; Gordon D. Fee, The First and Second Letters to the Thessalonians [NICNT] (Grand Rapids, MI: Eerdmans Publishing Co., 2009) 197-200. Morris [NICNT] notes, "...it is very hard to fit this passage into a secret rapture....it is difficult to understand how he (Paul) could more plainly describe something that is open and public". 145.

[18] *Power Healing*, 21.

[19] See *Power Healing* 20.

[20] See Donald Dayton, *Theological Roots of Pentecostalism* (Peabody, MA: Hendrikson Publishers, 1987) 21-28; D. William Faupel, *The Everlasting Gospel: The Significance of Eschatology in the Development of Pentecostal Thought* [Journal of Pentecostal Theology

Supplemental Series No. 10](London: Sheffield Academic Press, 1996) Ch. 2; Idem, "The Function of Models in the Interpretation of Pentecostal Thought", *Pneuma* (Spring, 1980) 51-71; Steven Jack Land, *Pentecostal Spirituality: A Passion for the Kingdom* [Journal of Pentecostal Theology Supplemental Series No. 1](London: Sheffield Academic Press, 1993) Ch. 2; Matthew K. Thompson, *Kingdom Come: Revisioning Pentecostal Eschatology* [Journal of Pentecostal Theology Supplemental Series No. 37] Ch. 1.

[21] See Larry Bertone "Seven Dispensations or Two-Age View of History: A Pauline Perspective" in *Perspectives in Pentecostal Eschatologies: World Without End* Ed. By Peter Althouse and Robby Waddell, (Eugene, OR: Pickwick Publishers, 2010) 91.

[22] This was primarily because some early Pentecostals saw tongues not merely as "spiritual" phenomena (i.e. Glossilalia) but as "natural" unlearned human languages (Xenolalia). For a discussion see Faupel, *Everlasting Gospel*, 220; Gary B. McGee, "'New World of Realities in Which We Live': How Speaking in Tongues Empowered Early Pentecostals". *Pneuma* Vol. 30 (No. 1 2008): 108-135.

[23] Faupel, "The Function of Models" 57.

[24] See Faupel's excellent discussion in *Everlasting Gospel*, 3-34.

[25] References to the "Full Gospel" are replete in early Pentecostalism; Dayton summarized much of the data by stating that there is a four-fold and five-fold form to this equation. The tenets of the five-fold form are as follows: 1. Justification by Faith, 2. Sanctification as a second work of Grace, 3. Healing of the body as guaranteed in the atonement, 4. The pre-millennial return of Christ, and 5. The Baptism of the Holy Spirit, evidenced by speaking in tongues. The four-fold form of the Full Gospel is the root of Aimee Semple McPherson's formula which became normative for many Pentecostals: Jesus is our Savior, Baptizer, Healer, and Coming King. See Dayton, 15-23; Faupel, *Everlasting Gospel,* 229-240.

[26] Steven Land, *Pentecostal Spirituality,* 51ff; William Faupel, in *Everlasting Gospel* cites numerous statements from the early Pentecostal newspaper, *The Apostolic Faith, which* recorded countless prophecies and exhortations that reflect this conviction. See chapter 6, especially pages 212ff. Of course this imminent expectation became problematic when they discovered that tongues speaking was not human language, and thus their missional "key" was thwarted, and Christ did not immediately return, as many had expected, which caused many to reframe their eschatology.

[27] During the so-called "Toronto Blessing" era of the Vineyard, Wimber and other Vineyard leaders would again utilize Edward's works such as his "Some

Thoughts Concerning the Present Revival" (1743). See *Vineyard Reflections* May/June 1994, where Wimber quotes Edwards' extensively.

[28] John Wimber "Learning from our Elders" in *Vineyard Reflections* Winter 1994, 1. Wimber continues, "Early on in the development of the Vineyard, I decided I wanted to be part of a church that embraced the best of conservative evangelical theology along with the Pentecostal experience. Thus the birth of the Vineyard".

[29] Both of these features tended to reveal the triumphalism and over-realized eschatology of the early Pentecostal movement that crystallized in most Pentecostal churches and denominations by Wimber's day. The doctrine of healing as guaranteed in the atonement especially troubled Wimber, as his experience and biblical study led him to believe that not all were healed. See *Power Healing,* 147ff when Wimber recounts an experience in 1983 where his close friend, the English Reverend David Watson, succumbed to liver cancer even after significant healing prayer by Wimber and many others. See also his discussion of "Healing in the Atonement" 152-56.

[30] Wimber, "The Five-Fold Ministry" *Vineyard Reflections* August 1997. See also Appendix A of *Power Evangelism*, which is largely adapted from the course material for MC501: Signs and Wonders and Church Growth. This material is included in the course syllabi.

[31] More will be said on this crucial distinction below in my discussion of Vineyard Pneumatology.

[32] Matthew Thompson's excellent work *Kingdom Come: Revisioning Pentecostal Eschatology* brilliantly argues this point. See also Dale M Coulter, "Pentecostal Visions of the End: Eschatology, Ecclesiology, and the Fascination of the Left Behind Series", *Journal of Pentecostal Theology* (14.1) 2005. 81-98; Faupel, "The Function of Models". In contrast to this view, some authors have argued that early Pentecostals were aware of the tensions with their burgeoning movement and dispensationalism: Larry McQueen contends that his examination of *The Apostolic Faith* reveals that "The alleged connections between classical dispensationalism and the eschatology articulated here are transformed in the light of the holistic and apocalyptic nature of early Pentecostal spirituality," "Early Pentecostal Eschatology in the Light of *The Apostolic Faith*, 1906-1908", in *Perspectives in Pentecostal Eschatologies,* 153.

Chapter 6:

[1] See note 6 below. Wimber had a very early experience with divine healing when his son Sean was instantly healed from an allergic reaction to bee stings. While his

theology had not yet made room for divine healing, Wimber instinctively prayed for his son, who was immediately healed. This episode, and Wimber's reflections on it, is recounted in chapter 1 of *Divine Healing*. Wimber's resistance to the operation of the charismata at the time was primarily due to, in his terms, a lack of reasonable and feasible healing models, rather than theological objections. See *Divine Healing*, chapter 2.

[2] A major influence on this theme was the work of James Kallas. In the MC 510 course, Wimber and Wagner included a section of Kallas' *The Significance of the Synoptic Miracles* hereafter *Significance* (Greenwich, CT: The Seabury Press, 1961) In this study citations drawn from the 2nd Ed. (Woodinville, WA: Sunrise, 2010). Other works by Kallas were included in the course bibliography, including *Jesus and the Power of Satan* (Philadelphia, PA: Westminster, 1968) hereafter *SPS*, *The Satanward View: A Study in Pauline Theology* (Philadelphia, PA: Westminster Press, 1966), and *The Real Satan* (Minneapolis, MN: Augsburg, 1975) hereafter *TRS*. Kallas is referenced numerous times in *Power Evangelism* and *Power Healing*. Dr. John White noted the influence of Kallas in MC 510 in a 1985 article, "MC 510: A Look Inside, Part I" in *First Fruits* (July 1985). Kallas' influence on Wimber is seen in multiple references in articles written for *First Fruits* and *Equipping the Saints;* for example see the January/February 1986 issue of *First Fruits* "The Kingdom of God: Establishing Christ's Rule" where Wimber cites *Jesus and the Power of Satan*.

[3] It is paramount to keep in mind that Wimber was primarily a practitioner, not a theorist, and thus his theological interests were primarily driven by practical and ecclesial concerns.

[4] Among many scholars, the following are noteworthy. First of note would be Dr. Peter Wagner, with whom Wimber taught MC 510 at Fuller, and had a lifetime friendship and collaboration. Dr. Don Williams, (Ph.D., Princeton) was a Presbyterian minister who joined Wimber in the early years of the Vineyard, and became a trusted theological source. See his *Signs, Wonders, and the Kingdom of God* (Ann Arbor, MI: Servant Books, 1989) hereafter *SWKG*. Another early confidant was Canadian psychiatrist Dr. John White, who submitted many articles to *First Fruits* and spoke at numerous Vineyard conferences. See White, *When the Spirit Comes with Power: Signs & Wonders among God's people* (Downers Grove, IL: Intervarsity Press, 1988). Dr. Peter H. Davids (New Testament, Manchester) was an early theological support for Wimber, and contributed research and articles for *First Fruits* and *Equipping the Saints*. Dr. Wayne Grudem (Ph.D., New Testament, Cambridge), Dr.

Jack Deere (Th.D., Old Testament, Dallas Theological Seminary) joined the Vineyard for a period of time and added significant support and theological legitimacy to Wimber and the Vineyard through difficult periods when Wimber's theology and practices were widely criticized by notable evangelicals. See Jackson, *Quest*, 156-168 for an overview of this period. Dr. Winn Griffin (D.Min., California Graduate School of Theology, 1984) was the editor of the Vineyard Publication *First Fruits* from 1984-87, and a research assistant to John Wimber. Numerous other academics befriended Wimber or joined the Vineyard movement; consult the relevant chapters in Jackson and in Carol Wimber, *TWIW*. Particularly notable is South African Dr. Derek Morphew (Ph.D., New Testament, University of Cape Town) who would become one of the more influential theological voices of the Vineyard over several decades.

[5] For example, in 2010, the Vineyard U.S.A. created an academic society aimed at increasing the depth of breadth of theological conservation in the movement. This society, the Society of Vineyard Scholars, held its first meeting in 2010, and has met yearly since. While based in North America, the group is a cross section of theologians, Scripture scholars, pastors, and movement leaders from Vineyards across the world.

[6] The critical point is Wimber's use of the Gospels as a model for ministry, whereas classic Pentecostals had tended to use Acts as their model for church activity. In *PH*, Wimber writes, "One of the most compelling reasons to pray for the sick is that Jesus healed many. *If He is our model of faith and practice*, we cannot ignore his healing ministry". (emphasis mine) 41. Carol Wimber recalls "John…would teach the Scriptures as if they were our instruction manuals. He talked about Word and Works, how we need to be word-workers" *TWIW*, 133. Don Williams aptly illustrates the connection between Wimber's view of the miracles as not merely authenticating the preaching of the Gospel in the ministry of Jesus and the Apostles, as traditional cessationists held, but that the miracles were an intrinsic feature of the coming of the Kingdom. If this is so, William reasons, than being "imitators of Christ" necessarily implies practicing the miraculous ministry as well. See *SWKG*, Chapter 9. This point will be elaborated in the chapter on Pneumatology.

[7] It is significant to note that Wimber held to a form of Spirit Christology that held that the miracles and acts of power performed by Jesus were empowered by the Spirit (a non-controversial point) but were to be understood, emulated, and repeated by the Church. That is to say, for Wimber, the miracles were not merely "proofs" of

Jesus' divinity, but more so, teachings in themselves, showing the disciples (and thus the primitive church, and the historical church) *how to* do the *works* of the kingdom of God.

[8] Examples of this pattern are numerous, Wimber often cited Matthew 4:23-25: "Jesus went throughout Galilee, teaching in their synagogues, preaching the good news of the Kingdom, and healing every disease and sickness among the people". Also Matthew 3:14-15, 10:7-8, 11:5; Luke 4:32-36, 5:40-42, 9:1-12; Mark 1:21-27, 2:1-13; Wimber saw the pattern repeated in the ministry of the Apostles in Acts, as evidenced by Peter's healing of the beggar at the Temple gate and subsequent sermon in chapter 3.

[9] Wimber clearly built much of his model for ministry on this insight, which has become enshrined in Vineyard vocabulary as "doing the word and the works". Carol Wimber relates the day that John connected this to his present day ministry in *TWIW*, 133-34: "It finally hit him. He read the story, the WORD, from the Scriptures, and THEN God did the WORKS!. 'Do you see it Carol? We teach the Word, then God does the work. Like TELL and SHOW or SHOW and TELL! I think I get it!'"

[10] *TWIWO*, 203-04. See also Don Williams, *SWKG* 127-28, "Jesus intends to reproduce himself in His disciples. He teaches them in order that they may become extensions of Himself". Williams also connects Paul's training as a Pharisee to his exhortations to believer's to "be Imitators of me, as I am an imitator of Christ" (I Corinthians 11). Williams cites Martin Hengel's *The Charismatic leader and His Followers* for support, but clearly much of modern New Testament research would support this conclusion. See F.F. Bruce's helpful discussion of Paul's training as a Pharisee in *Paul: Apostle of the Heart Set Free* (Grand Rapids, MI: Eerdmans, 1977), 44ff.

[11] One of Wimber's copies of Ladd's *Jesus and the Kingdom* is so marked, highlighted and cross-referenced that it is barely readable.

[12] Ladd, *ATNT* 45. Wimber quoted this passage verbatim in the MC 510 text and in *PE* 28.

[13] Wimber, *PE,* 30-31.

[14] Ibid., 31. Also Wimber audio teaching *KoG; Warfare.*

[15] *ATNT,* 48.

[16] This insight will be developed more completely in the chapter on the work of the Spirit.

[17] See *KoG III.*

[18] The significance of this insight for Wimber cannot be overemphasized, as for him, it solved numerous theological and practical puzzles. This mystery of the Kingdom helped to explain both the success and failures of his burgeoning power ministries of healing and deliverance from evil Spirits.

[19] Wimber, *PE*, 31-32; *KoG II*.

[20] See Morphew, *Breakthrough*, "Israel".

[21] The "ethical" or relational duties of the Kingdom were a strong concern for Wimber, nearly as much as his emphasis on healing and the supernatural. It is not that the so-called "supernatural" work supplanted the more pedestrian "ethics of the Kingdom"; rather the two both evidenced the rule of God in the lives of men.

[22] Recall Bultmann's famous quote "it is impossible to use electric light and the wireless and to avail ourselves of modern medical and surgical discoveries, and at the same time to believe in the New Testament world of demons and spirits" "The New Testament and Mythology" 5.

[23] Wimber writes of his early encounters with deliverance and demonic influence in *First Fruits*, November, 1984 and speaks of this in his teaching *KoG III*, where he notes his experience drove him to the scriptures and trusted theological sources to understand what his church was experiencing.

[24] See the footnote regarding the influence of Kallas. In the endnotes of chapter 3 in *PE* Wimber noted "much of this chapter is based on material gleaned from the writings of George Eldon Ladd and James Kallas". 40.

[25] Kallas takes the anti-supernatural worldview of Alan Richardson, Bultmann and Rudolph Otto to task throughout *The Significance of the Synoptic Miracles*. Kallas' thesis in this work is that the supernatural (especially the miracles) events recorded in the Gospels are intrinsic to understanding the ministry and person of Jesus and thus must be considered as "vitally important" historical events. Contra Bultmann and others in the demythologizing school, the supernatural is essential to the Gospel-hence we must "take the worldview of Jesus seriously" in order to understand his message. Kallas conceives of this project as "a strong protest against demythologizing" (149) and his entire concluding chapter is a polemic against

Bultmann's position, concluding with this assertion: "The Conquering Christ of the Gospels...is lost on Bultmann's sacrificial alter of adaptation" (150-51).

[26] Kallas, *TRS*, 31 ff.

[27] Ibid., 40ff.

[28] For an excellent exposition of demonology and exorcism in the New Testament period, as well as a helpful survey of the current literature on New Testament demonology, consult Graham H. Twelftree, *In the Name of Jesus: Exorcism among Early Christians* (Grand Rapids, MI: Baker, 2007). Slightly older but still helpful is Walter Wink's 3 volume study: *Naming the Powers: The Language of Power in the New Testament* The Powers vol. 1 (Philadelphia, PA: Fortress Press, 1984), *Unmasking the Powers: The Invisible Forces that Determine Human Existence* The Powers vol. 2 (Philadelphia, PA: Fortress Press, 1986), *Engaging the Powers: Discernment and Resistance in a World of Domination* The Powers vol. 3 (Philadelphia, PA: Fortress Press, 1992). Wimber notes *Naming the Powers* in the bibliography of *PH*.

[29] Kallas, *TRS*, 73. This theme shows up repeatedly and consistently in Wimber's writings.

[30] Other translations read "violent people have been raiding it" (NIV), or "violent take it by force", (NKJV).

[31] Wimber, audio teaching, *Warfare*.

[32] Kallas, *TRS*, 84-5. Wimber almost adopts Kallas phrasing verbatim in the *Warfare* audio.

[33] Kallas, *Significance*, 101-02. This section was included in the course readings for MC 510, and was highly impactful for Wimber. The section included in MC 510 was from the first printing. In a personal conversation with Bob Fulton, Wimber's brother-in-law, Mr. Fulton informed me that the influence of Kallas on Wimber has been underappreciated in the history of the Vineyard.

[34] Kallas, *TRS*, 91.

[35] Ibid., 91.

[36] Ibid., 93. Kallas states that Jesus retreats to Caesarea Philippi to "think through the issues anew". Kallas continues: "At Caesarea Philippi Jesus comes to recognize that efforts of the disciples will be sufficient (insufficient?) to topple the Satanic empire. No broadside attempts by them will cause Satan to crumble. He, Jesus, is the one who must do it! He is the one who must grapple with the most powerful weapon of Satan—death". Opt cited.

Wimber would have no doubt been uncomfortable with this low Christology in this early work of Kallas. Kallas echoes Schweitzer here, who wrote in *Quest* that

Jesus "does not expect to see them back in the present age", 358. Kallas does part with Schweitzer however, in that the latter sees this mission as one crucial mistaken belief of several that Jesus held; "There followed neither the sufferings, the outpouring of the Spirit, nor the Parousia of the Son of Man," 364.

[37] Luke's account of the return of the seventy unequivocally states "the seventy returned with joy, saying 'even the demons are subject to us in your name". (10:17)

[38] The significance of this cannot be understated for Wimber as he wrote and taught about it relentlessly. This concept of modeling or training formed the basis for his entire program of "Equipping the Saints". For example, Wimber uses Matthew 10 as his practical teaching model for the Vineyard in "Sent into the Harvest Field" *Equipping the Saints* Vol. 1, Number 5 (October 1987).

[39] Wimber spoke of his experience as a "WWII kid" giving him an understanding of skirmishes, battles, and campaigns- thus too, in the "battle" with Satan, there were greater and smaller conflicts in order and magnitude. See *KoG II.*

[40] Kallas, *Significance*, 112. Kallas seems to have a more positive view of these issues in *Significance*, reflecting his more mature understanding of Jesus' preaching on the kingdom of God.

[41] Wimber recounts the influence of Charles Kraft in *PH* 30. Kraft never joined Wimber's Fledgling movement, but served as a reliable source for Wimber for many years. See Kraft's contributions to *First Fruits* "Why the Vineyard Should move into Cross-Cultural Ministry", Nov/Dev 1985; *Equipping the Saints* "Shifting Worldviews, Shifting Attitudes", Vol. 1 No. 5 (1987); "Communicating and Ministering the Power of the Gospel Cross-Culturally: The Power of Gog for Christians who Ride Two Horses" in *The Kingdom and the Power* Ed. by Gary S. Grieg and Kevin Springer (Ventura, CA; Regal Books, 1993) 345-56. Wimber was especially influenced by Kraft's *Christianity and Culture: A Study in Dynamic Biblical Theologizing in Cross-Cultural Perspective* (Maryknoll, NY: Orbis Books, 1979), and *Christianity with Power* (Ann Arbor, MI: Vine Books, 1989). Both were referenced heavily in *Power Evangelism* Ch. 18, 21, 22. As noted above, Dr. C. Peter Wagner was also a tremendous influence in this time, primarily on Wimber's developing pneumatology. More will be said on this in following chapters.

[42] References to Jeremias are replete in Wimber's writings, See PP, 71. He frequently used Cullmann's "D-Day" analogy from *Christ and Time* (as an example see *PE* 55). For Wimber's use of Ridderbos, consult *PE,* 156.

Chapter 7

[1] Dr. Morphew is now the academic director of Vineyard Institute, an international educational organization designed to teach and develop leaders across the Vineyard worldwide. See www.vineyardinstitute.org.

---

[2] Fulton had started the Vineyard Bible Institute out of the Anaheim Vineyard in 1988, with a focus on providing Biblical teaching in a distance education format.

[3] Vineyard International Publishing, Cape Town, 1991. *Breakthrough* has sold over 6,500 copies of the monograph, another 1,900 through the study of the same name in the Vineyard Bible Institute program, and hundreds of DVD teaching sets of the same material. Considering the small number of Vineyard churches and members, they are influential numbers.

[4] See Morphew, *The Spiritual Spider We: A Study in Ancient and Contemporary Gnosticism* Available in electronic Kindle format from www.amazon.com.

[5] Ladd wrote in *TPOF*, "Although God is now the King, other references speak of the day when God shall become King, and shall rule over his people". 46.

[6] *Breakthrough*, 13.

[7] *Breakthrough*, 18.

[8] While the prophetic promise of the Kingdom and the "Day of the Lord" spoken of by the prophets is often discussed in twentieth century eschatology, the model of kingdoms in conflict in the Exodus narrative as Morphew conceives it had received little mention. Ladd considers the Sinai narrative as the beginning of the "kingdom" story. *TPOF*, 48. Kallas has little to say about the kingdoms in conflict in the Old Testament, as his focus is primarily the message of Jesus. However, it is clear that like Wimber and Kallas, Morphew sees much of the biblical narrative in terms of the "conflict" or warfare narrative.

[9] Ibid., 34.

[10] Ibid., 13, 57-65.

[11] Morphew also includes the parable of the nobleman in Luke 19:11-27 to belong to this set.

[12] Ibid., 64. While Jeremias' "sich realiserende Eschatologie" (eschatology in the process of realization) comes close to displaying this concept, and Jeremias certainly understood these parables as teaching a delay of the parousia (see the discussion on Jeremias above) he still struggled with the concept. See Jeremias, *Parables*, 49-51. However, Morphew makes it clear that Jeremias' understanding is preferable to Dodd or Schweitzer; who, in the case of Dodd virtually ignored the concept of delay, or in the case of Schweitzer, conflated delay with entirely future and apocalyptic.

While Ladd did not explicitly make use of "delay" language, he did think that these parables reinforced the message that the Gospels leave the reader "anticipating an imminent event and yet unable to date its coming". *TPOF*, 328. Ladd placed the emphasis here on the duties of the servants and the ethical demands of the Kingdom, and less on the "delay" of the master's coming.

[13] Morphew argues that "The fact is that none of these removals have any textual basis in the ancient manuscripts," although he does not go into detail in defending this statement. 64

[14] Ibid., 63. Thus, the growth parables would teach that the essential nature of the Kingdom is present even in the liminal form; in the tiny mustard seed, for example, as the seed takes hold and grows, the true nature of the organism becomes visible in more detail, but the essence was there in the seed.

[15] Ibid., 65. Morphew cites Cullmann's D-Day analogy for a word picture of the mystery. At the same time, Morphew would argue (with Ladd and Wimber) against the *konsequente* school that the Kingdom is established by *both* the work of men and God; that is to say, there *are actions* that men can accomplish that will further the Kingdom- it is not just a work of God, and God only, as Schweitzer seems to suggest.

[16] Ibid., 157.

[17] Ibid., 169 ff.

[18] Morphew finds the most congruence, as to be expected, with Evangelical authors such as Ben Witherington. However, he also highlights scholars like N.T. Wright, James Dunn, John Meier, and Graham Twelftree. 241ff.

[19] Morphew's book *Different but Equal? Going Beyond the Complementarian/Egalitarian Debate* (Cape Town: South Africa, Vineyard International Publishing, 2009) attempts to address the issue of gender role in church leadership by constructing a "Creation based inaugurated equality". This is one the first major attempts by a Vineyard scholar to resolve a theological problem via the inaugurated, enacted, eschatological framework. Morphew contends that as "the future kingdom transforms this-age gender relationships" we can accept the social context of the biblical passages that display (and even teach) patriarchy while at the same time, recognizing that they are not normative for today. However, in the eschaton, since male and female relationships will be transformed, and since according to inaugurated eschatology the "presence of the future," is breaking into this age, we should then look to the *future* to establish our norms, rather than giving the past pride of place. Morphew took a similar, though less fully developed approach in his work on a Christian response to Apartheid, *South Africa and the Powers Behind* available as an E-book.

Chapter 8

[1] For example, while Pentecostal denominations like the Assemblies of God were founding members of the National Association of Evangelicals in 1942, this inclusion was widely contested by many evangelicals. Pentecostals were viewed with a great deal of suspicion due to their charismatic practices by large numbers of Protestants until the Charismatic movement among traditional or "mainline" emerged in the 1960s.

[2] This was the standard dispensationalist position as stated by B.B. Warfield in his *Counterfeit Miracles* and C.I. Scofield in *The Scofield Reference Bible*. For the purposes of this study, *cessationism* will refer to those who believe that the "Charismatic" or miraculous gifts ceased with the death of the Apostles or early church. "Continuationism" will be used as contra cessationism in reference to the operation of the *charismata*; although "continuationist" is a more contemporary reference and not specifically employed by Dunn or Lloyd-Jones for example.

[3] I have been unable to find an evangelical representative of the Pentecostal second blessing doctrine, although some may well have existed. As we shall see, even ardent supporters of the continuing operation of the *Charismata* like Dr. D. Martyn Lloyd-Jones heavily modified the second blessing doctrine.

[4] Billy Graham, *The Holy Spirit* in *The Collected Works of Billy Graham* (New York: Inspirational Press, 1993)367-68. *The Holy Spirit* was originally published in 1978. All following quotations will be from this volume.

[5] Richard B. Gaffin, *Perspectives on Pentecost: Studies in New Testament Teaching on the Gifts of the Holy Spirit* (Phillipsburg, NJ: Presbyterian and Reformed Publishing Company, 1979)22.

[6] Gaffin, *Pentecost*, 22ff.

[7] B.B. Warfield, *Counterfeit Miracles* (New York: Charles Scribner and Sons, 1918, 1972) 23 hereafter *CM*. Warfield held that in the post-Apostolic age, the reported occurrence of miracles went from virtually non-existent to quite ubiquitous by the eighth and ninth centuries. (10) For Warfield, this increase in abundance in the apocryphal works were proof of their inauthenticity and the misuse of the miraculous to authenticate the Papal structure of the apostate Catholic Church; he calls these Apocryphal writings the ancient equivalent of Swift's *Gulliver's Travels*. Since the popularization of Warfield's work, and the subsequent adoption of the Scofield Reference Bible in Evangelicalism, the growth of cessationist literature was immense preceding Gaffin's work. Gaffin restates this argumentation in his selections in *Are the Miraculous Gifts for Today? Four Views* ed. by Wayne Grudem (Grand Rapids, MI:

Zondervan, 1996) especially his essay "A Cessationist View" where he restates this claim that the experience of Pentecost belongs to the *historia salutis* and thus is non-repeatable, 31. Perhaps the best review of this doctrine from a Pentecostal perspective is Jon Ruthven's *On the Cessation of the Charismata: The Protestant Polemic on Post-Biblical Miracles* (Tulsa, OK; Word and Spirit Press, 1993).

[8] Ruthven also collated an exhaustive list of cessationist monographs and articles which is extremely helpful for students of this doctrine. See for example *Cessation* 5n14 where he notes that the vast majority of Reformed Systematic theologies by Berkhof, Buswell, Chafer, Carl Henry, Hodge and Strong all support Warfield's position. Similarly helpful is Jack Deere's *Surprised by the Power of the Spirit* (Grand Rapids, MI: Zondervan, 1993) in which Deere traces his journey from a cessationist Dallas Theological Seminary professor to a staff position on John Wimber's Anaheim Vineyard.

[9] See Warfield, "Miracle" in *Dictionary of the Bible* Ed. J.D. Davis (Old Tappan, NJ: Revell, 1955, 1972) 482. This claim is repeated in Gaffin's rejoinder to Robert Saucy in Grudem's *Miraculous Gifts* where he softens Warfield's claim, and yet still contends that miraculous phenomenon accompanies "epochal" revelation and "revelation clusters about and is copiously given in connection with the climatic and decisive events of redemptive history" 150. John MacArthur argues this as well in *Charismatic Chaos* (Grand Rapids, MI: Zondervan, 1992) 112-14.

[10] Gaffin, *Pentecost,* 113. Graham attempts a similar distinction between "sign gifts" and "ordinary gifts. *The Holy Spirit,* 472ff.

[11] Graham, *The Holy Spirit,* 337. This is likely stemming from Graham's Dispensationalist reading of II Thess. 2:7 which speaks of the Holy Spirit restraining the power of evil.

[12] Ibid., 451.

[13] Ibid., 452-53.

[14] John R.W. Stott, *Baptism and Fullness: The Work of the Holy Spirit Today* (Downers Grove, IL: Intervarsity Press, 1964, 1978) 43. See Gaffin, "A Cessationist View" in Grudem's *Miraculous Gifts*, 31.

[15] Stott, *Baptism* , 98-99.

[16] Ibid., 118. Stott does allow for some occurrences of divine healing, but is skeptical of popular "healing ministries" that, unfortunately, so often dominated the discussion.

[17] Stott forcibly argued for a more experiential faith that evidenced the "fullness" of the Holy Spirit in the life of a Christian, even as he contended against the

Pentecostal "second blessing" doctrine. Graham as well pushed the point that "The Spirit-filled life is not abnormal; it is the normal Christian life. Therefore, to be filled with the Spirit…is intended for all, needed by all, and available to all," 416.

[18] Galatians 5:22-23. Graham dedicates 36 pages to his discussion of the fruit of the Spirit. *The Holy Spirit* 495-531.

[19] Romans 8:15-16, 26ff.

[20] John 16.

[21] Graham states, "The Spirit therefore witnesses in our hearts, convincing us of the truth of God's presence and assurance" 384. The eschatological presence of the Spirit as the "down payment" or "seal" of the Christian is found in Ephesians 1:14, 2 Cor. 1:21, 2 Cor. 5:5.

[22] As previously noted, many of the systematic theologies available to Evangelicals in the 1970s were written from a Dispensationalist or Reformed cessationist perspective. Even among non-dispensationalists, Pneumatology was an afterthought. In Millard Erickson's Systematic Theology (1983) scarce pages are devoted to the work of the Spirit. This text was in wide use at Fuller Seminary in the 1980s during and after Wimber taught the MC 510 course with Dr. Peter Wagner. Erickson's 3 volume collection of essays, *Readings in Christian Theology* (Grand Rapids, MI: Baker Books, 1973) have not a single essay dedicated to the work of the Spirit in over 1400 pages of text. Augustus Strong's *Systematic Theology* devotes two pages to the work of the Spirit as distinguished from the work of Christ. (Old Tappan, NJ: Revell, 1960, 21st printing). This lack of focus is acknowledged by many contributors to the collection of essays in *Who's Afraid of the Holy Spirit: An Investigation into the Ministry and Spirit of God Today* ed. By Daniel B. Wallace and M. James Sawyer (Dallas, TX: Biblical Studies Press, 2005), but especially in Dan Wallace's essay "The Uneasy Conscience of a Non-Charismatic Evangelical" where he admits the possibility of "bibliolatry" in his tradition (dispensationalism) that places cognitive knowledge of the Scriptures over and against experiential knowledge of the Spirit. In 1993 the President of Dallas Theological Seminary, Chuck Swindoll, created a minor stir in Evangelicalism by publishing his *Flying Closer to the Flame: A Passion for the Holy Spirit* (Dallas, TX: Word Books, 1993) that admitted his personal lack of appreciation for the Spirit's work, and encouraged Christians of all persuasions to more actively seek the influence of the Spirit in their lives. While Swindoll remained a cessationist, he strongly sought to make more space for cessationists to experience the Holy Spirit in other ways.

[23] Dunn, *Baptism*, 225.

[24] Ibid., 225-26. Dunn continued to follow through on these insights in later works that gave even greater emphasis on the role of the Spirit in the life of the believer. While not minimizing the differences between classic Pentecostalism and Dunn's account, Frank Macchia credits *Baptism in the Holy Spirit* for being "more Pentecostal" than Dunn even realized. See Macchia, "Salvation and Spirit Baptism: Another Look at James Dunn's Classic" *PNEUMA* Vol. 24, No.1 (Spring, 2002) 2.

[25] These claims are much in evident in Dunn's monumental *Jesus and the Spirit: A Study of the Religious and Charismatic Experiences of Jesus and the First Christians as Reflected in the New Testament* (Philadelphia: Westminster Press, 1975), a work that was highly influential for John Wimber; and in the collection of essays in volume II of *The Christ and the Spirit.*

[26] D. Martyn Lloyd-Jones, *Joy Unspeakable* (Wheaton, IL: Harold Shaw Publishers, 1984) 33. Subsequent citations will be from the combined volume *The Baptism and Gifts of the Spirit* Ed. by Christopher Catherwood (Grand Rapids, MI: Baker Books, 1996) which combines *Joy Unspeakable* and *The Sovereign Spirit*. The earlier works were collected sermons by Lloyd-Jones on topics related to the Holy Spirit and preached between 1964 and 1965. While Wimber was certainly familiar with *Joy Unspeakable*, as he cites is several times in *Power Healing*, I have been unable to ascertain whether he was familiar with Lloyd-Jones preaching before the 1984 publication of the book.

[27] Lloyd-Jones, *Baptism and Gifts*, 144-45.

[28] Ibid., 152. It is quite striking that this sermon from 1965 foreshadows Wimber's later emphasis on power evangelism.

[29] Ibid., 180. While Lloyd-Jones certainly made room for the experience of divine healing, he did not offer a "model" of how this should be done.

[30] In an extremely well-researched and enlightening two-volume biography of Lloyd-Jones, *David Martyn Lloyd-Jones: The Fight of Faith 1939-1981* (Edinburgh: Banner of Truth Trust, 1990), Iain Murray questions to what degree Lloyd-Jones actually taught or empowered his congregation to practice the gifts.

[31] While precise classifications are elusive, the present study is primarily concerned with those Evangelical leaders that were formative to Wimber's pneumatalogical development. At best, one could cautiously state that those evangelicals who enjoyed and pursued the *charismata* were likely *charismatics*.

[32] William Faupel has an excellent discussion of Perfectionist-Holiness roots of Pentecostalism in his *Everlasting Gospel* 60 ff. Other notable studies include Vinson Synan, *The Holiness-Pentecostal Movement in the United States* and Robert Mapes Anderson, *Vision of the Disinherited.*

---

[33] Faupel speaks of a "paradigm shift" which took place in the mid-nineteenth century regarding this change of language. Palmer herself is a superb example of the change to the "baptism of the Holy Spirit" phraseology. See Faupel, 80ff. Dayton notes "The Turn to Pentecostal Rhetoric" in his *Theological Roots* 71-80. According to Dayton, a significant move in this transition in language was the publication of Asa Mahan's *The Baptism of the Holy Ghost* in 1870. Marsden also makes note of this change in *Fundamentalism and American Culture* 74-75.

[34] Dayton's excellent discussion in *Theological Roots* provides a stellar overview of the various positions: sometimes overlapping, sometimes self-contradictory, often not consistent with Wesley's own accounts. Dayton overviews many of these

competing positions in chapter III, "The American Revival of Christian Perfection" in *Theological Roots* 63-80. Dayton also illustrates the shift in emphasis from "holiness" to "power" language in the conception of Spirit baptism, 93ff.

[35] Numerous accounts of tongue-speaking exist in revivalism and the holiness tradition, for example see the discussion in McGee, *Initial Evidence: Historical and Biblical Perspectives on the Pentecostal Doctrine of Spirit Baptism* (Peabody, MA: Hendrickson, 1991) 35-38; Paul G. Chappell, "Tongues as the Initial Evidence of Baptism in the Holy Spirit: A Pentecostal Perspective", *Criswell Theological Review* 4/1, (Fall 2006) 41-54.

[36] For the purposes of this paper, I shall refer to this classical Pentecostal conception of an "end times restoration of the gifts" as a restorationist pneumatology. The Pentecostal "latter days" eschatology was discussed in chapter 2. The later day restorationist theme was so dominant in early Pentecostalism that both a major publication from the earliest days of the movement The Latter Day Evangel, and a work contemporaneous to John Wimber, Vinson Synan's In the Latter Days: The Outpouring of the Holy Spirit in the Twentieth Century (Ann Arbor, MI: Servant Books, 1984) both use the Latter Days meme. Countless examples of the terminology could be cited.

[37] This idea came from Paul's admonition in I Corinthians that the gifts were a sign to unbelievers; Pentecostals connected their experience with the first Pentecost that spoke of judgment as well, as in Acts 2:40. Similarly, Pentecostals saw in the "coming judgment" themes in the preaching of John the Baptist a parallel with their own experience.

[38] The holiness four-fold pattern was salvation, healing, holiness, and the second coming of Christ. The four fold pattern in Pentecostalism would later be made famous in Sister Aimee Semple McPherson's phraseology, "Jesus is our Savior,

Baptizer, Healer, and soon coming King". The five-fold pattern of the holiness-influenced Pentecostals added Jesus as 'Sanctifier" to the four. See Allan Anderson, "Pentecostal Approaches to Faith and Healing" *International Review of Mission* Vol. XCI No. 363, 523-534. In the following years of Pentecostal history, numerous "four-fold" and "five-fold" patterns emerged. At his Bethel Bible Church in Topeka, Charles Parham instituted a five-fold gospel of new birth, second blessing sanctification, the baptism of the Holy Spirit evidenced by tongues, divine healing guaranteed in the atonement, and the rapture of the church.

[39] See Macchia, *Baptized in the Spirit: A Global Pentecostal Theology* (Grand Rapids, MI: Zondervan, 2006) 20. See Macchia's discussion on the centrality of Spirit baptism in classical Pentecostalism, and the waning of this influence among Pentecostal scholars in the last decades. Despite this declining lack of influence in the academy, Macchia contends that among Pentecostal pastors and laity the doctrine still holds a central place. pp 20-60.

[40] Philadelphia, The Westminster Press, 1970.

[41] Dunn, *Baptism,* 4.

[42] Dunn, *Baptism,* 5, 225.

[43] Dunn hints at this in his conclusion of *Baptism,* but develops this theme in his later writings. Numerous essays in his collection of writings on Pneumatology, *The Christ and the Spirit: Vol. 2 Pneumatology* (Grand Rapids, MI: Eerdmans, 1998) provide examples, but a notable point is made at the conclusion of his essay "Rediscovering the Spirit 2 (1992)" where he writes positively of the Pentecostal experience, and rhetorically asks "Indeed one many even dare to hope that some synthesis of Pentecostal experience with the older traditions will result in a new Christian presence which is both truer to the over-all balance of the New Testament and more suitable and adaptable to our fast changing world" P 90.

[44] Howard M. Ervin, *Conversion-Initiation,* 12.

[45] Ervin repeats this claim throughout, but most forcibly in his conclusion, 161-63.

[46] As Paul both *baptizes* them in water, and then lays hands on them for the reception of the Spirit, Dunn contends that the exact point that Luke makes is that Paul *did not consider them to be true Christians.* "The twelve Ephesians are therefore further examples of men who were not far short of Christianity, but were not yet Christians because they lacked the vital factor- the Holy Spirit". Dunn, *Baptism,* 88-89.

[47] Ervin, *Conversion-Initiation,* 55.

[48] Frank Macchia has made a more forceful recognition of the seriousness of this issue. He chides Pentecostals that they "need to face the elitism and exegetical problems implied in saying that large segments of the church have not received the Spirit as have the churches depicted in the Book of Acts". Macchia also concedes that the conversion-initiation is a "difficult issue" with numerous ambiguities, and thus is not easily resolved by either Dunn's or classical Pentecostal approaches. Macchia, "Salvation and Spirit Baptism" 4-5.

[49] Ervin, *Conversion-Initiation*, 70.

[50] New York: University Press of America, 1983.

[51] Hunter, *Spirit-Baptism*, 4.

[52] Ibid., 253ff.

[53] Ibid., 275. Hunter does urge caution in attempting to define an exact linear delineation of the process of salvation, as it is "often difficult to distinguish clearly 'parts' of the salvation experience".

[54] Ibid., 284.

[55] Ibid., 286-87. It is interesting that Hunter does not attempt to evade this charge, rather he accepts the situation as it is, and merely notes that if one accepts the biblical witness as it is, this is the conclusion one must come to. At the same time, he allows no room for spiritual pride on the part of the Pentecostal as the second blessing is as much a work of grace as is justification and regeneration.

[56] This thought also explains the Pentecostal hope that *xenolalia* or the sudden, functional speaking of an existing, but unknown human tongue would be the key to successful world missions and the great end-time harvest. See Mark Cartledge, "The Symbolism of Charismatic Glossolalia", *Journal of Empirical Theology* 12, 1(1991); Idem, *Speaking in Tongues: Multi-Disciplinary Perspectives* (London: Paternoster Press, 2006). This insight is also carried into modern Pentecostals by teachers like Roger Stronstad.

[57] While the other operative gifts such as prophecy, healing, working miracles, etc. were eagerly sought by Pentecostals, none of these garnered the epistemic status of immediate experience of the Spirit the way tongues did.

[58] Charles Parham, *A Voice Crying in the Wilderness* (Baxter Springs, KS: Robert L. Parham, 1944) 35. Quoted in Chappell, "Tongues as the Initial Evidence" 47.

[59] J. Roswell Flower, "Birth of the Pentecostal Movement," *Pentecostal Evangel* (November 26,1950): 3. Flower was an early leader of the Assemblies of God. Quoted in Chappell, "Tongues as the Initial Evidence" 47. Chappell notes that while not all strains of Pentecostalism adopted this distinction, it would become normative in most North American Pentecostal movements. A survey of the "Statements of

Fundamental Truths" of the Assemblies of God states "WE BELIEVE... The Initial Physical Evidence of the Baptism in the Holy Spirit is 'Speaking in Tongues,' as experienced on the Day of Pentecost and referenced throughout Acts and the Epistles". Retrieved from http://ag.org/top/Beliefs/Statement_of_fundamental_truths.

[60] Ervin, *Conversion-Initiation*, 72.

[61] Macchia, "Sighs Too Deep for Words: Towards a Theology of Glossolalia," *Journal of Pentecostal Theology* 1 (1992), 54. See also Simon Chan, "Evidential Glossolalia and the Doctrine of Subsequence", *Asian Journal of Pentecostal Studies* 2/2 (1999), 195-211. For the role of Parham and Seymour in the development of the doctrine, two essays in Gary B. McGee's *Initial Evidence* are informative: James Goff Jr's article "Initial Evidence in the Theology of Charles Fox Parham" and Cecil M. Robeck Jr.'s essay "William J. Seymour and 'The Bible Evidence'. Robeck notes that Seymour was especially influenced by the "long ending" of Mark, that explicitly states that the gospel message will be authenticated by "signs following". After the contentious separation of Parham and Seymour, Parham held to the initial evidence doctrine, and Seymour moved to a less doctrinaire position. Robeck posits that Seymour's position is more in common with the late twentieth century Charismatic position that with the classical Pentecostal view.

[62] Macchia, "Sighs Too Deep for Words", 55. Macchia constructs a rich understanding of Spirit Baptism and maintains an emphasis on tongues, but in an expanded context. He asserts that "Spirit baptism is not just about tongues. We cannot lock Spirit baptism into a glossolalic strait-jacket so that the former becomes inconceivable apart from the latter". Macchia's proposal came long after Wimber's time, and thus wasn't an alternative available to Wimber in his day.

[63] See Vinson Synan, "A Healer in the House? A Historical Perspective on Healing in the Pentecostal/Charismatic Tradition", *Asian Journal of Pentecostal Studies* 3/2, (2000), 191ff for a view on the significance of Cullis in the development of the doctrine and practice.

[64] The literature on healing in the Holiness tradition is immense; excellent overviews of the importation of the doctrine to Pentecostalism can be found in Faupel, *Everlasting Gospel*, chapter 5; Dayton, *Theological Roots* 122ff; Allan Anderson, "Pentecostal Approaches to Faith and Healing" *International Review of Mission* Vol. XCI No. 363 (2002); Synan, "A Healer in the House?, 189-201; Jonathan R. Baer, "Redeemed Bodies: The Functions of Divine Healing in Incipient Pentecostalism" *Church History* 70:4 (Dec 2001) 735-71; Paul Chappell, "Healing Movements" in

Dictionary of Pentecostal and Charismatic Movements ed. By Stanley Burgess, Gary McGee, Patrick Alexander (Grand Rapids, MI: Zondervan, 1988) 353-74; Steve Land, *Pentecostal Spirituality*, 18-19.

[65] This claim was notably made in Gordon's *The Ministry of Healing*.

[66] Synan notes that Parham visited Zion City, one of the healing homes established by Alexander Dowie near Chicago, and was thus led to establish a similar ministry in Topeka. Synan, "A Healer in the House?" 195. For more on Dowie's influence consult Faupel, *Everlasting Gospel*, 116-35; Baer, "Redeemed Bodies", 748ff.

[67] William J. Seymour, "Questions and Answers", *Apostolic Faith* January 1908. Quoted in Synan, "A Healer in the House?" 196.

[68] See for example the Fundamental Truths, and cardinal doctrines, of the Assemblies of God: "WE BELIEVE...Divine Healing of the Sick is a Privilege for Christians Today and is provided for in Christ's atonement (His sacrificial death on the cross for our sins). (1 of 4 cardinal doctrines of the AG). The Church of God in Cleveland, TN's "Declaration of Faith" states "We Believe... Divine healing is provided for all in the atonement". Anderson notes that some recent Pentecostals like Keith Warrington have softened the claim somewhat. Anderson, "Pentecostal Approaches", 530.

[69] The Charismatic renewal, or "second wave of the Holy Spirit" is widely understood to have began on April 3rd, 1960. The Reverend Dennis Bennett, of St. Mark's Episcopal Church in Van Nuys, California, confessed to his congregation that he had recently been baptized in the Holy Spirit, and spoken in tongues. He then invited all who desired this charismatic gift to come forward for prayer, with many responding. Unlike the Pentecostals of an earlier generation, those experiencing this renewal did not desire to form new churches or denominations, but rather, they sought to remain in their churches and parishes, continue in the beliefs and practices of their church families, but with the addition of a dynamic, continual charismatic experience of the Holy Spirit. The diverse expression was soon labeled the "charismatic movement" which spread into historical mainline denominations (such as Lutheran, Episcopal, Methodist, etc.) and Evangelical congregations. John Wimber would form many close friendships with leaders or the Charismatic movement.

Chapter 9

[1] Wimber speaks of this in his teaching "Born Again and Baptized in the Holy Spirit", available at Wimber.org.

[2] Ibid.

[3] Wimber, *The Holy Spirit and the Church* (1977) available from Vineyard Resources.

[4] Wimber certainly held an orthodox Trinitarian theology, and certainly understood the issues related to the hypostatic union of the divine persons. His primary interest was practical of course (the *ministry* of the Christ) and how he (Wimber) could "replicate" this ministry, more so than carefully explicating *theological* concerns in Trinitarian terms. Wimber seemed to be quite comfortable with a Spirit Christology, even if he did not recognize it as such. A helpful presentation of Spirit Christology is Ralph Del Colle, *Christ and the Spirit: Spirit-Christology in Trinitarian Perspective,* (Oxford: Oxford University Press, 1994). A full examination of Wimber's Christology would be fruitful, but beyond the scope of this project.

[5] Wimber, *The Holy Spirit's Work in Believer's* (1986) available from Wimber.org.

[6] Wimber, *PP,* 136.

[7] Ibid., 136.

[8] That is, in Wimber's view, there was no explicit profession of faith before the Holy Spirit fell. Wimber, *Baptism in the Holy Spirit* (1991), from Wimber.org. This realization was significant for Wimber as in his ministry, he had seen this phenomenon countless times- in the Calvary Chapel and Vineyard churches, and in many worldwide conferences and ministry experiences, they had situations where individuals were overcome with the power of the Spirit, and later, made professions of faith and were baptized. Seeing this occurrence in Acts was more evidence for Wimber that there indeed, was no scriptural "pattern" for the Spirit's work.

[9] Ibid. Wimber also takes note that in Acts 4 after the healing at the temple gate, the *same people have the same experience* they had in Acts 2. In the case of Acts 8, Wimber would agree with Pentecostals, contra Dunn, that the Spirit was bestowed on believers *subsequent to* conversion; however he draws the conclusion that this simply is another datum point to illustrate his conviction that there is no explicit pattern or process that we should expect in the complex of Spirit baptism.

[10] Wimber, *PP,* 137.

[11] Wimber, *Baptism in the Holy Spirit.*

[12] Wimber, *Baptism in the Holy Spirit,* quoted from Clark Pinnock,

[13] Wimber cites Stott as a source several times in *Power Points.*

[14] Wimber understood this dynamic in terms of spiritual maturity, and what the believer may be taught in respect to the gifts. See *PP*, 148-49.

[15] See Wimber's exposition of I Corinthians 14:23-25 in *PP* 157ff.

[16] R.A. Torrey, *Divine Healing* (Grand Rapids, MI: Baker Book House, 1974) 53. Quoted in Wimber, *PH*, 154.

[17] Wimber's relationship with Watson is well chronicled in Carol Wimber, *TWIW* and in *PH*.

[18] See *PH* 149-156.

[19] Wimber, *PH*, 155ff. Wimber cites J. Sidlow Baxter and Collin Brown in support of his position.

[20] Wimber, *PH,* 156-57. This thought is echoed in many Vineyard influenced authors, see for example Ken Blue, *Authority to Heal: Answers for everyone who has prayed for a sick friend* (Downers Grove, IL: Intervarsity Press, 1987) 90; Williams, *Signs and Wonders*, 139; Morphew, *Breakthrough* 183-87.

[21] This phrase has become an idiomatic expression in some vineyard circles to express this dynamic of healing in the eschatological tension.

[22] Once again, this is also because Wimber understood that followers of Christ were commanded to pray for the sick, thus the practice of healing was an act of obedience. His "clinic" times, when he demonstrated the process of praying for healing, not only shocked many at Fuller Seminary in MC 510, but also was a surprise to many who came into his churches later with the constitutional view.

[23] A "constitutional" view would hold that a believer held the office of healer, as one would hold the office of pastor, apostle, or elder. For reasons why Wimber rejected this view, see *Power Points,* 147-50.

[24] For example, in *The Way in is the Way On*, Wimber states "I maintain the evangelical position that the born-again experience is the consummate charismatic experience", 220.

[25] Wimber, *The Holy Spirit's Work in Believers* (1986), retrieved from Wimber.org.

[26] This insight is the basis of Wimber's reasoning as to why the gifts may or may not manifested in an individual's life, and explains his perspective that the gifts can be taught, practiced, and improved upon. This is a major departure from the constitutional view. In this view, a Christian either "had" the gift of healing, or they didn't. Thus *teaching* the practice of healing to the body would be highly illogical. However, in his position outlined above, it's quite sensible to teach and practice the gifts, as a person's cooperation and information contributed to enacting the potential gift. Wimber's extensive healing model is comprehensively discussed in *Power Healing*

Part III, "An Integrated Model of Healing: Principles, Values, and Practices", 169-235.

27 Wimber, "Healing" audio teachings, "Healing the demonized" retrieved from www.wimber.org.

28 Wimber, *PH,* 101.

29 Wimber, *PH,* 103. Wimber was often challenged by Evangelicals when he taught that Christians could be influenced by demonic beings. His conception of how demons could influence or partially control Christian believers is detailed in *Power Healing* 114ff. In short, Wimber held that Christians could be significantly influenced by demons; however, as they were sealed with the Spirit at conversion, the term "possession" was a misnomer. Wimber often chose the simple term "demonized" to include the possible influence on both Christians and nonbelievers.

30 Wimber, *PP,* 157.

31 Wimber, "Introducing Prophetic Ministry", *ETS* Vol. 3, No.4 (Fall, 1989).

32 Ibid., 6.

33 See the relevant chapters in Jackson, *Quest,* chapters 10-14, relating to the so-called "Kansas City prophets" era of the Vineyard. Significant in Wimber's turn was the prophetic word of Paul Cain that Wimber's son Sean would return to the faith; Carol Wimber discusses this episode in detail in *TWIW,* 178-80. Wimber's initial enthusiasm for the inclusion of these prophets in the movement is illustrated by his articles in *Equipping the Saints* "Introducing Prophetic Ministry," where he says of Paul Cain, "he had a proven, mature, prophetic ministry".

34 Jackson relates that in a Vineyard pastor's conference in 1995, Wimber confessed that his leading the movement into the prophetic era was a mistake. *Quest,* 234.

35 Carol Wimber, *TWIW* 180-81.

36 In "The Movement I would build" Wimber put it this way: "at one time in the Vineyard we had an 'everybody can play' attitude. Everybody can worship. Everybody can pray. Everybody can prophesy. Everybody can heal...and on and on". Carol Wimber, *TWIW* 181.

37 Wimber, *PH,* 59 ff.

38 Wimber at one point stated "I do not hold healing services so much as equipping seminars, where everyone learns how to exercise the power that God makes available to us". *PH,* 171. He also explained the format of these seminars, "each session at my healing seminar is divided into three parts: worship, instruction, and a clinic. In the clinic participants observe trained members of a healing team

pray for the sick while I describe what is happening and why certain things are done," 176.

[39] *PP,* 150.

[40] Ibid., 159.

[41] John Wimber, "Releasing Lay People", *ETS*, Vol. 3 No. 4, July-August 1986, 13. Wimber understood such events as the sending out the twelve (Matt. 12) and the seventy (Luke 10) and the miracle of the feeding of the five thousand (Matt. 14), as just several examples of "training" that exemplified this claim, but even more so, saw the entire three year ministry of Jesus as an extended training period for the disciples.

[42] Romans 8:23.

[43] This is another example of Wimber's amusing idioms used to illustrate theological or practical concepts.

[44] See Wimber's poignant recollection of the effect Watson's death had on him in *PH* 147-49.

[45] Fee, *God's Empowering Presence,* 573.

[46] Ephesians 1:14. Wimber often echoed the words of James Dunn's statement "ἀρραβών means more than "guarantee"; as "First Installment" or "down-payment" the ἀρραβών is part of and the same as the whole". Dunn, "Spirit and Kingdom," 134. See also 2 Cor. 5:5 where the Spirit is a "guarantee" of the fulfillment of God's blessing on the believer, even in the midst of bodily decay and suffering.

[47] Christensen, *Welcome Holy Spirit,* 75.

[48] Wimber, "Warfare in Kingdoms", available from www.wimber.org.

Chapter 10

[1] Wimber, *PH,* 4. This event occurred in 1964.

[2] Carol Wimber's account of this incident is found in *TWIW* 75ff .

[3] Wimber, *PH,* 50-51.

[4] Ibid., 51.

[5] Carol Wimber, *TWIW,* 154. In these accounts she is retelling stories kept in a journal of a woman on the trip.

[6] Wimber, *PH,* 199ff.

[7] Wimber was expectant that physical and emotional phenomena would occur, as "often they indicate that the Holy Spirit is manifesting His presence on someone, and we can *learn to recognize what they mean". PH,* 181, 212-16.

[8] Wimber maintained that this "clinical" approach did not distract or derail the

free moving of the Spirit, but rather, provided an increased opportunity for all to learn and understand how to better pray for the sick.

[9] White, "A Look Inside part II" 24. White provides a detailed account of a total healing of a football player who had a ruptured Achilles tendon, who came up to the front of the class on crutches and left completely healed with little pain and a nearly full range of motion. White also discusses these physical manifestations in *When the Spirit Comes with Power* 90ff.

[10] See for example Wimber's Signs and Wonders conferences, the DVD recordings of which are available from www.vineyardresources.org.

[11] Wimber, *PH, 200, 204.* Wimber suggested that there should be a "testing" of the word by asking for some form of confirmation from the Spirit.

[12] Much of the evidence of this comes once again, from Wimber's "narrating" the ministry occurring in the conference.

[13] Numerous accounts state that at times the intercessor has been quite certain that a particular word or impression was valid, but the giving of the word had little discernable effect on the person. Wimber speaks of this mystery in his *Healing* teaching resource, "A Position on Healing", CD 3, www.vineyardresources.org.

[14] Wimber, *PE,* 74. This author has been told numerous first-hand account of this form of phenomenon by Vineyard members, involving words, pictures, symbols or letters 'written' on a person, in the space around a person, or on a physical object (i.e. a wall).

[15] This concept is the general message of Wimber's *Power Evangelism.* We shall see this phenomenon repeated in the following accounts by Jack Deere, Gary Best, Alexander Venter and Robby Dawkins among others.

[16] Wimber encouraged his churches to understand this experience in light of the already-not yet eschatology, in much the same way that healing is imperfect and not "guaranteed" in the atonement, exact prophetic 'accuracy" or "foretelling" is not perfect either. The best defense (from a Vineyard perspective) of this understanding of how prophecy functions in the church is Wayne Grudem's *The Gift of Prophecy in the New Testament Church and Today* (Wheaton, IL: Crossway Books, 2000).

[17] Wimber and others would refer to these events as "power encounters," "divine appointments," "power healings," and the like.

[18] Wimber, *PH,* 52.

[19] Wimber understood "deliverance from spirits" to be a form of spiritual "healing".

[20] Wimber, *PE* 48-49.

²¹ For example see *PE, 161-67; PH* 85, 97; Carol Wimber *TWIW* 154; White, *When the Spirit Comes with Power,* 201; Williams, *Signs, Wonders and the Kingdom of God* 140-41. Also see the following discussions of Gary Best and Alexander Venter.

²² This does not insinuate that the more 'clinical' or three-person intercessory forms were *replaced* or superseded by the more "spectacular" forms, only that there was a new increase in emphasis on the large scale experiences, as they occurred in stadiums and with enormous crowds.

²³ Consult Jackson's *Quest* for a detailed history of the relationship between Kansas City Metro Fellowship and the Vineyard.

²⁴ See Kevin Springer, "Paul Cain: A New Breed of Man" in *ETS* Vol. 3 No. 4, (1989), 11-13.

²⁵ Jack Deere, *Surprised by the Power of the Spirit* (Grand Rapids, MI: Zondervan, 1993) 39ff. Dr. Jack Deere was a Professor at Dallas Seminary and a confirmed cessationist when he invited Dr. John White to speak at his church. Dr. White had fully embraced Wimber's ministry style by this time, and introduced Deere to the ministry of John Wimber and the Vineyard. Deere later became a staff member of the Anaheim Vineyard. See also Deere's *Surprised by the Voice of God* (Grand Rapids, MI: Zondervan, 1996).

²⁶ Deere states that the woman's name was Linda Tidwell and that her previous diagnosis and remediation were confirmed by medical doctors, Ibid., 40.

²⁷ Ibid., 69-70.

²⁸ Perhaps the most dramatic example is Cain's prophecy that Wimber's son Sean, who was mired in a destructive lifestyle, would "return" to the faith and be healed from his addictions. Carol Wimber discusses this extensively in *TWIW* 178-79. Carol claimed that a reason they were so willing to embrace the prophetic ministry of Cain and Jones were events like this that they personally experienced; thus it was difficult to reject the reality of the ministry.

²⁹ See for example Mike Bickle, *Growing in the Prophetic: A Practical, Biblical Guide to Dreams, Visions, and Spiritual Gifts* (Lake Mary, FL: Charisma House, 1996); Jack Deere, *Surprised by the Voice of God* 144-50, 287; John Paul Jackson, "Prophetic Reformation", *ETS* Vol. 7 No. 4 (Fall 1993); David Pytches, *Some Say it Thundered: A Personal Encounter with the Kansas City Prophets* (Nashville, TN: Thomas Nelson, 1991).

³⁰ For example, in wake of claims made by Paul Cain, there was an investigation made by a Charismatic pastor named Ernie Gruen who accused many of the "Kansas City Prophets" of inaccuracies, excesses and abuse of ministry. This investigation was made public in *Equipping the Saints*; see especially Wimber's article from the Fall,

1990 (Vol. 4 No. 4) issue "A Response to Ernie Gruen", 13-15. This entire issue was dedicated to issues related to the prophetic and Metro Vineyard in Kansas City. Jackson also chronicles the accusations and counter-accusations between Gruen, Mike Bickle, Wimber and others in *Quest* 216ff. Gruen's paper "Documentation of the Aberrant Practices and Teachings of the Kansas City Fellowship (Grace Ministries)" can be found reproduced in numerous places in digital format on the internet.

[31] See the discussion of this event in Carol Wimber, *TWIW* 146-48; Jackson, *Quest*, 72ff.

[32] The Toronto Blessing was given a number of monikers by participants and critics alike. I refer to the "Toronto Experience" or the "Toronto blessing", "outpouring" etc. as those are the terms used by Wimber, John Arnott, and others in general reference to the charismatic renewal that began in Toronto, but was experienced in all of the United States, Canada and many places in the world.

[33] Guy Chevreau, *Catch the Fire* (Toronto, Canada: HarperCollins, 1994) 13; John Arnott, *The Father's Blessing* (Orlando, FL: Creation House, 1994); John Wimber, "Board Report: " Why I respond to phenomena" ; Highly critical of these ministries and their influence on the "Toronto Blessing" is James Beverly, *Holy Laughter and the Toronto Blessing* (Grand Rapids, MI: Zondervan, 1994); idem, Revival *Wars: A Critique of Counterfeit Revival* (Toronto, Canada: Evangelical Research Ministries, 1997). A more cautious but generally positive response can be found in Margaret M. Poloma's sociological analysis, "Inspecting the Fruit of the 'Toronto Blessing': A Sociological Perspective", *PNEUMA: The Journal of the Society for Pentecostal Studies* Vol. 20, No. 1 (Spring, 1998) 43-70, and her fuller treatment, *Main Street Mystics: The Toronto Blessing and Reviving Pentecostalism* (Walnut Creek, CA: AltaMira Press, 2003). Frank D. Macchia's "The 'Toronto Blessing': No Laughing Matter", *Journal of Pentecostal Theology* 8, (1996), 3-6 is more cautious as well. Also consult Martyn Percy, "Adventure and Atrophy in a Charismatic Movement: Returning to the 'Toronto Blessing'", *Journal of Contemporary Religion* Vol. 20, No. 1 (2005) 71-90; Jon Bialecki, "The Kingdom and its Subjects: Charisms, Language, Economy, and the Birth of a Progressive Politics in the Vineyard" Ph.D. Dissertation, Anthropology, University of California, San Diego, 2009.

[34] Chevreau, *Catch the Fire*, 14.

[35] In typical Vineyard parlance, this became known in the reports about the renewal as "carpet time". The phenomenon is frequently recorded in revival and Pentecostal history designated by the Pentecostal phrase "being slain in the Spirit".

See John Wimber, "Vineyard Reflections" (May/June 1994), available from Vineyard Institute as *Wimber Letters II*.

[36] In the Cane Ridge, Kentucky revival of 1800-01 these physical manifestations were called "the jerks". These bodily movements believed to be in response to the presence of the Spirit gave both the Quakers and the Shakers their monikers. Similar physical manifestations were evidenced in the ministry of Jonathan Edwards, Wesley, and Azuza street. See "Cane Ridge", and numerous references to "slain in the Spirit" in *Dictionary of Pentecostal and Charismatic Movements* edited by Stanley Burgess.

[37] Stephan Witt, "Where the Spirit of the Lord is, There is Freedom", *ETS* (Fall, 1994), 13. The characterization of this as drunkenness was a common refrain. This was immediately connected to the response of Peter at Pentecost in Acts 2, "we are not drunk as you suppose".

[38] Ibid., 14.

[39] Chevreau, *Catch the Fire*, 27.

[40] Ibid., 147-204.

[41] Guy Chevreau, *Share the Fire: The Toronto Blessing and Grace-Based Evangelism* (Shippensburg, PA: Revival Press, 1997).

[42] Consult Jackson, *Quest,* for a discussion of the fallout from the Toronto era, and the number of churches that disaffiliated with the movement after 1996-97.

[43] Gary Best, *Naturally Supernatural: Joining God in His Work* (Cape Town, South Africa: Vineyard International Publishing, 2005).

[44] Best, *Naturally Supernatural* 47.

[45] Ibid., 54-57.

[46] For example he includes numerous accounts of prophetic "words' connected to physical healings, including legs being lengthened (77, 79) arthritis and hearing (88), an injured arm (108), and a damaged knee (124). He also catalogs occurrences of 'deliverances" from demonic oppression (198, 202, 205) and a precise prophetic word of a woman's name (similar to John Wimber's account) that had a profound impact on the penitent.

[47] Venter is the author of *Doing Church, Doing Healing* (Cape Town, South Africa: Vineyard International Publishing, 1998), and *Doing Reconciliation: Racism, Reconciliation, and Transformation in Church and World* (Cape Town, South Africa: Vineyard International Publishing, 2004), which is a theological reflection on his work in the anti-apartheid movement. Venter served as Wimber's research assistant in 1982, and was the principal editor of the material that Wimber used for MC 510,

some of this material written for Wimber was copy written by Venter and included in *Doing Healing*. Venter discusses his relationship with Wimber pages 8-12.

[48] See for example Venter's discussion of inaugurated eschatology in pages 74-79, 189 ff. Venter also develops a relatively sophisticated psychological anthropology in the context of how sickness, disease, and demonic influences may harm a person.

[49] Not that Venter's work has supplanted *Power Healing* or other Wimber's teachings, but since Venter still travels widely to the U.S. and the U.K., his work and ministry is simply more current than *Power Healing*.

[50] *Doing Healing*, 192. Venter gives numerous examples of these elements, such as seeing an image of "sticky spider web" which symbolized a besetting sin (220), a vision of a girl in a darkened room symbolizing fear and isolation (237), an "electric current" felt by a man healed from curvature of the spine and a shortened leg (262).

[51] Venter, *Doing Healing*, 205. He states, "the presenting problem is often a symptom of deeper issues, so we take time with the person to heal the related causes with a view to restoring *Shalom* to the person" See also 210-211.

[52] Idem, 205.

[53] Idem, 309-312.

[54] Robby Dawkins, *Do What Jesus Did: A Real-life Field Guide to Healing the Sick, Routing Demons and Changing Lives Forever* (Minneapolis, MN: Chosen Books, 2013).

[55] Ibid., 46-7.

[56] Ibid., 48.

[57] In recent years Dawkins and some of his Vineyard associates have become the subject of a number of documentary films, including *Finger of God*, *Father of Lights* and *Furious Love* filmed and produced by Darren Wilson. All of these are available at www.robbydawkins.com.

[58] In *Power Healing* Wimber refers to these changed mental or psychological states as "inner healing" or "healing of emotions", 79-81.

[59] Dawkings, *Do What Jesus Did* 70-71. He refers to these manifestations as a "sympathy pain" or a "temporary, prophetic manifestations of pain or discomfort someone else is experiencing from a condition he or she has that needs healing", 113. Wimber spoke often of this in his teachings on healing as well.

[60] Ibid., 69.

[61] Many accounts of charismatic phenomenon can be found on the Vineyard U.S.A. website, and on numerous other sites such as Vineyard United Kingdom. In keeping with Wimber's desire to "equip the saints" many of these stories are of men and women who are not professional ministers, but lay people "doing the stuff" in the Vineyard idiom.

Chapter 11:

[1] There were also other studies done in order to ascertain the effectiveness of Wimber's prayer model. For an example, consult Dr. David Lewis *Healing: Fiction, Fantasy or Fact?* (London: Hodder and Stoughton, 1989) which is an examination of Wimber's ministry trips to London in 1985. Dr. Lewis is a Royal Anthropological institute member who conducted interviews and issued questionnaires to over 2000 participants in order to collect sociological data on healing, prophetic "words" and other charismatic phenomena.

[2] Wimber, Best, and Dawkins all relate situations that fit this pattern.

[3] Vineyard authors frequently cited the experience of Jonathan Edwards (Wimber, *Power Healing*, "Board Report", Deere, *Surprised by the Power of the Spirit* , Chevreau, *Catch the Fire*). Wimber was especially fond of the accounts of phenomenon cited in Wesley's Journals (*PE* 59, 228ff as examples), along with John White (*Spirit* 75-79) and Deere (*Power of the Spirit* 88). Also frequently cited were the words of Charles Finney, "the Holy Spirit descended upon me in a manner that seemed to go through me, body and soul. I could feel the impression, like a wave of electricity, going through and through me. Indeed it seemed to *come in waves and waves of liquid love*; for I could not express it in any other way". Charles Grandison Finney, Memoirs of Reverend Charles G. Finney Written By Himself (New York: A.S. Barnes, 1876), 13–23.

[4] Venter also cautions that "words" should always be given in humility due to the "already-not yet" nature of the kingdom.

[5] Venter, *Healing*, 300.

[6] Ibid., 304. Wimber also cautioned regarding the possibility of deception, see for example *The Way in is the Way On*, 244-47.

[7] Venter lists scriptures from Jeremiah 23:9, Nehemiah 8, 2 Chronicles 5, and Acts 2 as samples of extreme physical responses to the presence of God's Spirit. Certainly more scriptures could be cited to defend the human physical response to the power of God.

[8] Venter also makes the stimulating contention that it is no surprise that these extreme reactions in the human body could occur, as "we experience resurrection power in our bodies" and "if the *full* resurrectional power of the Spirit came on us, our bodies would explode or be transfigured into glorified bodies, like Jesus' glorified body". 306.

[9] Ibid., 308. Wimber as well places emphasis on the "fruit" of the experience, evidenced by statements such as this from *The Way in is the Way On:* "So my question

to someone after they've shaken, fallen down, or made a noise is this: 'Do you love Jesus more? Do you believe in Him more? Are you more committed to Him? If the answer is "Yes!" then praise the Lord!'" 250.

[10] Wimber, *PH, 223.

Chapter 12

[1] This would especially be in mind when we consider Wimber's overall "Warfare" conception of the ministry of healing; that is, the Christian is conscripted into ever-present conflict with the "forces of Satan" seeking to destroy or corrupt God's creation.

[2] Wimber was fond of saying, in his homespun idiom, "sometimes the Spirit comes in power, and sometimes we drink coffee and call it a night".

[3] Dr. Peter Davids writes that suffering can occur from conflict with the world (Romans 8:18), in identification with the suffering of Christ (Philippians 3:10), or as a means of developing "Christian endurance" (Romans 5:3), in "Suffering, Endurance and Relief", *ETS* Vol. 3, No. 4, (July-August 1986). Wimber wrote that "God uses our suffering to fulfill his purposes and bring maturity to our lives". "Why Christians Suffer" *ETS* Vol. 2 No. 1, (Winter 1988) 14. Also consult John Wimber, *Kingdom Suffering: Why do People Suffer* (1990) booklet available from www.vineyardresources.com.

[4] Wimber, *PH,* 163-65; Venter, *Doing Healing* chapter 19, "Ministering Healing to the Dying and the Dead", 282-96. Wimber's foundational experience for this was his friend Gunnar Payne, who experienced the traumatic loss of both of his children, and yet did not renounce his faith in the midst of his suffering. See Wimber, "Why Christians Suffer", 2.

[5] Wimber, "Season of New Beginnings", *ETS* (Fall, 1994), 5.

Chapter 13

[1] Rudolf Bultmann, *History and Eschatology.* Gifford Lectures 1955. (Edinburgh: University Press, 1957).

[2] In his essay "Saul's armor: the problem and the promise of Pentecostal theology today" Pneuma. 2001. 23: (1 Spring) 115-146, D. Lyle Dabney says of Pentecostals " They have failed to take themselves seriously as a movement with an implicit theological trajectory of their own, and thus have neglected to ask the hard questions of their own beliefs and practices and then to pursue the disciplined task of rendering an account of their faith to Christian and non-Christian alike". 125.

[3] Dr. Derek Morphew provides a Vineyard appraisal of the so-called "Third Quest", including the Jesus Seminar, in *Breakthrough* 240-49. Other kingdom studies such as Bruce Chilton's *Pure Kingdom: Jesus' Vision of God* offer valid insights, but in the case of Chilton's thesis that the message of the kingdom being God's self-disclosure - "God in strength" - one struggles to ascertain just what his thesis may offer to a practicing church, especially a church of pneumatological experience like the Vineyard. Supremely helpful for gaining context on the Third Quest is Part One of James D.G. Dunn's *Jesus Remembered: Christianity in the Making Volume I* (Grand Rapids, MI: Eerdmans, 1993).

[4] Wright's first two volumes, *The New Testament and the People of God* and *Jesus and the Victory of God* are most helpful for kingdom studies, but the idea resurfaces throughout the series. The Fourth volume in the series is *Paul and the Faithfulness of God* (London/Minneapolis: Fortress, 2013).

[5] Wright has also had a tremendous influence on the Vineyard movement's close cousin, the New Wine renewal movement in Anglicanism. Wright embraces the modern-day operation of the *charismata*, including healing, and was a strong advocate for Vineyard-style ministry while he was the Bishop of Durham.

[6] Wright uses this grounding in other fascinating ways as well. For example, his predisposition towards the present-future tension implicit in the kingdom is evident in his rejection of certain formulations of Q that suggest a "realized" Early Q, and a "future" tensed Late Q. *NTPG*, 439-40.

[7] See especially *Jesus and the Victory of God* chapter 10.

[8] Wright, *JVG* 451.

[9] Wright, *JVG*, 469, commenting on Luke 11:20/Matthew 12:28.

[10] (London: HarperOne, 2008).

[11] Wright, *Surprised by Hope* 211. Wright here speaks of space in spiritual and material terms, as a "coming together" of heaven and earth, i.e. a theology of place rooted in a good creation.

[12] Ibid., 97. Wright repeatedly uses the term "good creation" as a refutation of the Gnostic association of matter with evil.

[13] See for example retired Vineyard Pastor Tri Robinson's book *Saving God's Green Earth: Rediscovering the Church's Responsibility to Environmental Stewardship* (Norcross, GA: Ampelon, 2006).

[14] See especially N.T. Wright, How God Became King: The Forgotten Story of the Gospels (New York: HarperCollins, 2012).

[15] (Grand Rapids, MI: Baker Academic, 2011). Keener is currently a member of a Vineyard church in Kentucky.

[16] Ibid., 1.

[17] For example, on pages 752-56 he charts a number of accounts where he was either present, or close trusted (even academic) friends participated in the healing event.

[18] Ibid., 225. Keener also reveals how in many cases, especially regarding medicine, diet, and health, the West has begun to recognize the wisdom and authenticity of majority world practices, 229ff.

[19] Ibid., 255.

[20] Graham Twelftree, *Jesus the Miracle Worker: A Historical and Theological Study*. (Illinois: InterVarsity Press, 1999); *Paul and the Miraculous: A Historical Reconstruction*. (Grand Rapids, MI: Baker Academic, 2013.

[21] A helpful source here for the Vineyard would be Stanley J. Grentz, *Theology for the Community of God* (Grand Rapids, Eerdmans, 1994) 478ff. Grentz is familiar to many Vineyard pastors, is solidly Evangelical, and his thought has much in connection with inaugurated eschatology.

[22] Derek Morphew, *Breakthrough*, 150-51.

[23] Max Weber, *The Sociology of Religion* (Boston, MA: Beacon Press, 1993) 98. Weber's thesis has been challenged on many fronts. Yves Congar argues in his *I Believe in the Holy Spirit* that institutional structure and charismatic vitality are not mutually exclusive, as charism and institution" are "two types of activity" that 'lead to the same end". He concludes, "they are, in other words, complementary", Vol. I, 11. See also the essay in the Third volume, "The Life of the Church as One Long Epiclesis" where Congar expands on the relationship between institution and charismatic expression.

[24] This would be a weakness of Grentz's approach for the Vineyard; while he does have an understanding of the church as the eschatological people of God, he also tends to limit the mission of the church to evangelism, edification and service. This obviously is insufficient for the Vineyard conception of the mission of the church, which sees its mandate for ministry in scriptures such as Isa. 61 & Luke 4. See Grentz, *Theology*, 502ff. If the mission of the church is limited to these practices, as Grentz seems to indicate, it would not be adequate for a Vineyard ecclesiology, or for that matter, a Pentecostal or Charismatic one as well.

[25] For example, on baptism, the statement reads "We believe that Jesus Christ has committed two ordinances to the church: water baptism and the Lord's Supper. Both are available to all believers".

286

[26] This is the fundamental contention of Alexander Venter's book *Doing Church*, written as an organizational manual for Vineyard churches. For a practice-oriented movement like the Vineyard, it could be argued that *Doing Church* is the most developed "practical" ecclesiology in the Vineyard, whereas the movement still needs a formal *theological* exposition of ecclesiology.

[27] One could argue that historically, the centered-set, relational model *has worked*, in that during the Kansas City prophets era, the Toronto Blessing, and the contentious women in ministry discussions, the essential identity of the Vineyard survived intact, and those expressions outside of that identity found themselves at a relational distance. This author recognizes that this perspective is one written from the "victors" as it were, and thus may be open to critique from those who lost relationship or affiliation with the Vineyard in this time.

[28] For example where the role of women in ministry might be decided in progressive, secular cultures like the modern west, this is by no means settled in emerging Vineyard contexts.

[29] For an excellent discussion of these issues, see Allan G. Johnson, *Privilege, Power and Difference* (Boston, Mass.: McGraw-Hill, 2006).

[30] For example, nationally supported justice-focused conferences were held in Winnipeg, Canada in 1996, in Columbus, Ohio in 2006, along with smaller regional conferences and meetings. Also, in 2009 the Vineyard created an anti-slavery task force, which has blossomed into the Vineyard Justice Network, which includes such arenas as poverty, human trafficking, the environment, and racial justice. The Winnipeg Vineyard now offers a School of Justice focusing on the issue of enacting the justice of the kingdom, see http://vineyardschoolofjustice.org.

[31] For an introduction to justice issues from a Vineyard perspective, see Quinton Howitt, *Christianity and the Poor*, CreateSpace Independent Publishing Platform (July 1, 2011).

[32] As previously considered in the discussion of Derek Morphew's *Breakthrough*.

[33] Deuteronomy 10;18, 16:18, 24:17, 27:19, 33:21.

[34] Gen. 18:19.

[35] 1 Kings 3:11.

[36] Isaiah 42:1-4.

[37] Matthew 12:18-20.

[38] John 10:10.

[39] For example, see Vineyard pastor Rich Nathan's *Who is My Enemy? Welcoming People the Church Rejects* (Grand Rapids, MI: Zondervan, 2002).

[40] This is one of the claims of Alexander Venter's recent work, *Doing Reconciliation* (Cape Town, South Africa: Vineyard International Publishing, 2009).

[41] A potential dialogue partner here may be Dr. Mitri Raheb's *Faith in the Face of Empire: The Bible Through Palestinian Eyes* (New York: Orbis Books, 2014).

[42] Statistics according to the United Nations, www.un.org.

[43] For example, the Columbus, Ohio Vineyard and its senior pastor Rich Nathan have become active participants in National conversations on immigration, even testifying before Congress on their experience assisting immigrants as a congregation.

[44] The various United Nation reports on women's rights are helpful here, such as "UN Women: Annual Report 2013-2014"; "Baseline Study of UN Women's Anti-Human Trafficking Programme", (2013); "Making Women's Voice and Votes Count: Baseline Report – 2013".

[45] There are a number of La Vina Latino congregations in the U.S. and a number of large city churches that have made racial diversity a major concern. The Vineyard USA created a task force for racial diversity as well.

[46] (Downers Grove, IL: Intervarsity, 2013). More of her writing can be found at www.christenacleveland.com

[47] Ibid., 166.

[48] I borrow this phraseology from Dr. Calvin DeWitt of the Au Sable Institute, the "father" of present-day Christian environmentalism. Dr. DeWitt has been a frequent speaker at Vineyard churches and conferences. See the work of the Au Sable Institute at www.ausable.org. Formative for Vineyard pastors interested in environmental issues has been DeWitt's *Earth-Wise: A Biblical Response to Environmental Issues* 2nd Edition (Grand Rapids, MI: Faith Alive Publishers, 1994, 2007). Creation care is a central concern in the Vineyard Justice Network initiative as well.

[49] This is a key argument of DeWitt's presentation. Also see Vineyard Pastor Tri Robinson, *Saving God's Green Earth: Rediscovering the Church's Responsibility to Environmental Stewardship* (Norcross, GA: Ampelon, 2006). Also consult Christopher Vena, *Beyond Stewardship: Toward An Agapeic Environmental Ethic* Ph.D. Dissertation, Marquette University, 2009.

[50] See Charles Taylor's *Sources of the Self* and *The Secular Age*.

[51] This is a concept I first heard presented by Dr. Derek Morphew in *Breakthrough*.

[52] Karl Barth's insights in *Church Dogmatics* III.2 §43 have influenced much of the discussion on these points in contemporary theological anthropology.

---

[53] David Kelsey addresses these paradoxes posed by an "eschatological" anthropology in his *Eccentric Existence: A Theological Anthropology – 2 Volumes.* (Louisville, KT: Westminster John Knox Press, 2009). Kelsey is conversant with the modern and late modern cross pressures and complexities involved in advancing a suitable anthropology, as well as understanding that rooting anthropology in a doctrine of creation (especially the traditional starting locus of Genesis 1-3) without pointing towards eschatological realization is short sighted. Kelsey locates his starting point not at the traditional creation narratives in the first chapters of Genesis, but in the creation accounts in Wisdom literature. Kelsey's work may be a valued partner for a Vineyard theologian reflecting on theological anthropology. See also Kelsey's "The Human Creature" in *The Oxford Handbook of Systematic Theology* John Webster, Kathryn Tanner, Iain Torrance, eds., (Oxford: Oxford University Press, 2007) 122ff.

[54] Thiselton, *The Hermeneutics of Doctrine*, (Grand Rapids, MI: Eerdmans, 2007), Idem, *Interpreting God and the Postmodern Self*, (Edinburgh: T&T Clark, 1995); Stanley Grenz, *The Social God and the Relational Self: A Trinitarian Theology of the Imago Dei*, (Lousville, KT: Westminster John Knox, 2001); Amos Yong, *Theology and Down Syndrome: Reimaging Disability in Late Modernity* (Waco, TX: Baylor University Press, 2007).

[55] Yong, *Theology and Down Syndrome*, 185.

[56] Yong's insights into the eschatological nature of disabled persons provide fascinating insights here. Rather than conceive of our redemptive bodies from ableist preconceptions of "perfected" bodies, might we imagine pneumatological bodies that maintain continuity with their pre-resurrected persons, even to the degree of severely impaired physical and cognitive "impairments"? While much of this future state is an unfathomable mystery, Yong's proposals are certainly worth considering for the Vineyard theologian, especially given their theology of healing written primarily from an ableist perspective. Thiselton also places a great deal of stress on embodiment as an essential component of a Biblical anthropology.

[57] From 1987 until 2009 the Vineyard published a monthly publication for worship leaders called *Worship Update* . John Wimber did a great deal of teaching related to the theology and practice of worship; his 1989 teaching *Worship* can be obtained on DVD from www.vineyardresources.com. Other Vineyard influencers include worship leader Andy Park, whose *To Know You More: Cultivating the Heart of the Worship Leader* (Downers Grove, IL: Intervarsity Press, 2002) focuses more on the ministerial aspects of worship pastors than theology of worship. Former Vineyard

worship leader Dan Wilt has written a great deal about worship, including a theology of worship on a popular level. His work can be found at www.danwilt.com.

[58] Yet another idiomatic expression of Wimber's that reflected this sensibility was his "Sometimes we experience the power of the Spirit, and sometimes we quit and drink coffee".